# Delphi High Performance

Build fast Delphi applications using concurrency, parallel
programming and memory management

**Primož Gabrijelčič**

**BIRMINGHAM - MUMBAI**

# Delphi High Performance

**Commissioning Editor:** Merint Mathew
**Acquisition Editor:** Nitin Dasan
**Content Development Editor:** Nikhil Borkar
**Technical Editor:** Jijo Maliyekal
**Copy Editor:** Safis Editing
**Project Coordinator:** Ulhas Kambali
**Proofreader:** Safis Editing
**Indexer:** Mariammal Chettiyar
**Graphics:** Tania Dutta
**Production Coordinator**: Deepika Naik

First published: February 2018

Production reference: 1230218

Published by Packt Publishing Ltd.
Livery Place
35 Livery Street
Birmingham
B3 2PB, UK.

ISBN 978-1-78862-545-6

www.packtpub.com

`mapt.io`

Mapt is an online digital library that gives you full access to over 5,000 books and videos, as well as industry leading tools to help you plan your personal development and advance your career. For more information, please visit our website.

## Why subscribe?

- Spend less time learning and more time coding with practical eBooks and Videos from over 4,000 industry professionals

- Improve your learning with Skill Plans built especially for you

- Get a free eBook or video every month

- Mapt is fully searchable

- Copy and paste, print, and bookmark content

## PacktPub.com

Did you know that Packt offers eBook versions of every book published, with PDF and ePub files available? You can upgrade to the eBook version at `www.PacktPub.com` and as a print book customer, you are entitled to a discount on the eBook copy. Get in touch with us at `service@packtpub.com` for more details.

At `www.PacktPub.com`, you can also read a collection of free technical articles, sign up for a range of free newsletters, and receive exclusive discounts and offers on Packt books and eBooks.

# Contributors

## About the author

**Primož Gabrijelčič** started coding in Pascal on 8-bit micros in the 1980s and he never looked back. In the last 20 years, he was mostly programming high-availability server applications used in the broadcasting industry. A result of this focus was the open sourced parallel programming library for Delphi—OmniThreadLibrary. He's also an avid writer and has written several hundred articles, and he is a frequent speaker at Delphi conferences where he likes to talk about complicated topics, ranging from memory management to creating custom compilers.

# About the reviewers

**Stefan Glienke**, since his very first steps with Turbo Pascal in school, was passionate about programming. In his spare time, he worked at a software company using Visual Basic and started learning C++ and Delphi and decided to start an apprenticeship as a software developer after graduation.

Over the years, he developed an interest in software architecture and began helping fellow developers improve their skills, participating in several open source projects, such as Spring4D. He is also the author of TestInsight.

Stefan has worked as reviewer on the books *Coding in Delphi* and *Dependency Injection in Delphi*.

> *I'd like to thank Primoz for writing this incredible book and suggesting me as a technical reviewer. I'd also like to thank Nitin Dasan and Ulhas Kambali from Packt for their help and patience. Also, big thanks go to my parents who helped me with my relocation, which was happening at the same time as I was doing this review.*

**Bruce McGee** is the founder of Glooscap Software, a software development and consulting company in Toronto, Ontario. He is also a long-time Delphi user, which he continues to work with every day.

# Packt is searching for authors like you

If you're interested in becoming an author for Packt, please visit `authors.packtpub.com` and apply today. We have worked with thousands of developers and tech professionals, just like you, to help them share their insight with the global tech community. You can make a general application, apply for a specific hot topic that we are recruiting an author for, or submit your own idea.

# Table of Contents

# Preface

Performance matters!

I started programming on 8-bit micros, and boy, was that an interesting time! Memory was typically not a problem as we didn't write big programs, but they certainly weren't running fast, especially if you run them with a built-in BASIC interpreter. It is not surprising that I quickly learned assembler and spent lots of early years shifting bits and registers around. So did almost everybody else who wanted to release a commercial application written for one of those computers. There were, more or less, no games and applications written in BASIC simply because they would run too slow and nobody would use them.

Time has changed; computers are now fast—incredibly fast! If you don't believe me, check the code examples for this book. A lot of times, I had to write loops that spin over many million iterations so that the result of changing the code would be noticed at all. The raw speed of processors has also changed the software development world. Low-level languages such as assembler and C mostly gave way to more abstract approaches—C#, C++, Delphi, F#, Java, Python, Ruby, JavaScript, Go, and so on. The choice is yours. Almost anything you write in these languages runs fast or at least *fast enough*.

Computers are so fast that we sometimes forget the basic rule—performance matters. Customers like programs that operate so fast that they don't have to think about it. If they have to wait 10 seconds for a form to appear after clicking on a button, they won't be very happy. They'll probably still use the software, though, provided that it works for them and doesn't crash. On the other hand, if you write a data processing application that needs 26 hours for a job that executes daily, you'll certainly lose them.

I'm not saying that you should switch to assembler. Low-level languages are fast, but coding in them is too slow for modern times, and the probability of introducing bugs is just too high. High-level languages are just fine, but you have to know how to use them. You have to know what is fast and what not and—preferably—you should take this into account when designing the code.

This book will walk you through the different approaches that will help you write better code. Writing fast code is not the same as optimizing a few lines of your program to the extreme. Most of the time, that is in fact the completely wrong approach! However, I'm getting ahead of myself. Let the book speak for itself.

# Who this book is for

This book was written for all Delphi programmers out there. You will find something interesting inside, whether you are new to programming or a seasoned old soul. I'm talking about basic stuff, about strings and arrays, lists and objects, but I'm also discussing parallel programming, memory manager internals, and object linking. There is also plenty of dictionaries, pointers, algorithmic complexities, code inlining, parameter passing, and what not.

So, whoever you are, dear reader, I'm pretty sure you'll find something new in this book. Enjoy!

# What this book covers

Chapter 1, *About Performance*, talks about performance. We'll dissect the term itself and try to find out what users actually mean when they say that a program is performing (or not performing) well. Then, we will move into the area of algorithm complexity. We'll skip all the boring mathematics and just mention the parts relevant to programming. We will also look at different ways of finding the slow (non-performant) parts of the program, from pure guesswork to measuring tools of a different sophistication, homemade and commercial.

Chapter 2, *Fixing the Algorithm*, examines a few practical examples where changing an algorithm can speed up a program dramatically. In the first part, we'll look at graphical user interfaces and what we can do when a simple update to TListBox takes too long. The second part of the chapter explores the idea of caching and presents a reusable caching class with very fast implementation. In the last part, we'll revisit some code from Chapter 1, *About Performance*, and make it faster, again, by changing an algorithm.

Chapter 3, *Fine-Tuning the Code*, deals with lots of small things. Sometimes, performance lies in many small details, and this chapter shows how to use them to your advantage. We'll check the Delphi compiler settings and see which ones affect the code speed. We'll look at the implementation details for built-in data types and method calls. Using a correct type in a right way can mean a lot. Of course, we won't forget about the practical side. This chapter will give examples of different optimization techniques, such as extracting common expressions, using pointers to manipulate data, and implementing parts of the solution in assembler. At the end, we'll revisit the code from Chapter 1, *About Performance*, and make it even faster.

Chapter 4, *Memory Management*, is all about memory. It starts with a discussion on strings, arrays, and how their memory is managed. After that, we will move to the memory functions exposed by Delphi. We'll see how we can use them to manage memory. Next, we'll cover records—how to allocate them, how to initialize them, and how to create useful dynamically-allocated generic records. We'll then move into the murky waters of memory manager implementation. I'll sketch a very rough overview of FastMM, the default memory manager in Delphi. First, I'll explain why FastMM is excellent and then I'll show when and why it may slow you down. We'll see how to analyze memory performance problems and how to switch the memory manager for a different one. In the last part, we'll revisit the SlowCode program and reduce the number of memory allocations it makes.

Chapter 5, *Getting Started with the Parallel World*, moves the topic to parallel programming. In the introduction, I'll talk about processes and threads, and multithreading and multitasking to establish some common ground for discussion. After that, you'll start learning what not to do when writing parallel code. I'll explain how the user interface must be handled from background threads and what problems are caused by sharing data between threads. Then, I'll start fixing those problems by implementing various kinds of synchronization mechanisms and interlocked operations. We'll also deal with the biggest problem synchronization brings to the code—deadlocking. As synchronization inevitably slows the program down, I'll explain how to achieve the highest possible speed using data duplication, aggregation, and communication. At the end, I'll introduce two third-party libraries that contain helpful parallel functions and data structures.

Chapter 6, *Working with Parallel Tools*, focuses on a single topic, Delphi's TThread class. In the introduction, I'll explain why I believe that TThread is still important even in this modern age. I will explore different ways in which TThread based threads can be managed in your code. After that, I'll go through the most important TThread methods and properties and explain what they're good for. In the second part of the chapter, I'll extend TThread into something more modern and easier to use. Firstly, I'll add a communication channel so that you'll be able to send messages to the thread. After that, I'll implement a derived class designed to handle one specific usage pattern and show how this approach simplifies writing parallel code to the extreme.

Chapter 7, *Exploring Parallel Practices*, moves the multithreaded programming to more abstract terms. In this chapter, I'll discuss modern multithreading concepts: tasks and patterns. I'll look into Delphi's own implementation, Parallel Programming Library, and demonstrate the use of TTask/ITask. We'll look at topics such as task management, exception handling, and thread pooling. After that, I'll move on to patterns and talk about all Parallel Programming Library patterns: Join, Future, and Parallel For. I will also introduce two custom patterns—Async/Await and Join/Await—and finish the chapter with a discussion on the Pipeline pattern from OmniThreadLibrary.

Chapter 8, *Using External Libraries*, admits that sometimes Delphi is not enough. Sometimes the problem is too complicated to be efficiently solved by a human. Sometimes Pascal is just lacking the speed. In such cases, we can try finding an existing library that solves our problem. In most cases, it will not support Delphi directly but will provide some kind of C or C++ interface. This chapter looks into linking with C object files and describes typical problems that you'll encounter on the way. In the second half, I'll present a complete example of linking to a C++ library, from writing a proxy DLL to using it in Delphi.

Chapter 9, *Best Practices*, wraps it all up. In this last chapter, I'll revisit all the important topics I explored in previous chapters. At the same time, I'll drop in some additional tips, tricks, and techniques.

# To get the most out of this book

Although you can read this book in bed or on the beach, you will need a computer and Delphi to play with the code examples. The code was written in Delphi 10.2 Tokyo, but it should also work without a problem in the older versions. I did use some modern features in demos—and dedicated a chapter to Parallel Programming Library that was introduced in Delphi XE7—so anything older than that is hit and miss.

This book does not refer to any functionality specific to the Enterprise edition. You'll be able to test all the code with the entry-level professional edition.

# Download the example code files

You can download the example code files for this book from your account at www.packtpub.com. If you purchased this book elsewhere, you can visit www.packtpub.com/support and register to have the files emailed directly to you.

You can download the code files by following these steps:

1. Log in or register at `www.packtpub.com`.
2. Select the **SUPPORT** tab.
3. Click on **Code Downloads & Errata**.
4. Enter the name of the book in the **Search** box and follow the onscreen instructions.

Once the file is downloaded, please make sure that you unzip or extract the folder using the latest version of:

- WinRAR/7-Zip for Windows
- Zipeg/iZip/UnRarX for Mac
- 7-Zip/PeaZip for Linux

The code bundle for the book is also hosted on GitHub at `https://github.com/PacktPublishing/Delphi-High-Performance/`. In case there's an update to the code, it will be updated on the existing GitHub repository.

We also have other code bundles from our rich catalog of books and videos available at `https://github.com/PacktPublishing/`. Check them out!

# Conventions used

There are a number of text conventions used throughout this book.

`CodeInText`: Indicates code words in text, database table names, folder names, filenames, file extensions, pathnames, dummy URLs, user input, and Twitter handles. Here is an example: "A string parameter `value` is present in a string list."

A block of code is set as follows:

```
function IsPresentInList(strings: TStrings; const value: string): Boolean;
var
  i: Integer;
begin
  Result := False;
  for i := 0 to strings.Count - 1 do
    if SameText(strings[i], value) then
      Exit(True);
end;
```

**Bold**: Indicates a new term, an important word, or words that you see onscreen. For example, words in menus or dialog boxes appear in the text like this. Here is an example: "Go to **Options** | **Options**, then select **General** | **Search directory**."

 Warnings or important notes appear like this.

 Tips and tricks appear like this.

# Get in touch

Feedback from our readers is always welcome.

**General feedback**: Email `feedback@packtpub.com` and mention the book title in the subject of your message. If you have questions about any aspect of this book, please email us at `questions@packtpub.com`.

**Errata**: Although we have taken every care to ensure the accuracy of our content, mistakes do happen. If you have found a mistake in this book, we would be grateful if you would report this to us. Please visit `www.packtpub.com/submit-errata`, selecting your book, clicking on the Errata Submission Form link, and entering the details.

**Piracy**: If you come across any illegal copies of our works in any form on the Internet, we would be grateful if you would provide us with the location address or website name. Please contact us at `copyright@packtpub.com` with a link to the material.

**If you are interested in becoming an author**: If there is a topic that you have expertise in and you are interested in either writing or contributing to a book, please visit `authors.packtpub.com`.

# Reviews

Please leave a review. Once you have read and used this book, why not leave a review on the site that you purchased it from? Potential readers can then see and use your unbiased opinion to make purchase decisions, we at Packt can understand what you think about our products, and our authors can see your feedback on their book. Thank you!

For more information about Packt, please visit packtpub.com.

# 1
# About Performance

*"My program is not fast enough. Users are saying that it is not performing well. What can I do?"*

These are the words I hear a lot when consulting on different programming projects. Sometimes the answer is simple, sometimes hard, but almost always the critical part of the answer lies in the question. More specifically, in one word - **performing**.

What do we mean when we say that a program is performing well? Actually, nobody cares. What we have to know is what **users** mean when they say that the program is **not** performing well. And users, you'll probably admit, look at the world in a very different way than we programmers.

Before starting to measure and improve the performance of a program, we have to find out what users really mean by the word **performance**. Only then can we do something productive about it.

We will cover the following topics in this chapter:

- What is performance?
- What do we mean when we say that a program performs well?
- What can we tell about the code speed by looking at the algorithm?
- How does the knowledge of compiler internals help us write fast programs?
- Why is it better to measure than to guess?
- What tools can we use to find the slow parts of a program?

# What is performance?

To better understand what we mean when we say that a program is *performing* well, let's take a look at a user story. In this book, we will use a fictitious person, namely Mr. Smith, Chief of Antarctica Department of Forestry. Mr. Smith is stationed in McMurdo Base, Antarctica, and he doesn't have much real work to do. He has already mapped all the forests in the vicinity of the station and half of the year it is too dark to be walking around and counting trees, anyway. That's why he spends most of his time behind a computer. And that's also why he is very grumpy when his programs are not performing well.

Some days he writes long documents analyzing the state of forests in Antarctica. When he is doing that, he wants the document editor to *perform* well. By that he actually means that the editor should work *fast enough* so that he doesn't feel any delay (or *lag*, as we call the delay when dealing with user input) while typing, preparing graphs, formatting tables, and so on.

In this scenario, performance simply means *working fast enough* and nothing else. If we speed up the operation of the document editor by a factor of two, or even by a factor of ten, that would make no noticeable improvement for our Mr. Smith. The document editor would simply stay *fast enough* as far as he is concerned.

The situation completely changes when he is querying a large database of all of the forests on Earth and comparing the situation across the world to the local specifics of Antarctica. He doesn't like to wait and he wants each database query to complete in as short a time as possible. In this case, performance translates to **speed**. We will make Mr. Smith a happier person if we find a way to speed up his database searches by a factor a ten. Or even a factor of five; or two. He will be happy with any speedup and he'd praise us up to the heavens.

After all this hard work, Mr. Smith likes to play a game. While the computer is thinking about a next move, a video call comes in. Mr. Smith knows he's in for a long chat and he starts resizing the game window so that it will share the screen with a video call application. But the game is thinking hard and is not processing user input and poor Mr. Smith is unable to resize it, which makes him unhappy.

In this example, Mr. Smith simply expects that the application's user interface will **respond** to his commands. He doesn't care if the application takes some time to find the next move, as long as he can do with the application what he wants to. In other words, he wants a user interface that doesn't **block**.

# Different types of speed

It is obvious from the previous example that we don't always mean the same thing when we talk about a program's speed. There is a **real speed**, as in the database example, and there is a **perceived speed**, hinted at in the document editor and game scenario. Sometimes we don't need to improve the program speed at all. We just have to make it not stutter while working (by making the user interface responsive at all times) and users will be happy.

We will deal with two types of performance in this book:

- Programs that react quickly to user input
- Programs that perform computations quickly

As you'll see, the techniques to achieve the former and the latter are somehow different. To make a program react quickly, we can sometimes just put a long operation (as was the calculation of the next move in the fictitious game) into a background thread. The code will still run as long as in the original version but the user interface won't be blocked and everybody will be happy.

To speed up a program (which can also help with a slowly-reacting user interface), we can use different techniques, from changing the algorithm to changing the code so that it will use more than one CPU at once to using a hand-optimized version, either written by us or imported from an external library.

To do anything, we have to know which part of the code is causing a problem. If we are dealing with a big legacy program, problematic part may be hard to find. In the rest of this chapter, we will look at different ways to locate such code. We'll start by taking an educated **guess** and then we'll improve that by **measuring** the code speed, first by using home-grown tools and then with a few different open source and commercial programs.

# Algorithm complexity

Before we start with the dirty (and fun) job of improving program speed, I'd like to present a bit of computer science theory, namely the **Big O** notation.

You don't have to worry, I will not use pages of mathematical formulas and talk about *infinitesimal asymptotics*. Instead, I will just present the essence of the Big O notation, the parts that are important to every programmer.

In the literature and, of course, on the web, you will see expressions such as *O(n)*, *O(n^2)*, *O(1)* and similar. This fancy-looking notation hides a really simple story. It tells us how much slower the algorithm will become if we increase the data size by a factor of **n**.

The *n^2* notation means "*n* to the power of two", or $n^2$. This notation is frequently used on the internet because it can be written with the standard ASCII characters. This book uses the more readable variant $O(n^2)$.

Let's say we have an algorithm with complexity of **O(n)**, which on average takes T seconds to process input data of size *N*. If we increase the size of the data by a factor of 10 (to *10\*N*), then the algorithm will (on average) also use 10 times more time (that is, *10\*T*) to process the data. If we process 1,000 times more data, the program will also run 1,000 times slower.

If the algorithm complexity is **O($n^2$)**, increasing the size of the data by a factor of 10 will cause the algorithm to run *$10^2$* or 100 times longer. If we want to process 1,000 times more data, then the algorithm will take *$1,000^2$* or a million times longer, which is quite a hit. Such algorithms are typically not very useful if we have to process large amounts of data.

Most of the time, we use the Big O notation to describe how the computation **time** relates to the input data size. When this is the case, we call the Big O notation **time complexity.** Nevertheless, sometimes the same notation is used to describe how much **storage** (memory) the algorithm is using. In that case, we are talking about a **space complexity**.

You may have noticed that I was using the word **average** a lot in the last few paragraphs. When talking about the algorithm complexity, we are mostly interested in the average behavior, but sometimes we will also need to know about the worst behavior. We rarely talk about best behavior because users don't really care much if the program is sometimes faster than average.

Let's look at an example. The following function checks whether a string parameter `value` is present in a string list:

```
function IsPresentInList(strings: TStrings; const value: string): Boolean;
var
  i: Integer;
begin
  Result := False;
  for i := 0 to strings.Count - 1 do
    if SameText(strings[i], value) then
      Exit(True);
end;
```

What can we tell about this function? The best case is really simple—it will find that the `value` is equal to `strings[0]` and it will exit. Great! The best behavior for our function is *O(1)*. That, sadly, doesn't tell us much as that won't happen frequently in practice.

The worst behavior is also easy to find. If the `value` is not present in the list, the code will have to scan all of the `strings` list before deciding that it should return `False`. In other words, the worst behavior is *O(n)*, if the *n* represents the number of elements in the list. Incidentally (and without proof), the average behavior for this kind of search is also *O(n)*.

 The Big O limits don't care about constant factors. If an algorithm would use *n/2* steps on average, or even just *0.0001 * n* steps, we would still write this down as *O(n)*. Of course, a *O(10 * n)* algorithm is slower than a *O(n)* algorithm and that is absolutely important when we fine-tune the code, but no constant factor *C* will make *O(C * n)* faster than *O(log n)* if *n* gets sufficiently large.

There are better ways to check whether an element is present in some data than searching the list sequentially. We will explore one of them in the next section, *Big O and Delphi data structures*.

While the function of *n* inside the *O()* notation can be anything, there are some *O* functions that appear constantly in standard programming problems. The following table shows those Big O limits and the most common examples of problems that belong to each class:

| Time complexity | Common examples of problems with that time complexity |
|---|---|
| *O(1)* | Accessing array elements |
| *O(log n)* | Search in an ordered list |
| *O(n)* | Linear search |
| *O(n log n)* | Quick sort (average behavior) |
| $O(n^2)$ | Quick sort (worst behavior), naive sort (bubblesort, insertion sort, selection sort) |
| $O(c^n)$ | Recursive Fibonacci, travelling salesman problem using dynamic programming (*c* is some numeric constant) |

If we care about program performance, then *O(1)* algorithms are of special interest to us as they present algorithms which don't get slower (at least not noticeably) when we increase the problem size. We'll see an example of such *O(1)* algorithms in the next section.

When we deal with algorithms that search in some datasets, we usually try to make them behave as *O(log n)*, not *O(n)*, as the former slows down much, much slower than the latter.

Another big class of problems deals with sorting the data. While the naive approaches sort in $O(n^2)$, better algorithms (such as mergesort and quicksort) need on average just *O(n log n)* steps.

The following image shows how the time complexity for these typical limits (we have used $2^n$ as an example of a more generic $c^n$) grows when we increase the problem size up to 20-fold:

Most frequently encountered Big-O limits

We can see that *O(1)* and *O(log n)* grow very slowly. While *O(n log n)* grows faster than *O(n)*, it also grows much slower than $O(n^2)$, which we had to stop plotting when data was increased nine-fold.

The $O(2^n)$ starts slowly and looks like a great solution for small data sizes (small *n*), but then it starts rising terribly fast, much faster than $O(n^2)$.

The following table shows how fast *O(n log n)* and $O(n^2)$ are growing if we compare them with *O(n)* and how quickly $O(2^n)$ explodes.

The **data** column shows the data size increase factor. The number 10 in this column, for example, represents input with 10 times more elements than in the original data:

| Data size | O(1) | O(log n) | O(n) | O(n log n) | O(n²) | O(2ⁿ) |
|-----------|------|----------|------|------------|-------|-------|
| 1 | 1 | 1 | 1 | 1 | 1 | 1 |
| 2 | 1 | 2 | 2 | 4 | 4 | 2 |
| 10 | 1 | 4 | 10 | 43 | 100 | 512 |
| 20 | 1 | 5 | 20 | 106 | 400 | 524,288 |
| 100 | 1 | 8 | 100 | 764 | 10,000 | $10^{29}$ |
| 300 | 1 | 9 | 300 | 2,769 | 90,000 | $10^{90}$ |

We can see from this table that *O(log n)* algorithms present a big improvement over *O(n)* algorithms (8 versus 100 times increase in time when data increases 100-fold). We can also see that the *O(2ⁿ)* quickly becomes completely unmanageable.

The last cell in this table is particularly interesting. There are different estimates for the number of elementary particles (electrons, protons, neutrons, and so on) in the visible universe, but they all lie somewhere around $10^{90}$. Suppose we have a computer which can solve an *O(2ⁿ)* in a reasonable time. If we would increase the input data by a factor of just 300, then we would need $10^{90}$ computers to solve the new problem in the same time. That is as much as the number of particles in the visible universe!

Don't use algorithms which have time complexity *O(2ⁿ)*. It won't end well.

# Big O and Delphi data structures

Delphi's **Run-Time Library (RTL)** contains many **data structures** (classes that are specifically designed to store and retrieve data), mostly stored in System.Classes and System.Generics.Collection units that greatly simplify everyday work. We should, however, be aware of their good and bad sides.

Every data structure in the world is seeking a balance between four different types of data access: accessing the data, inserting the data, searching for data, and deleting data. Some data structures are good in some areas, others in different ones, but no data structure in this world can make all four operations independent of data size.

When designing a program, we should therefore know what our needs are. That will help us select the appropriate data structure for the job.

The most popular data structure in Delphi is undoubtedly TStringList. It can store a large amount of strings and assign an object to each of them. It can—and this is important—work in two modes, **unsorted** and **sorted.** The former, which is a default, keeps strings in the same order as they were added while the latter keeps them alphabetically ordered.

This directly affects the speed of some operations. While accessing any element in a string list can always be done in a constant time (*O(1)*), adding to a list can take *O(1)* when the list is not sorted and *O(log n)* when the list is sorted.

Why that big difference? When the list is unsorted, Add just adds a string at its end. If the list is, however, sorted, Add must first find a correct insertion place. It does this by executing a *bisection search*, which needs *O(log n)* steps to find the correct place.

The reverse holds true for searching in a string list. If it is not sorted, IndexOf needs to search (potentially) the whole list to find an element. In a sorted list, it can do it much faster (again by using a bisection) in *O(log n)* steps.

We can see that TStringList offers us two options - either a fast addition of elements or a fast lookup, but not both. In a practical situation, we must look at our algorithm and think wisely about what we really need and what will behave better.

To sort a string list, you can call its Sort method or you can set its Sorted property to True. There is, however, a subtle difference that you should be aware of. While calling Sort sorts the list, it doesn't set its internal *is sorted* flag and all operations on the list will proceed as if the list is unsorted. Setting Sorted := True, on the other hand, does both - it sets the internal flag and calls the Sort method to sort the data.

To store any (non-string) data, we can use traditional TList and TObjectList classes or their more modern generic counterparts, TList<T> and TObjectList<T>. They all always work in an **unsorted** mode and so adding an element takes *O(1)* while finding and removing an element takes *O(n)* steps.

All provide a `Sort` function which sorts the data with a quicksort algorithm (*O(n log n)* on average) but only generic versions have a `BinarySearch` method, which searches for an element with a bisection search taking *O(log n)* steps. Be aware that `BinarySearch` requires the list to be sorted but doesn't make any checks to assert that. It is your responsibility to sort the list before you use this function.

If you need a very quick element lookup, paired with a fast addition and removal, then `TDictionary` is the solution. It has methods for adding (`Add`), removing (`Remove`) and finding a key (`ContainsKey` and `TryGetValue`) that, on average, function in a constant time, *O(1)*. Their worst behavior is actually quite bad, *O(n)*, but that will only occur on specially crafted sets of data that you will never see in practical applications.

I've told you before that there's no free lunch and so we can't expect that `TDictionary` is perfect. The big limitation is that we can't access the elements it is holding in a direct way. In other words, there is no `TDictionary[i]`. We can walk over all elements in a dictionary by using a `for` statement, but we can't access any of its elements directly. Another limitation of `TDictionary` is that it does not preserve the order in which elements were added.

Delphi also offers two simple data structures that mimic standard queue—`TQueue<T>`—and stack—`TStack<T>`. Both have very fast *O(1)* methods for adding and removing the data, but they don't offer any bells and whistles—there is no direct data access, we cannot search for data, and so on. We can only insert (`Enqueue` in queue or `Push` in stack) and remove (`Dequeue` and `Pop`) data.

To help you select the right tool for the job, I have put together a table showing the most important data structures and their most important methods, together with average and (when they differ from the average) worst-case time complexities:

| Data structure | Operation | Average | Worst |
|---|---|---|---|
| **TStringList** | Direct access | O(1) | |
| | Add | O(1) / O(*log n*) | |
| | Insert | O(1) | |
| | Delete | O(1) | |
| | IndexOf | O(*n*) / O(*log n*) | |
| | Sort | O(*n log n*) | O(*n²*) |
| **TList, TObjectList** | Direct access | O(1) | |

| | | | |
|---|---|---|---|
| | Add | O(1) | |
| | Insert | O(1) | |
| | Delete | O(1) | |
| | Remove | O(n) | |
| | IndexOf | O(n) | |
| | Sort | O($n \log n$) | O($n^2$) |
| **TList<T>, TObjectList<T>** | Direct access | O(1) | |
| | Add | O(1) | |
| | Insert | O(1) | |
| | Delete | O(1) | |
| | Remove | O($n$) | |
| | IndexOf | O($n$) | |
| | BinarySearch | O($\log n$) | |
| | Sort | O($n \log n$) | O($n^2$) |
| **TDictionary** | Direct access | Not possible | |
| | Add | O($1$) | O($n$) |
| | Remove | O($1$) | O($n$) |
| | TryGetValue | O($1$) | O($n$) |
| | ContainsKey | O($1$) | O($n$) |
| | ContainsValue | O(n) | |
| **TQueue<T>** | Direct access | Not possible | |
| | Enqueue | O(1) | |
| | Dequeue | O(1) | |
| **TStack<T>** | Direct access | Not possible | |
| | Push | O(1) | |
| | Pop | O(1) | |

*The table shows the time complexity of the most important operations on built-in Delphi data structures. Complexity for the worst case is only listed if it differs from the average complexity.*

# Data structures in practice

Enough with the theory already! I know that you, like me, prefer to talk through the code. As one program explains more than a thousand words could, I have prepared a simple demo project: `RandomWordSearch`.

This program functions as a very convoluted random word generator. When started, it will load a list of 370,101 English words from a file. It will also prepare three internal data structures preloaded with these words:

Random word generator

The program shows three buttons to the user. All three run basically the same code. The only difference is the test function which is passed to the centralized word generator as a parameter:

```
procedure TfrmRandomWordSearch.FindGoodWord(const wordTest:
TWordCheckDelegate);
var
  word: string;
  isWordOK: boolean;
  time: TStopwatch;
begin
  time := TStopwatch.StartNew;
  repeat
    word := GenerateWord;
    isWordOK := wordTest(word);
  until isWordOK or (time.ElapsedMilliseconds > 10000);
```

```
   if isWordOK then
      lbWords.ItemIndex := lbWords.Items.Add(Format('%s (%d ms)', [word,
time.ElapsedMilliseconds]))
   else
      lbWords.ItemIndex := lbWords.Items.Add('timeout');
end;
```

The core of the `FindGoodWord` method can be easily described:

1.  Generate a random word by calling `GenerateWord`.
2.  Call the test function `wordTest` on that word. If this function returns `False`, repeat *Step 1*. Otherwise show the word.

The code is a bit more complicated because it also checks that the word generation part runs for at most 10 seconds and reports a timeout if no valid word was found in that time.

The random word generator `GenerateWord` is incredibly simple. It just appends together lowercase English letters until the specified length (settable in the user interface) is reached:

```
function TfrmRandomWordSearch.GenerateWord: string;
var
  pos: integer;
begin
  Result := '';
  for pos := 1 to inpWordLength.Value do
    Result := Result + Chr(Ord('a') + Random(Ord('z') - Ord('a') + 1));
end;
```

Let's now check the data preparation phase. The not very interesting (and not shown here) `OnCreate` handler loads data from a file into a `TStringList` and calls the `LoadWords` method:

```
procedure TfrmRandomWordSearch.LoadWords(wordList: TStringList);
var
  word: string;
begin
  FWordsUnsorted := TStringList.Create;
  FWordsUnsorted.Assign(wordList);

  FWordsSorted := TStringList.Create;
  FWordsSorted.Assign(wordList);
  FWordsSorted.Sorted := True;

  FWordsDictionary := TDictionary<string,boolean>.Create(wordList.Count);
  for word in wordList do
    FWordsDictionary.Add(word, True);
```

```
end;
```

The first data structure is an unsorted `TStringList`, `FWordsUnsorted`. Data is just copied from the list of all words by calling the `Assign` method.

The second data structure is a sorted `TStringList`, `FWordsSorted`. Data is firstly copied from the list of all words. The list is then sorted by setting `FWordsSorted.Sorted :=`
`True`.

The last data structure is a `TDictionary`, `FWordsDictionary`. A `TDictionary` always stores **pairs** of keys and values. In our case, we only need the **keys** part as there is no data associated with any specific word, but Delphi doesn't allow us to ignore the **values** part and so the code defines the value as a `boolean` and always sets it to `True`.

Although the dictionaries can grow, they work faster if we can initially set the number of elements that will be stored inside. In this case that is simple—we can just use the length of the `wordList` as a parameter to `TDictionary.Create`.

The only interesting part of the code left is `OnClick` handlers for all three buttons. All three call the `FindGoodWord` method, but each passes in a different test function.

When you click on the **Unsorted list** button, the test function checks whether the word can be found in the `FWordsUnsorted` list by calling the `IndexOf` function. As we will mostly be checking non-English words (remember, they are just random strings of letters), this `IndexOf` will typically have to compare all 307,101 words before returning $-1$:

```
procedure TfrmRandomWordSearch.btnUnsortedListClick(Sender: TObject);
begin
  FindGoodWord(
    function (const word: string): boolean
    begin
      Result := FWordsUnsorted.IndexOf(word) >= 0;
    end);
end;
```

When you click on the **Sorted list** button, the test function calls `FWordsSorted.IndexOf`. As this `TStringList` is sorted, `IndexOf` will use a binary search that will need at most *log(307101) = 19* (rounded up) comparisons to find out that a word is not found in the list. As this is much less than 307.101, we can expect that finding words with this approach will be much faster:

```
procedure TfrmRandomWordSearch.btnSortedListClick(Sender: TObject);
begin
  FindGoodWord(
    function (const word: string): boolean
    begin
      Result := FWordsSorted.IndexOf(word) >= 0;
    end);
end;
```

A click on the last button, **Dictionary**, calls `FWordsDictionary.ContainsKey` to check if the word can be found in the dictionary, and that can usually be done in just one step. Admittedly, this is a bit of a slower operation than comparing two strings, but still the `TDictionary` approach should be faster than any of the `TStringList` methods:

```
procedure TfrmRandomWordSearch.btnDictionaryClick(Sender: TObject);
begin
  FindGoodWord(
    function (const word: string): boolean
    begin
      Result := FWordsDictionary.ContainsKey(word);
    end);
end;
```

If we use the terminology from the last section, we can say that the *O(n)* algorithm (unsorted list) will run much slower than the *O(log n)* algorithm (sorted list), and that the *O(1)* algorithm (dictionary) will be the fastest of them all. Let's check this in practice.

Start the program and click on the **Unsorted list** button a few times. You'll see that it typically needs few hundred milliseconds to a few seconds to generate a new word. As the process is random and dependent on CPU speed, your numbers may differ quite a lot from mine. If you are only getting *timeout* messages, you are running on a slow machine and you should decrease the **Word length** to 3.

If you increment the **Word length** to 5 and click the button again, you'll notice that the average calculation time will grow up to a few seconds. You may even get an occasional *timeout*. Increase it to 6 and you'll mostly be getting timeouts. We are clearly hitting the limits of this approach.

Prepare now to be dazed! Click on the **Sorted list** button (while keeping the **Word length** at 6) and words will again be calculated blazingly fast. On my computer, the code only needs 10 to 100 milliseconds to find a new word:

Testing with different word length and with first two algorithms

To better see the difference between a sorted list and a dictionary, we have to crank up the word length again. Setting it to 7 worked well for me. The sorted list needed from a few 100 milliseconds to a few seconds to find a new word while the dictionary approach mostly found a new word in under 100 milliseconds.

Increase the **Word length** to 8 and the sorted list will start to time out while the dictionary will still work. Our O(*1*) approach is indeed faster than the O(*log n*) code:

Comparing sorted list (first six words and the two after "timeout") with the dictionary approach (next five and last two).

While the knowledge of algorithms and their complexity is useful, it will not help in every occasion. Sometimes you already use the best possible algorithm but your program is still too slow. At such times, you'll want to find the slow parts of the program and speed them up with whatever trick possible. To do that, you have to find them first, which is the topic of the rest of this chapter.

# Mr. Smith's first program

While I was talking about theory and data structures and best practices, our friend Mr. Smith read everything about polar forests on the internet and then got really bored. In a moment of sheer panic—when he was thinking about watching videos of cute kittens for the whole polar night—he turned to programming. He checked various internet sources and decided that Delphi is the way to go. After all, he could use it to put together a new game for iOS *and* Android and make lots of money while waiting for the sun to show up!

As he didn't have any programming literature on the Antarctic base, he learned programming from internet resources. Sadly, he found most of his knowledge on Experts Exchange and Yahoo Answers and his programs sometimes reflect that.

As of this moment, he has written one working program (and by working I mean that it compiles), but he is not really sure what the program actually does. He only knows that the program is a bit slow and because of that he named it SlowCode.

His program is a console mode program which upon startup calls the Test method:

```
procedure Test;
var
  data: TArray<Integer>;
  highBound: Integer;
begin
  repeat
    Writeln('How many numbers (0 to exit)?');
    Write('> ');
    Readln(highBound);
    if highBound = 0 then
      Exit;

    data := SlowMethod(highBound);
    ShowElements(data);
  until false;
end;
```

That one, at least, is easy to grasp. It reads some number, passes it to something called SlowMethod (hmm, Mr. Smith really should work on naming techniques), and then passes the result (which is of type TArray<Integer>) to a method called ShowElements. When the user types in 0, the program exits.

Let's check the ShowElements function:

```
function SlowMethod(highBound: Integer): TArray<Integer>;
var
  i: Integer;
  temp: TList<Integer>;
begin
  temp := TList<Integer>.Create;
  try
    for i := 2 to highBound do
      if not ElementInDataDivides(temp, i) then
        temp.Add(i);
    Result := Filter(temp);
  finally
    FreeAndNil(temp);
  end;
end;
```

The code creates a list of integers. Then it iterates from a value 2 to the value that was entered by the user and for each value calls `ElementInDataDivides`, passing in the list and the current value. If that function returns `True`, the current value is entered into the list.

After that, `SlowMethod` calls the `Filter` method which does something with the list and converts it into an array of integers which is then returned as a function result:

```
function ElementInDataDivides(data: TList<Integer>; value: Integer):
boolean;
var
  i: Integer;
begin
  Result := True;
  for i in data do
    if (value <> i) and ((value mod i) = 0) then
      Exit;
  Result := False;
end;
```

The `ElementInDataDivides` function iterates over all the numbers in the list and checks if any element in the list divides the `value` (with the additional constraint that this element in the list must not be equal to the `value`).

Let's check the last part of the puzzle—the `Filter` function:

```
function Reverse(s: string): string;
var
  ch: char;
begin
  Result := '';
  for ch in s do
    Result := ch + Result;
end;
function Filter(list: TList<Integer>): TArray<Integer>;
var
  i: Integer;
  reversed: Integer;
begin
  SetLength(Result, 0);
  for i in list do
  begin
    reversed := StrToInt(Reverse(IntToStr(i)));
    if not ElementInDataDivides(list, reversed) then
    begin
      SetLength(Result, Length(Result) + 1);
      Result[High(Result)] := i;
```

```
      end;
    end;
  end;
```

This one again iterates over the list, reverses the numbers in each element (changes 123 to 321, 3341 to 1433, and so on) and calls `ElementInDataDivides` on the new number. If it returns `True`, the element is added to the returned result in a fairly inefficient way.

I agree with Mr. Smith—it is hard to tell what the program does. Maybe it is easiest to run it and look at the output:

It looks like the program is outputting prime numbers. Not all prime numbers, just some of them. (For example, 19 is missing from the list, and so is 23.) Let's leave it at that for the moment.

# Looking at code through the Big O eyes

We can tell more about the program, about its good and bad parts, if we look at it through the eyes of time complexity, in terms of the Big O notation.

We'll start where the code starts—in the `SlowMethod` method. It has a loop iterating from 2 to the user-specified upper bound, `for i := 2 to highBound do`. The size of our data, or *n*, is therefore equal to `highBound` and this `for` loop has time complexity of *O(n)*:

```
for i := 2 to highBound do
  if not ElementInDataDivides(temp, i) then
    temp.Add(i);
```

Inside this loop, the code calls `ElementInDataDivides` followed by an occasional `temp.Add`. The latter will execute in O(1), but we can't say anything about the `ElementInDataDivides` before we examine it.

This method also has a loop iterating over the `data` list. We can't guess how many elements are in this list, but in the short test that we just performed, we know that the program writes out 13 elements when processing values from 2 to 100:

```
for i in data do
  if (value <> i) and ((value mod i) = 0) then
    Exit;
```

For the purpose of this very rough estimation I'll just guess that the `for i in data do` loop also has a time complexity of O(*n*).

In `SlowMethod` we therefore have an O(*n*) loop executing another O(*n*) loop for each element, which gives us a O($n^2$) performance.

The `SlowMethod` then calls the `Filter` method which also contains O(*n*) for loop calling `ElementInDataDivides`, which gives us O($n^2$) complexity for this part:

```
for i in list do
begin
  reversed := StrToInt(Reverse(IntToStr(i)));
  if not ElementInDataDivides(list, reversed) then
  begin
    SetLength(Result, Length(Result) + 1);
    Result[High(Result)] := i;
  end;
end;
```

There's also a conversion to string, some operation on that string, and conversion back to the integer `StrToInt(Reverse(IntToStr(i)))`. It works on all elements of the list ($O(n)$) but in each iteration it processes all characters in the string representation of a number. As a length of the number is proportional to *log n*, we can say that this part has complexity of $O(n \log n)$, which can be ignored as it is much less than the $O(n^2)$ complexity of the whole method.

There are also some operations hidden inside `SetLength`, but at this moment we don't know yet what they are and how much they contribute to the whole program. We'll cover that area in `Chapter 4`, *Memory Management*.

The `SlowMethod` therefore consists of two parts, both with complexity $O(n^2)$. Added together, that would give us $2*n^2$, but as we ignore constant factors (that is, 2) in the Big O notation, we can only say that the time complexity of `SlowMethod` is $O(n^2)$.

So what can we say simply by looking at the code?

- The program probably runs in $O(n^2)$ time. It will take around 100 times longer to process 10,000 elements than 1,000 elements.
- There is a conversion from the integer to the string and back (`Filter`), which has complexity of only $O(n \log n)$ but it would still be interesting to know how fast this code really is.
- There's a time complexity hidden behind the `SetLength` call which we know nothing about.
- We can guess that most probably the `ElementInDataDivides` is the most time-consuming part of the code and any improvements in this method would probably help.
- Fixing the terrible idea of appending elements to an array with `SetLength` could probably speed up a program, too.

As the code performance is not everything, I would also like to inform Mr. Smith about a few places where his code is less than satisfactory:

- The prompt *How many numbers* is misleading. A user would probably expect it to represent the number of numbers outputted, while the program actually wants to know how many numbers to test.
- Appending to `TArray<T>` in that way is not a good idea. Use `TList<T>` for temporary storage and call its `ToArray` method at the end. If you need `TArray<T>`, that is. You can also do all processing using `TList<T>`.

- `SlowMethod` has two distinctive parts - data generation, which is coded as a part of `SlowMethod`, and data filtering, which is extracted in its own method, `Filter`. It would be better if the first part is extracted into its own method, too.
- Console program, really? Console programs are good for simple tests, but that is it. Learn VCL or FireMonkey, Mr. Smith!

We can now try and optimize parts of the code (`ElementInDataDivides` seems to be a good target for that) or, better, we can do some measuring to confirm our suspicions with hard numbers.

In a more complicated program (what we call a *real life*), it would usually be much simpler to measure the program performance than to do such analysis. This approach, however, proves to be a powerful tool if you are using it while designing the code. Once you hear a little voice nagging about the time complexities all the time while you're writing a code, you'll be on the way to becoming an excellent programmer.

# Don't guess, measure!

There is only one way to get a good picture about the fast and slow parts of a program—by measuring it. We can do it manually, by inserting time-measuring calls in the code, or we can use specialized tools. We have a name for measuring—**profiling**—and we call specialized tools for measuring **profilers**.

In the rest of this chapter, we'll look at different techniques of measuring the execution speed. First we will measure the now familiar program, `SlowCode`, with a simple software stopwatch and then we'll look at a few open source and commercial profilers.

Before we start, I'd like to point out a few basic rules that apply to all profiling techniques:

- Always profile **without** the debugger. The debugger will slow the execution in unexpected places and that will skew the results. If you are starting your program from the Delphi IDE, just press *Ctrl+Shift+F9* instead of *F9*.
- Try not to do anything else on the computer while profiling. Other programs will take the CPU away from the measured program which will make it run slower.
- Take care that the program doesn't wait for user action (data entry, button click) while profiling. This will completely skew the report.

- Repeat the tests a few times. Execution times will differ because Windows (and any other OS that Delphi supports) will always execute other tasks besides running your program.
- All the above especially holds for multithreaded programs, which is an area explored in Chapters 5 to 7.

# Profiling with TStopwatch

Delphi includes a helpful unit called System.Diagnostics, which implements a TStopwatch record. It allows us to measure time events with a better precision than 1 millisecond and has a pretty exhaustive public interface, as shown in the code fragment below:

```
type
  TStopwatch = record
  public
    class function Create: TStopwatch; static;
    class function GetTimeStamp: Int64; static;
    procedure Reset;
    procedure Start;
    class function StartNew: TStopwatch; static;
    procedure Stop;
    property Elapsed: TTimeSpan read GetElapsed;
    property ElapsedMilliseconds: Int64 read GetElapsedMilliseconds;
    property ElapsedTicks: Int64 read GetElapsedTicks;
    class property Frequency: Int64 read FFrequency;
    class property IsHighResolution: Boolean read FIsHighResolution;
    property IsRunning: Boolean read FRunning;
  end;
```

To use a stopwatch, you first have to create it. You can call TStopwatch.Create to create a new **stopped** stopwatch or TStopwatch.StartNew to create a new **started** stopwatch. As TStopwatch is implemented as a record, there's no need to destroy a stopwatch object.

When a stopwatch is started, it is measuring time. To start a stopwatch, call the Start method and to stop it, call the Stop method. The IsRunning property will tell you if the stopwatch is currently started. Call the Reset method to reset the stopwatch to zero.

The TStopwatch contains a few functions that return the currently measured time. The most precise of them is ElapsedTicks, but as there is no built-in (public) function to convert this into standard time units, this function is hard to use. My recommendation is to just use the ElapsedMilliseconds property which will give you elapsed (measured) time in milliseconds.

For a simple demo, this code will return 1,000 or a bit more:

```
function Measure1sec: int64;
var
  sw: TStopwatch;
begin
  sw := TStopwatch.StartNew;
  Sleep(1000);
  Result := sw.ElapsedMilliseconds;
end;
```

Let's now use this function to measure the SlowMethod method.

First, you have to add the System.Diagnostics unit to the uses list:

```
uses
  System.SysUtils,
  System.Generics.Collections,
  System.Classes,
  System.Diagnostics;
```

Next, you have to create this stopwatch inside SlowMethod, stop it at the end, and write out the elapsed time:

```
function SlowMethod(highBound: Integer): TArray<Integer>;
var
 // existing variables
 sw: TStopwatch;
begin
  sw := TStopwatch.StartNew;

  // existing code

  sw.Stop;
  Writeln('SlowMethod: ', sw.ElapsedMilliseconds, ' ms');
end;
```

We can use this code to verify the theory that `SlowCode` has time complexity $O(n^2)$. To do this, we have to measure the execution times for different counts of processed numbers (different values entered at the *How many numbers* prompt).

I did some testing for selected values from 10,000 to 1,000,000 and got the following numbers:

| Highest number | Execution time [ms] |
|---|---|
| 10,000 | 15 |
| 25,000 | 79 |
| 50,000 | 250 |
| 75000 | 506 |
| 100,000 | 837 |
| 250,000 | 4,515 |
| 500.000 | 15564 |
| 750,000 | 30,806 |
| 1,000,000 | 54,219 |

If you repeat the tests, you will of course measure different values, but the growth rate should be the same.

For a quick confirmation, I have plotted a **Scatter Chart** of this data in Excel and the result surely looks like a square function. To be more sure, I have added a **power trendline** which created a function in the form of $n^c$, where $c$ was a constant that Excel has calculated from the data. In the case of my specific measurements, this *fitting* function was $y = 10^{-6} * x^{1.7751}$, which is not that far from $x^2$:

Curve fitting in Excel (left) and Wolfram Alpha (right)

Next, I repeated this *curve fitting* process on the wonderful Wolfram Alpha (`www.wolframalpha.com`) where you can find a *Regression Calculator Widget,* a tool designed specifically for this task. I entered measurements into the widget and it calculated a fitting function of $4.76372\times10^{-8} * x^2 + 0.0064733 * x - 143.666$. If we ignore all unimportant factors and constants, the only part left is $x^2$. Another confirmation for our analysis!

Now we know how the program behaves in global terms, but we still have no idea of which part of the code is the slowest. To find that out, we also have to measure execution times of the `ElementInDataDivides` and `Filter` methods.

These two methods are called multiple times during the execution of the program so we can't just create and destroy a stopwatch each time `Filter` (for example) is executed. We have to create a global stopwatch, which is a bit inconvenient in this program because we have to introduce a global variable.

If you check the `SlowCode_Stopwatch` program, you'll see that it actually creates three global stopwatches, one for each of the functions that we want to measure:

```
var
  Timing_ElementInData: TStopwatch;
  Timing_Filter: TStopwatch;
  Timing_SlowMethod: TStopwatch;
```

All three stopwatches are created (but not started!) when the program starts:

```
Timing_ElementInData := TStopwatch.Create;
Timing_Filter := TStopwatch.Create;
Timing_SlowMethod := TStopwatch.Create;
```

When the program ends, the code logs elapsed time for all three stopwatches:

```
Writeln('Total time spent in SlowMethod: ',
  Timing_SlowMethod.ElapsedMilliseconds, ' ms');
Writeln('Total time spent in ElementInDataDivides: ',
  Timing_ElementInData.ElapsedMilliseconds, ' ms');
Writeln('Total time spent in Filter: ',
  Timing_Filter.ElapsedMilliseconds, ' ms');
```

In each of the three methods, we only have to *Start* the stopwatch at the beginning and *Stop* it at the end:

```
function Filter(list: TList<Integer>): TArray<Integer>;
  // existing variables
begin
  Timing_Filter.Start;

  // existing code

  Timing_Filter.Stop;
end;
```

The only tricky part is the `ElementInDataDivides` function which calls `Exit` as soon as one element divides the `value` parameter. The simplest way to fix that is to wrap the existing code in a `try .. finally` handler and to stop the stopwatch in the `finally` part:

```
function ElementInDataDivides(data: TList<Integer>; value: Integer):
boolean;
var
  i: Integer;
begin
  Timing_ElementInData.Start;
  try
    Result := True;
    for i in data do
      if (value <> i) and ((value mod i) = 0) then
        Exit;
    Result := False;
  finally
    Timing_ElementInData.Stop;
  end;
```

```
end;
```

If you run the program and play with it for a while and then exit, you'll get a performance report. In my case, I got the following result:

We now know that most of the time is spent in `ElementInDataDivides`, but we don't know how many calls to it were made directly from `SlowMethod` and how many from the `Filter` method. To find that out, we have to add two new global variables and some more code:

```
var
  Generate_ElementInData_ms: int64;
  Filter_ElementInData_ms: int64;

function SlowMethod(highBound: Integer): TArray<Integer>;
var
  i: Integer;
  temp: TList<Integer>;
begin
  Timing_SlowMethod.Start;
  temp := TList<Integer>.Create;
  try

    Timing_ElementInData.Reset;
    for i := 2 to highBound do
      if not ElementInDataDivides(temp, i) then
        temp.Add(i);
    Generate_ElementInData_ms := Generate_ElementInData_ms +
      Timing_ElementInData.ElapsedMilliseconds;

    Timing_ElementInData.Reset;
    Result := Filter(temp);
    Filter_ElementInData_ms := Filter_ElementInData_ms +
      Timing_ElementInData.ElapsedMilliseconds;
```

```
finally
  FreeAndNil(temp);
end;
Timing_SlowMethod.Stop;
end;
```

The code (which can be found in the `SlowCode_Stopwatch2` program) now resets the `Timing_ElementInData` stopwatch before the data generation phase and adds the value of the stopwatch to `Generate_ElementInData_ms` afterwards. Then it resets the stopwatch again for the `Filter` phase and adds the value of the stopwatch to `Filter_ElementInData_ms` afterwards.

At the end that will give us the cumulative execution time for `ElementInDataDivides` called directly from `SlowMethod` in `Generate_ElementInData_ms` and the cumulative execution time for `ElementInDataDivides` called from `Filter` in `Filter_ElementInData_ms`.

A test run with an upper bound of 100,000 produced the following output:

Now we can be really sure that almost all the time is spent in `ElementInDataDivides`. We also know that approximately 75% of the time it is called directly from `SlowMethod` and 25% of the time from the `Filter` method.

We are now ready to optimize the program. We can either improve the implementation to make it faster, or replace it with a faster algorithm, or both.

But first, let's see what *profilers* can tell us about our program.

# Profilers

Measuring the speed of a program by inserting special code into the program by hand is perfect if you want to measure a very specific part of the code, but becomes cumbersome if you don't know exactly which part of the program you should focus on. In such cases, it is best to use specialized software - profilers.

Profilers can measure all kinds of parameters. Sure, they are mostly used for measuring execution speed, at a method or even on a line level, but they can do much more. They can display the *call tree* - a graph showing how methods call one another. They can show memory usage in a program so you can quickly find the one method which is constantly eating the memory. They can show you the *coverage* of your tests so you can see which code was tested and which not. And much more.

They do that magic in two ways, by *sampling* or *instrumentation*.

Sampling profiling looks at the state of your program at regular intervals (for example, 100 times per second) and each time checks which line of the code is currently being executed. Statistically, it will predominantly *see* lines of code that are executed most of the time.

Sampling profiling will give us only a rough overview of behavior inside the program but it will do that without affecting the program speed, and because of that is excellent for taking a first look at some code.

Instrumenting profiles do their magic by changing—*instrumenting*—the code. They are, in fact, doing almost exactly the same kind of changing the code as we did by inserting the stopwatch calls.

There are two ways to do instrumentation. The profiler can change the source code or it can change the program binary. Source instrumenting profilers are rare because they are less safe to use (there's always the possibility that a compiler will mess up the source) and because you have to recompile the code after it is instrumented (modified by the profiler).

Most of the instrumenting profilers on the market modify the binary code, which is a bit more tricky to implement but doesn't require a recompilation and cannot destroy the source code.

The advantage of instrumentation over sampling is that the former can collect everything that is going on inside the program and not just a few samples here and there. The disadvantage is that instrumentation reduces the speed of the program. Although instrumenting profilers take extra care to optimize the code that is inserted into your program, executing this code in many instrumented methods can still take a long time.

The other problem is the amount of collected data. A short and fast method which is called 100,000 times in 1 second will generate 100,000 data samples in an instrumenting profiler and only 100 samples in a sampling profiler (provided that it samples the code 100 times a second).

Because of all that, instrumenting profilers are best used once we already know on which part(s) of the program we want to focus.

I'll end this chapter with an overview of four profilers, two open source and free (AsmProfiler and Sampling Profiler) and two commercial (AQTime and Nexus Quality Suite), to make it easier for you to choose the best fit for your situation. These four profilers are, of course, not your only options. If you need a very precise profiling of short methods, check out ProDelphi (`www.prodelphi.de`). And if you need a high-end tool that will not only profile your application but help it optimize to its fullest potential, take a look at Intel's VTune Amplifier (`software.intel.com/en-us/intel-vtune-amplifier-xe`).

# AsmProfiler

AsmProfiler is a 32-bit instrumenting and sampling profiler written by André Mussche. Its source, along with Windows exe, can be found at `https://github.com/andremussche/asmprofiler`. Although the latest version was released in 2016, it works well with the newest Delphi at the time of writing this book, 10.2 Tokyo.

The sampling and instrumenting profilers are used in a different way, so I'll cover them separately.

To use AsmProfiler you first have to unpack the release ZIP into some folder on your disk. That will create two subfolders—`Sampling` and `Instrumenting`. To start the sampling profiler, start `AsmProfiling_Sampling` from the `Sampling` folder and then click **Start profiling**.

AsmProfiler has two ways of starting a profiling session. You can start the program manually, click **Select process** in AsmProfiler, and select your program from the list of running processes. Alternatively, you can click **Select exe**, browse to the compiled EXE of your program, and then click **Start process now**, which will start the program or click **Start sampling** which will start the program and also start sampling the code.

The reasoning behind the two different ways of starting the program is that mostly you want to profile a specific part of the program, so you would load it into the profiler, navigate to the specific part, click **Start sampling**, do the required steps in your program, click **Stop sampling**, and analyze the results. Sometimes, however, you would want to profile the very startup of the program so you would want sampling to start immediately after your program is launched. The following screenshot shows the initial AsmProfiler screen:

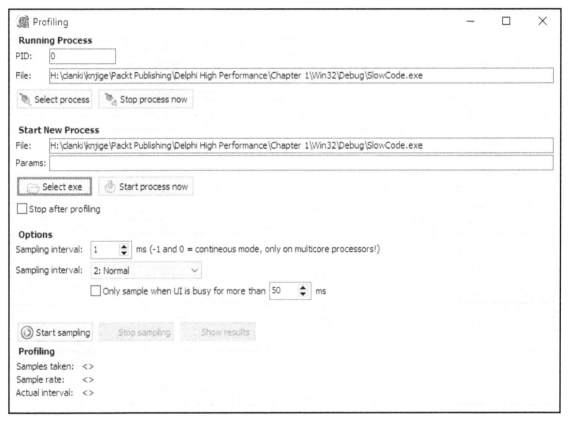

Starting profiling session in AsmProfiler

Sampling options can be configured in the **Options** group. You can set the sampling interval—how many milliseconds will pass between two samples. Setting this value to 4, for example, will generate 250 (1000/4) samples per second.

Setting the sampling interval to 0 enables a continuous sampling mode which still leaves some time to threads running on the same CPU. (The sampling code calls `Sleep(0)` between taking two samples.) Setting it to −1 causes the samples to be taken as fast as possible. In effect, AsmProfiler will use one CPU core for itself.

You can also set the priority of sample-taking threads from the default, **Normal**. I will discuss threads and priorities in `Chapter 5`, *Getting Started with the Parallel World*.

After you have taken the samples and clicked **Stop sampling**, click the **Show results** button to analyze the results.

If you want to compare your results with mine, here are steps to produce the results (as shown in the following screenshot):

1. Start AsmProfiler.
2. Click **Select exe** and select the `SlowCode.exe`.
3. Click **Start process now**.
4. Click **Start sampling**.
5. Enter `100,000` into the program.
6. Click **Stop sampling**.
7. Enter `0` into the program to exit.
8. Click **Show results**.
9. Click **Results** on the **Sampling Results** form.

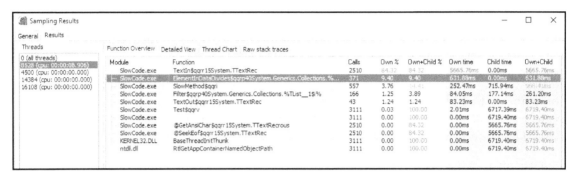

Result of a test run profiled with AsmProfiler's Sampling profiler

AsmProfiler displays results organized by threads, but it automatically highlights the main thread so you don't have to care about that detail if your program doesn't use multithreading.

In the result grid, it shows the module (main EXE or DLL), name of the function, how many times the code was found to be in this function, and times (absolute and percentage) the code spent in that function (**Own**), in all functions called from it (**Child**), and both in that function and in all functions called from it (**Own+Child**).

If we sort results by the time spent only in the function (**Own time**), we'll see that function `TextIn$qqrr15System.TTextRec` comes to the top. This a function that reads console input (in the `Readln` statement) and we can safely ignore it.

The next one on the list, `ElementInDataDivides$qqrp40...`, is the one that interests us. We can see that it was sampled 371 times (*Calls*) and that it needed 0.6 seconds to execute. If you switch to the **Detailed view** tab and select this function, you'll see in the **Parent calls (called by...)** panel that it was called 258 times from `SlowMethod` and 113 times from the `Filter` method. In reality, of course, it was called many more times, but most of them were not *seen* by the sampling profiler.

In this view, we can also see how many times each line of some method was hit, which will give us a good idea about where the program spends most of the time. Unfortunately, we cannot sort the data on different criteria:

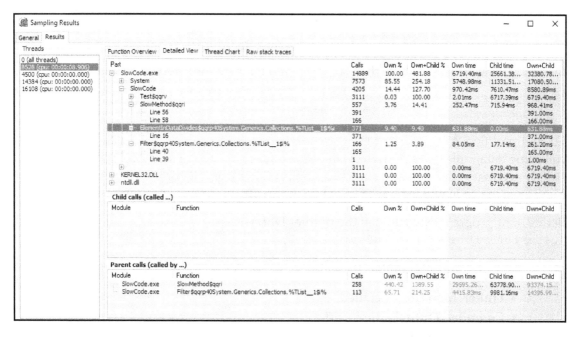

Detailed view showing information for each line of the program

The names of the methods in these outputs are very weird, but that is how the Delphi compiler calls these methods internally. The part after the $ encodes the parameter types. This process is called **name mangling** (and the part after $ is sometimes referred to as a **decoration**) and it enables us to use overloaded methods with the same name and different parameters—internally they all have different names.

For example, the function `SlowMethod(highBound: Integer)` is internally known as `SlowMethod$qqri`. The `qqr` part specifies the *fastcall* calling convention (it describes how parameters are passed to the function in registers and on stack) and `i` identifies one `integer` parameter.

AsmProfiler's instrumenting profiler requires a bit more work. Firstly, you have to copy `AsmProfiler.dll` from the `Instrumenting` subfolder into a folder on the Windows environment path or into the `exe` folder. Secondly, you have to copy `Instrumenting\API\_uAsmProfDllLoader.pas` into Delphi's library path, into your project's folder or add this folder to your project's search path.

Thirdly, you have to add the *_uAsmProfDllLoader* unit to your project and call the following code. This will show the profiler's main form on the screen:

```
if _uAsmProfDllLoader.LoadProfilerDll then
  _uAsmProfDllLoader.ShowProfileForm;
```

To start profiling, call `_uAsmProfDllLoader.StartProfiler(False);`. To stop collecting data, call `_uAsmProfDllLoader.StopProfiler;`. These two calls are not strictly necessary. You can also start and stop profiling from the profiler's user interface. Modifying the code will, however, give you more control over the profiling process.

Before your program exits, unload the profiler DLL with `_uAsmProfDllLoader.UnLoadProfilerDll;`.

Make sure that your program has the following compiler options correctly set:

- **Linker, Map file = detailed**
- **Compiler, Optimization = off**
- **Compiler, Stack frames = on**

The instrumenting profiler requires your program to process messages which makes it mostly useless when used in Mr. Smith's program, as it is spending most of the time inside a `Readln` call (and is not processing messages). As I still wanted to show you how this profiler works, I have converted `SlowCode` into a more modern VCL version, `SlowCode_VCL`.

At first I wanted to start/stop profiling right in `SlowMethod`:

```
function TfrmSlowCode.SlowMethod(highBound: Integer): TArray<Integer>;
var
  i: Integer;
  temp: TList<Integer>;
begin
  _uAsmProfDllLoader.StartProfiler(False);

  // existing code

  _uAsmProfDllLoader.StopProfiler;
```

```
end;
```

That attempt, however, misfired, as AsmProfiler didn't want to show profiling results for
`SlowCode`. It turned out to be better to move the start/stop calls out of this method and into
the method which calls `SlowCode`:

```
procedure TfrmSlowCode.btnTestClick(Sender: TObject);
var
  data: TArray<Integer>;
begin
  outResults.Text := '';
  outResults.Update;

  _uAsmProfDllLoader.StartProfiler(False);
  data := SlowMethod(inpHowMany.Value);
  _uAsmProfDllLoader.StopProfiler;

  ShowElements(data);
end;
```

A version of the program, ready for profiling with the AsmProfiler, is stored in
the `SlowCode_VCL_Instrumented` project. You will still have to download AsmProfiler
and store `AsmProfiler.dll` and `_uAsmProfDllLoader.pas` into appropriate places.

When you start the program, a small form will appear alongside the program's main form.
From here you can start and stop profiling, select items (methods) that should be profiled
(**Select items**), and open results of the profiling session (**Show results**):

AsmProfiler's instrumenting profiler

We are interested only in three methods, so click the **Select items** button, select the ElementInDataDivides, Filter and SlowMethod methods, and click **OK**:

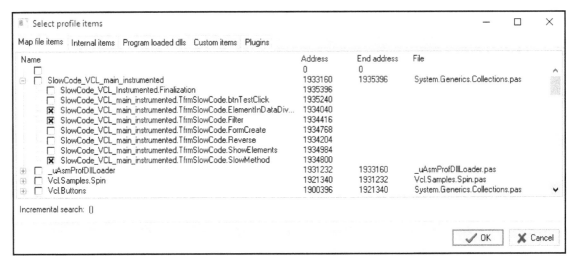

Selecting methods to be profiled

Next, enter 100000 into the **How many numbers** field and click the **Test** button. You don't have to start and stop the profiler, as the program will do that. When the values are calculated and displayed on the screen, click the **Show results** button. Don't close the profiled program as that would close the profiler form, too.

The result form of the instrumenting profiler is very similar to the equivalent form of the sampling profiler. The most interesting feature is the **Unit overview** tab, which combines detailed timing information and a call tree:

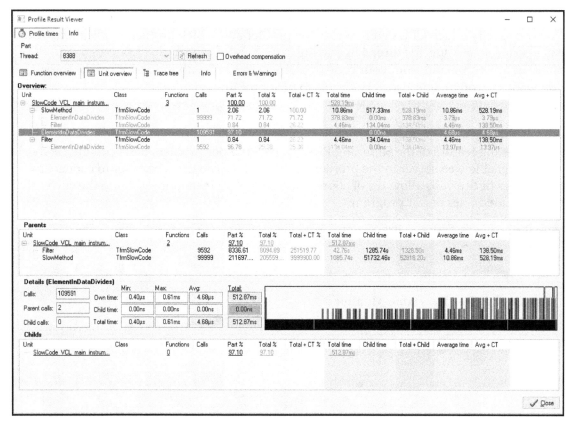

Unit overview display

We can see that `ElementInDataDivides` is in fact called 99,999 times directly from the `SlowMethod` and only 9,592 times from the `Filter` method, not 258 and 113 times, as shown by the sampling profiler.

AsmProfiler gives a good combination of a global overview and detailed analysis, although it is rough around the edges and requires more effort on your part than more polished commercial profilers.

# Sampling Profiler

The Sampling Profiler is, as its name suggests, a sampling profiler for Delphi, written by Eric Grange. You can find it at `www.delphitools.info`. Although it officially supports only Delphi 5 to XE4, it will function well with applications written in modern Delphis.

The strongest part of the Sampling Profiler is its configurability for multithreaded sampling. You can specify which CPUs will execute the profiler and which profiled application. You can also focus on a specific thread by issuing a `OutputDebugString('SAMPLING THREAD threadID')` command from your code (replace `threadID` with the real ID of the thread you want to profile). It is also very simple to turn profiling on or off by calling `OutputDebugString('SAMPLING ON')` and `OutputDebugString('SAMPLING OFF')`.

An interesting feature of the Sampling Profiler, which other profilers don't provide, is the ability to enable web server in the profiler. After that, we can use a browser to connect to the profiler (if firewalls allow us, of course) and we get an instant insight into the currently most executed lines of our program:

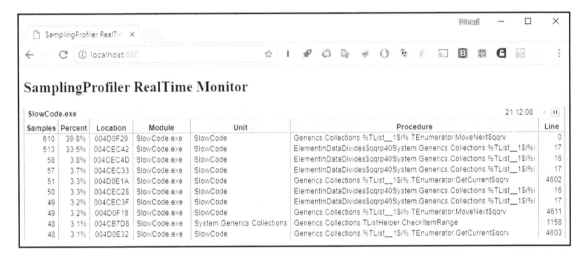

Live status view from remote location

The weakest point of the Sampling Profiler is its complete inability to select methods that are of interest to us. As we can see in the following screenshot, we get some methods from `Generics.Collections` mixed between methods from `SlowCode`. This only distracts us from our task—trying to find the slow parts of `SlowCode`.

Saying all that, I must admit that the display of profiling results is really neatly implemented. The results view is simple, clean, and easy to use:

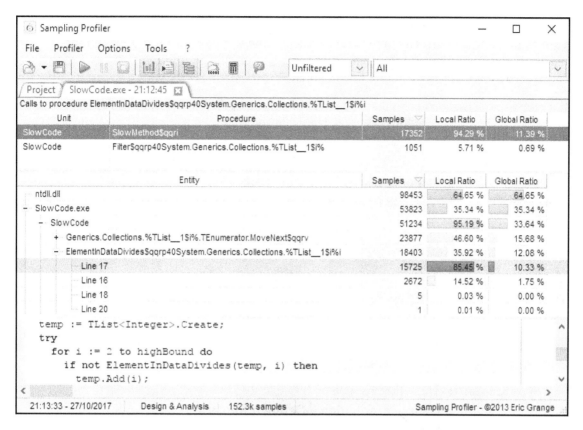

Simple and effective result view

The Sampling Profiler would be a perfect solution for occasional profiling if it would only allow us to select topics of interest.

# AQTime

AQTime is a performance and memory profiler for C/C++, Delphi, .NET, Java, and Silverlight, produced by SmartBear Software. It supports 32- and 64-bit applications and can be found at www.smartbear.com.

Previously, a special Standard version of AQTime was included with RAD Studio, C++Builder, and Delphi. This offer was only available for releases XE to XE8 and the licensing was not renewed after that. If you want to use AQTime with any other Delphi release, you have to buy AQTime Professional.

For testing purposes, you can install a trial version of AQTime Professional, which will only allow you to run five profiling sessions. Dedicate some time to testing and use your five sessions wisely!

AQTime Professional supports all Delphi version from 2006 to Tokyo and you can even use it in Visual Studio, which is a great plus for multiplatform developers. It contains a variety of profilers—from the *performance profiler* (binary instrumentating profiler) and the *sampling profiler*, to the *coverage profiler* (to see which parts of the program were executed) and more specific tools such as *BDE SQL profiler*, *static analysis* (a code analysis tool which is not really a profiler), and more.

It integrates nicely into the Delphi IDE but you can also use it as a standalone application. That gives you more flexibility during the profiling and result analysis and that's why I also used the standalone AQTime Professional for the examples.

To prepare your program for profiling, make sure that the following compiler options are set:

- **Compiler, Stack frames = on**
- **Compiler, Debug information = Debug information**
- **Compiler, Local symbols = true**
- **Linker, Debug information = true**

In order for AQTime to be able to find the source file for your project, you have to specify a search path. Go to **Options** | **Options**, then select **General** | **Search directory**, and add all the folders with your source files.

Next you can choose to profile all units, but unless you are using a sampling profiler this will slow down the execution in a typical program a lot. It is better to select just a few units or, as in our example, just a few methods.

The easiest way to do that is to create a new *profiling area* and the easiest way to do that is to select one or more methods in the left tree (use *Shift+click* and *Ctrl+click*), then right-click and select **Add selected to | New profiling area**. After that you can add additional methods to that profiling area by right-clicking and selecting **Add selected to | Existing profiling area**, or simply with drag-and-drop.

When creating a new profiling area, you also have to choose whether to profile on a method or on a line level by checking or unchecking the **Collect info about lines** checkbox:

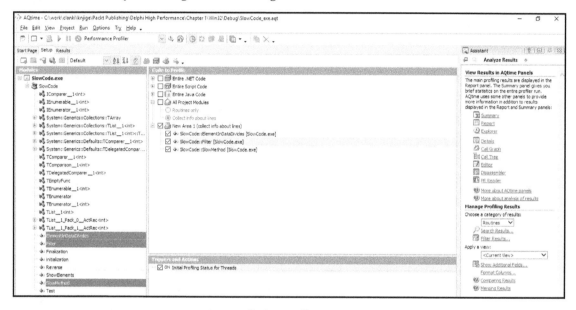

Creating new profiling area

Then start the program from AQTime—or select the **AQTime | Run with profiling** menu from Delphi, do the necessary steps you want to profile, and exit. AQTime will show the profiling results. Similarly to all other profilers, it will show a grid with measured methods, net time spent in each, time with children, and a **hit count**—an indicator showing how many times the method executed.

More interesting info is hiding in the lower panel. There is a very detailed *Call Graph*, which displays a call tree for the selected method, and a very useful *Editor* panel, which shows the source together with the *hit count* information for each line:

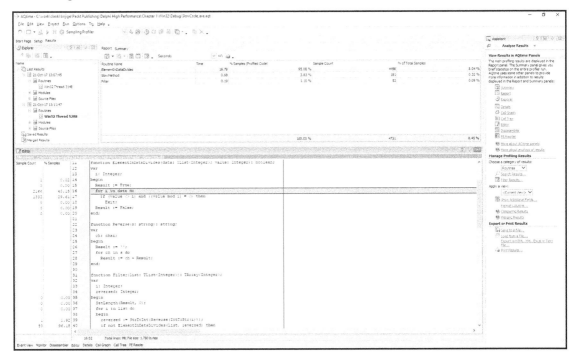

Editor view showing hit count for instrumented methods

AQTime is a great tool provided that you stay away from the very limited Standard edition and go directly for the Professional.

# Nexus Quality Suite

**Nexus Quality Suite** (**NQS**) is a successor to the long-defunct TurboPower's SleuthQA, published by NexusQA Pty Ltd. It supports 32- and 64-bit applications written in Delphi from 5 to 10.2 Tokyo. You can find it at www.nexusdb.com.

The trial version has fewer limitations than AQTime's. Some functions are disabled and some are limited in the quantity of collected data. Still, the program is not so limited that you wouldn't be able to test it out.

NQS integrates into Delphi's *Tools* menu and extends it with all the profilers it brings to Delphi. Of the most interest to us are **Method Timer**, an instrumenting profiler working at a method level, and **Line Timer**, an instrumenting profiler working at a line level. There is also a **Block Timer**, an instrumenting profiler working on a block level (a `for` loop, for example), which was not working correctly at the time of writing this book and so I wasn't able to test it. That's really bad luck, as there are no other profilers working on a block level and it would be really interesting to compare it with more standard approaches.

A few other tools are also interesting from the profiling viewpoint. **Coverage Analyst** will help you analyze code coverage, which is an important part of unit testing. After all, you definitely want to know whether your unit tests test all of the methods in a unit or not.

Also interesting is **CodeWatch**, which hunts for bugs in the code by looking for memory and resource leaks.

All these profilers, with the exception of CodeWatch, are available in 32-bit and 64-bit versions, although the 64-bit operation is not as stable as in the 32-bit counterparts. I was only able to use Line Timer in 32-bit mode, for example, while Method Timer worked flawlessly in 32-bit and 64-bit modes.

Both Method Timer and Line Timer require no special preparation. You just have to have debug information turned on in the linker options.

When you start the Method Timer, a profiler window opens. Click on the **Routines** button to select methods to profile. To change the profiling status of a method, double-click its name or right-click and select **Profile Status | Enable Profile Status For Selected**.

When you are done, press *F9* to start the program, go through the steps that you want to profile, and exit the program.

The program will then display basic timing information including net time per method and *gross time* (what other programs call "time with children"). If you click on a method, the lower two panes will display information about methods that called the current method and methods that were called from the current method.

If you double-click on a method, another window will appear showing the source code for the selected method but without any information about the profiling results:

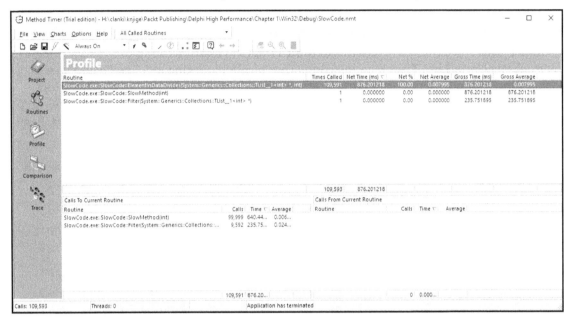

Method Timer result window

Line Timer has a similar user interface. First you select the methods to be profiled in the *Routines* view, then you run the program, and at the end examine the results in the **Line Times** window.

This profiler has a display that is a bit different from other profilers that support line-level profiling. It is not grouped by methods, but by line numbers. This gives us an immediate overview of the most critical part of the code, but is hard to integrate into a bigger picture.

As in the Method Timer, a double-click on a line in the results grid opens up an editor window which displays the source code, together with the time spent in each profiled line and the number of times this line was executed:

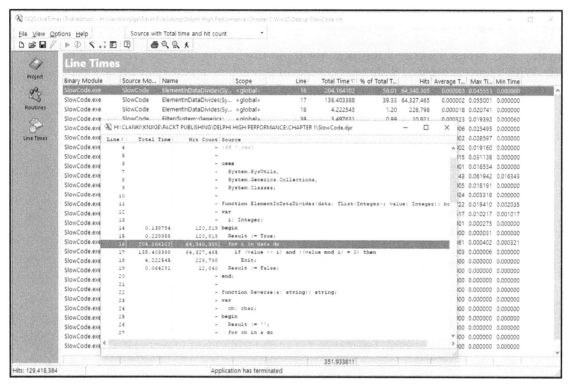

Line Timer with built-in code display

Nexus Quality Suite is a nice set of tools and we can only hope that its stability will improve with future releases.

# Summary

This chapter provided a broad overview of the topics we'll be dealing with in this book. We took a look at the very definition of performance. Next we spent some time describing the Big O notation for describing time and space complexity and we used it in a simple example.

In the second part of the chapter, we looked into the topic of profiling. We used a manual approach and specialized tools—profilers—to find the slowest part of a simple program.

In the next chapter, I'll briefly return to the topic of selecting the correct algorithm for the job. With a few examples, I'll show you how an algorithm can make or break a program's performance.

# 2
# Fixing the Algorithm

In the previous chapter, we explored the concept of *performance* and looked at different scenarios where we would like to make the program faster. The previous chapter was largely theoretical, but now is the time to look at it in a more practical way.

There are two main approaches to speeding up a program:

- Replace the algorithm with a better one.
- Fine-tune the code so that it runs faster.

I spent lots of time in the previous chapter discussing the *time complexity* simply to make it clear that a difference between two algorithms can result in impressive speed-up. It can be much more than a simple constant factor (such as a 10-times speed-up). If we go from an algorithm with bad time complexity (say, $O(n^2)$) to an algorithm with a better behavior ($O(n \log n)$, for example), then the difference in speed becomes more and more noticeable when we increase the size of the data.

Saying all that, it should not be surprising that I prefer the first approach (fixing the algorithm) to the second one (fine-tuning the code). To continue this point, this chapter will deal with several practical examples on speeding up the code by changing the algorithm.

Firstly, we will look at user interfaces. As we can't speed up VCL or Windows by fine-tuning the code (simply because we cannot modify that code), any speed-up in user interface responsiveness can only be a result of a better algorithm.

After that, I'll introduce the concept of *caching*. This approach can help you when everything else fails. Maybe it is not possible to change an algorithm, but introducing a cache of frequently-calculated values can still improve the code speed drastically.

As implementing a fast cache is quite a tricky business, I'll also present a generic cache class which you can use freely in your own code.

Before concluding the chapter, I'll look at Mr. Smith's `SlowCode` example and try to speed it up by implementing a better algorithm.

We will cover the following topics in this chapter:

- Writing responsive user interfaces
- How to update VCL and FMX controls without waiting
- Speeding up functions by introducing caching
- How to implement a reusable generic caching class
- How to analyze and improve an unknown algorithm

# Responsive user interfaces

A user's first contact with any program is always the user interface. A good UI can make or break a program. Leaving the user interface design aside (as I am not qualified to speak about that), I will focus on just one fact.

Users hate user interfaces that are not **responsive**.

In other words, every good user interface must react quickly to a user's input, be that a keyboard, mouse, touchpad, or anything else.

What are the tasks that can make a user interface unresponsive? Basically, they all fall into one of two categories:

1. A program is running a slow piece of code. While it is running, the UI is not responding.
2. Updating the user interface itself takes a long time.

The problems from the first category fall into two subsets—functions that have non-blocking (asynchronous) alternative and functions that don't.

Sometimes we can replace the slow function with another one that runs *asynchronously*. For example, instead of using a standard function for reading from a file, we can use the Windows Asynchronous File I/O API. File reading will then occur in parallel with our program and we will be notified of successful or unsuccessful reads via some other mechanism.

Often, however, this is not possible (there is no alternative for the slow function) or the asynchronous version is too complicated to implement. In that case, we can execute the slow code in a thread. This will be covered in chapters 5 to 7.

An excellent candidate for the multithreaded approach is the file reading example. True, Windows offers an asynchronous API for that, but it is quite complicated and tricky to implement correctly. Pushing a read operation into a thread is simpler **and** cross-platform compatible, if that is important for your application.

The second category (updating the UI takes a long time) is typically solved with a simple solution: *Do less updating!* Delphi/Windows controls are typically very fast and they only fail when we want them to do too many operations in a short time.

We will now focus on that category. I'll show a few examples of overabundant updates and give solutions for faster code.

# Updating a progress bar

Almost any change to VCL controls can cause one or more Windows messages to be sent to the operating system. That takes time, especially as the program waits for the operating system to process the message and return an answer. This can happen even if nothing has changed in the user interface.

The next demonstration will show how an abundance of messages can slow down the execution speed. I must admit that the code in the ProgressBar demo is a bit contrived. Still, I assure you that I have seen similar code running in production.

This demo simulates reading a large file block by block. (The code doesn't really open and read the file; it just runs a loop which would do the reading.) For each read block, a progress bar is updated.

For speed comparison, this progress bar update is done in two ways. In the first, slow approach, the Max property of the progress bar is set to the size of the file we are reading. After each block, the progress bar's Position is set to the number of bytes read so far:

```
function TfrmProgressBar.Test0To2G: Integer;
var
  total: Integer;
  block: Integer;
  sw: TStopwatch;
begin
  sw := TStopwatch.StartNew;
  ProgressBar1.Max := CFileSize;
  ProgressBar1.Position := 0;

  total := 0;
  while total < CFileSize do begin
```

```
    block := CFileSize - total;
    if block > 1024 then
      block := 1024;
    // reading 'block' bytes
    Inc(total, block);

    ProgressBar1.Position := total;
    ProgressBar1.Update;
  end;
  Result := sw.ElapsedMilliseconds;
end;
```

This code runs slow for two reasons. Firstly, setting the `Position` property sends a message `PBM_SETPOS` to Windows and that is a relatively slow operation when compared with non-graphical program code. Secondly, when we call `Update`, Windows API function `UpdateWindow` gets called. This function repaints the progress bar even if its position didn't change and that takes even more time. As all this is called 1,953,125 times it adds up to a considerable overhead.

The second, faster approach, sets `Max` to 100. After each block, the progress is calculated in *percentage* with `currPct := Round(total / CFileSize * 100);`.
The `Position` property is updated only if this percentage differs from the current progress bar's position.

As reading the `Position` property also sends one message to the system, the current position is stored in a local variable, `lastPct`, and a new value is compared to it:

```
function TfrmProgressBar.Test0To100: Integer;
var
  total: Integer;
  block: Integer;
  sw: TStopwatch;
  lastPct: Integer;
  currPct: Integer;
begin
  sw := TStopwatch.StartNew;
  ProgressBar1.Max := 100;
  ProgressBar1.Position := 0;
  lastPct := 0;

  total := 0;
  while total < CFileSize do begin
    block := CFileSize - total;
    if block > 1024 then
      block := 1024;
    // reading 'block' bytes
```

```
    Inc(total, block);

    currPct := Round(total / CFileSize * 100);
    if currPct > lastPct then
    begin
      lastPct := currPct;
      ProgressBar1.Position := currPct;
      ProgressBar1.Update;
    end;
  end;
  Result := sw.ElapsedMilliseconds;
end;
```

File size is set to **2,000,000,000** bytes, or 1.86 GB. That is a lot, but completely reasonable for a video file or database storage. The block is set to 1024 to amplify the problem. With a more reasonable size of 65536 bytes, the difference is less noticeable.

As you can see, the second example contains more code and is a bit more complex. The result of those few additional lines is, however, more than impressive.

When you start the test program and click on a button, it will first run the slow code followed by the fast code. You will see a noticeable difference in display speed. This is also confirmed by the measurements:

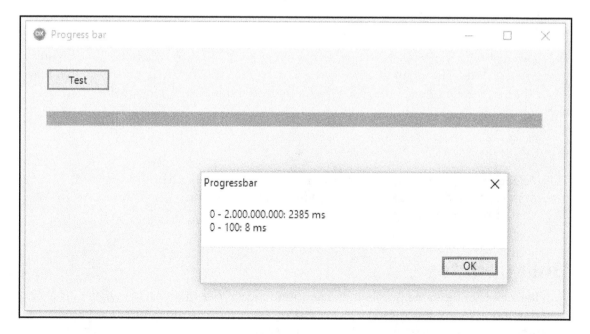

If you ran the demo code, you have probably noticed that the message showing the timing results is displayed *before* the progress bar finishes its crawl towards the full line. This is caused by a feature introduced in Windows Vista.

In Windows XP and before, updates to the progress bar were immediate. If you set Max to 100, Position to 0 and then a bit later updated Position to 50, the progress bar display would jump immediately to the middle. Since Vista, every change to the progress bar is animated. Changing Position from 0 to 50 results in an animation of the progress bar going from the left side to the middle of the control.

This makes for a nicer display but sometimes—as in our example—causes weird program behavior. As far as I know, there is only one way to work around the problem.

When I said that *every* change results in an animation, I lied a bit. In reality, animation is only triggered if you *increase* the position. If you *decrease* it, the change is displayed immediately.

We can therefore use the following trick. Instead of setting the Position to the desired value—ProgressBar1.Position := currPct;—we do that in two steps. Firstly we set it a bit too high (this causes the animation to start) and then we correctly position it to the correct value (this causes an immediate update):

```
ProgressBar1.Position := currPct+1;
ProgressBar1.Position := currPct;
```

This leaves us with the problem of forcing the progress bar to display a full line when all processing is done. The simplest way I can find is to decrease the Max property so that it is lower than the current Position. That also causes an immediate update to the progress bar:

```
ProgressBar1.Position := ProgressBar1.Max;
ProgressBar1.Max := ProgressBar1.Max - 1;
```

This technique of minimizing the number of changes also applies to multithreaded programs, especially when they want to update the user interface. I will return to it in Chapter 7, *Exploring Parallel Practices*.

# Bulk updates

Another aspect of the same problem of overabundance of messages occurs when you want to add or modify multiple lines in a TListBox or TMemo. The demonstration program, BeginUpdate, demonstrates the problem and shows possible solutions.

Let's say we have a listbox and we want to populate it with lots of lines. The demo program displays 10,000 lines, which is enough to show the problem.

A naive program would solve the problem in two lines:

```
for i := 1 to CNumLines do
  ListBox1.Items.Add('Line ' + IntToStr(i));
```

This, of course, works. It is also unexpectedly slow. 10,000 lines is really not much for modern computers so we would expect this code to execute very quickly. In reality, it takes 1.4 seconds on my test machine!

We could do the same with a TMemo. The result, however, is a lot more terrible:

```
for i := 1 to CNumLines do
  Memo1.Lines.Add('Line ' + IntToStr(i));
```

With the memo we can see lines appear one by one. The total execution time on my computer is a whopping 12 seconds!

This would make both listbox and memo unusable for displaying a large amount of information. Luckily, this is something that the original VCL designers anticipated, so they provided a solution.

If you look into the code, you'll see that both TListBox.Items and TMemo.Lines are of the same type, TStrings. This class is used as a base class for TStringList and also for all graphical controls that display multiple lines of text.

The TStrings class also provides a solution. It implements methods BeginUpdate and EndUpdate, which turn visual updating of a control on and off. While we are in *update* mode (after BeginUpdate was called), visual control is not updated. Only when we call EndUpdate will Windows redraw the control to the new state.

BeginUpdate and EndUpdate calls can be nested. Control will only be updated when every BeginUpdate is paired with an EndUpdate:

```
ListBox1.Items.Add('1');   // immediate redraw
ListBox1.BeginUpdate;      // disables updating visual control
ListBox1.Items.Add('2');   // display is not updated
ListBox1.BeginUpdate;      // does nothing, we are already in *update* mode
ListBox1.Items.Add('3;);   // display is not updated
ListBox1.EndUpdate;        // does nothing, BeginUpdate was called twice
ListBox1.Items.Add('4');   // display is not updated
ListBox1.EndUpdate;        // exits update mode, changes to ListBox1 are
                           // displayed on the screen
```

Adding `BeginUpdate`/`EndUpdate` to existing code is very simple. We just have to wrap them around existing operations:

```
ListBox1.Items.BeginUpdate;
for i := 1 to CNumLines do
  ListBox1.Items.Add('Line ' + IntToStr(i));
ListBox1.Items.EndUpdate;

Memo1.Lines.BeginUpdate;
for i := 1 to CNumLines do
  Memo1.Lines.Add('Line ' + IntToStr(i));
Memo1.Lines.EndUpdate;
```

If you click on the second button in the demo program you'll see that the program reacts much faster. Execution times on my computer were 48 ms for `TListBox` and 671 ms for `TMemo`. This second number still seems suspicious. Why does `TMemo` need 0.7 seconds to add 10,000 lines if changes are not painted on the screen?

To find an answer to that we have to dig into VCL code, into the `TStrings.Add` method:

```
function TStrings.Add(const S: string): Integer;
begin
  Result := GetCount;
  Insert(Result, S);
end;
```

Firstly, this method calls `GetCount` so that it can return the proper index of appended elements. Concrete implementation in `TMemoStrings.GetCount` sends two Windows messages even when the control is in the *updating* mode:

```
Result := SendMessage(Memo.Handle, EM_GETLINECOUNT, 0, 0);
if SendMessage(Memo.Handle, EM_LINELENGTH, SendMessage(Memo.Handle,
  EM_LINEINDEX, Result - 1, 0), 0) = 0 then Dec(Result);
```

After that, `TMemoStrings.Insert` sends three messages to update the current selection:

```
if Index >= 0 then
begin
  SelStart := SendMessage(Memo.Handle, EM_LINEINDEX, Index, 0);
  // some code skipped ... it is not executed in our case
  SendMessage(Memo.Handle, EM_SETSEL, SelStart, SelStart);
  SendTextMessage(Memo.Handle, EM_REPLACESEL, 0, Line);
end;
```

All that causes five Windows messages to be sent for each appended line and that slows the program down. Can we do it better? Sure!

To speed up `TMemo`, you have to collect all updates in some secondary storage, for example in a `TStringList`. At the end, just assign the new memo state to its `Text` property and it will be updated in one massive operation.

The third button in the demo program does just that:

```
sl := TStringList.Create;
for i := 1 to CNumLines do
  sl.Add('Line ' + IntToStr(i));
Memo1.Text := sl.Text;
FreeAndNil(sl);
```

This change brings execution speed closer to the listbox. My computer needed only 75 ms to display 10,000 lines in a memo with this code.

An interesting comparison can be made by executing the same code in the `FireMonkey` framework. Graphical controls in `FireMonkey` are not based directly on Windows controls, so effects of `BeginUpdate/EndUpdate` may be different.

The program `BeginUpdateFMX` in the code archive does just that. I will not go through the whole process again, but just present the measurements. All times are in milliseconds:

| framework | update method | TListBox | TMemo |
|-----------|---------------|----------|-------|
| **VCL** | direct update | 1444 | 12231 |
| | BeginUpdate | 48 | 671 |
| | Text | N/A | 75 |
| **FireMonkey** | direct update | 8760 | 406 |
| | BeginUpdate | 44 | 137 |
| | Text | N/A | 131 |

We can see that `BeginUpdate/EndUpdate` are also useful in the `FireMonkey` framework.

> If a class implements `BeginUpdate/EndUpdate`, use it when doing bulk updates.

In the next part, we'll see how we can replace a `TListBox` with an even faster solution if we are programming with the VCL framework.

# Virtual display

A long time ago Mike Lischke wrote a great Delphi component—Virtual TreeView. He stopped supporting it a long time ago, but the component found a new sponsor and a place on GitHub: `https://github.com/Virtual-TreeView`.

Virtual TreeView supports the VCL framework in Delphi XE3 and later. There are also versions of code that support older Delphis, but you'll have to look around for them. To use it, you have to download the source and recompile two included packages. That will add three new components to Delphi. This example will use the most useful of them, `TVirtualStringTree`.

Alternatively, you can install Virtual TreeView with the Delphi's GetIt Package Manager if you are using Delphi XE8 or newer.

The `VirtualTree` demo compares `TListBox` with `TVirtualStringTree` where the latter is used in different ways. Although `TVirtualStringTree` is very flexible and designed to display tree structures, we can also use it as a very fast listbox, as I will do in this example. To use it as a listbox, you should **remove** options `toShowRoot` and `toShowTreeLines` from the component's `TreeOptions.PaintOptions` property.

Before you start using Virtual TreeView, go through the included demos. They show all the power of this component.

This demo compares two different modes of operation. One is adding lots of lines in one operation. We already know that we should use `BeginUpdate/EndUpdate` in this case.

The other mode is adding just one line to the list. As this is hard to measure precisely, the operation is repeated 100 times.

Virtual TreeView is different from other components included with Delphi. It operates on a *view/model* principle. The component itself just displays the data (presents a *view* on the data) but doesn't store it internally. Data itself is stored in a storage that we have to maintain (a *model*). Virtual TreeView only stores a short reference that helps us access the data.

The first thing that we must do before we can use the component is to decide how large this *reference to data* is and set the `NodeDataSize` property accordingly.

Typically, we'll use an integer index (4 bytes), or an object or interface (4 bytes on Win32 and 8 bytes on Win64). We can also store larger quantities of data in this area, but that kind of defeats the view/model separation principle. In this example, I'll use a simple integer so NodeDataSize is set to 4.

The simplest way to use TVirtualStringTree is to use the AddChild method to add a new *node* (display line) and pass a *user data* (reference to model) as a parameter:

```
VirtualStringTree1.BeginUpdate;
for i := 1 to 10000 do begin
  idx := FModel1.Add('Line ' + IntToStr(i));
  VirtualStringTree1.AddChild(nil, pointer(idx));
end;
VirtualStringTree1.EndUpdate;
```

The code uses global FModel1: TStringList for data storage. It firstly adds the data to the model FModel1.Add and sets the index of this data (idx) as user data for the newly-created node (AddChild).

The first parameter to AddChild is a reference to the node's parent. As we are not displaying a tree structure but a list, we simply set it to nil (meaning that there is no parent). The second parameter represents user data. AddChild supports only pointer user data so we have to cast our parameter accordingly.

We also have to take care of retrieving the data from the model so it can be displayed on the screen. For that, we have to write OnGetText event handler. This event is called once for each column of each **visible** line. It is not called for lines that are not visible on the screen.

The code must firstly call Node.GetData to get the *user data* associated with the node. To be more precise, GetData returns a **pointer** to user data. As we know that our user data is just an integer, we can cast this pointer to PInteger to access the value (index into the FModel1 string list):

```
procedure TfrmVTV.VirtualStringTree1GetText(Sender: TBaseVirtualTree;
  Node: PVirtualNode; Column: TColumnIndex; TextType: TVSTTextType;
  var CellText: string);
begin
  CellText := FModel1[PInteger(Node.GetData)^];
end;
```

If you run the demonstration program and click the **Add 10.000 lines** button, you'll see that listbox needs more time for the operation (68 ms in my case) than Virtual TreeView (16 ms). Quite nice!

Clicking the second button, **Add 1 line 100 times**, shows something completely different. In this case, listbox is a lot faster (17 ms) than the Virtual TreeView (184 ms).

I must admit that I didn't expect that so I did some digging around. As it turns out, TVirtualStringTree **sorts** its data on each call to AddChild (unless we called BeginUpdate before that!) This may be useful if you are using a multi-column view where data can be sorted on the selected column, but in our case it only destroys the performance.

The fix for that is very simple. Just remove the toAutoSort option from the component's TreeOptions.AutoOptions property.

I cleared this flag in the second TVirtualStringTree and the result is obvious. Adding 100 lines now takes 17 ms instead of 184 ms and is on par with the listbox.

The third TVirtualStringTree pushes the whole virtual aspect to the max. Instead of initializing nodes in code (by calling AddChild), we just tell the component how many nodes it must display by setting the RootNodeCount property and the component will call the OnInitNode event handler for each node that is currently **visible on the screen**. In this mode, not only painting but the initialization is executed on demand!

```
for i := 1 to 10000 do
  FModel3.Add('Line ' + IntToStr(i));
VirtualStringTree3.RootNodeCount := VirtualStringTree3.RootNodeCount +
10000;
```

This approach is only feasible if we can somehow determine the part of the model that is associated with the given node in the OnInitNode handler. The only information we have at that moment is the node's index in the list (the Node.Index property). The first node gets index 0, second index 1, and so on. Luckily, that is exactly the same as the index into the TStringList so we can just use the SetData method to set the user data:

```
procedure TfrmVTV.VirtualStringTree3InitNode(Sender: TBaseVirtualTree;
  ParentNode, Node: PVirtualNode;
  var InitialStates: TVirtualNodeInitStates);
begin
  Node.SetData(pointer(Node.Index));
end;
```

In addition to SetData and GetData there are also generic versions of those functions, GetData<T> and SetData<T>, which are of tremendous use if we want to use user data as a storage for an object or an interface. The code implements all necessary reference counting so that interfaces are correctly managed.

This on-demand initialization approach speeds the program up even more. The addition of 10,000 lines now takes only 3 ms. The speed when adding lines one by one is not affected, though:

VirtualTree demo showing different approaches to managing the TVirtualStringTree component

This concludes my foray into user interface land. The second part of this chapter will deal with an aspect of algorithmic improvement which we usually ignore—caching. And at the very end I will return to Mr. Smith's code from `Chapter 1`, *About Performance*, and make it run much faster.

# Caching

Our good friend Mr. Smith has improved his programming skills considerably. Currently, he is learning about recursive functions and he programmed his first recursive piece of code. He wrote a simple seven-liner which calculates the $n^{th}$ element in the *Fibonacci* sequence:

```
function TfrmFibonacci.FibonacciRecursive(element: int64): int64;
begin
  if element < 3 then
    Result := 1
  else
    Result := FibonacciRecursive(element - 1) +
              FibonacciRecursive(element - 2);
end;
```

I will not argue with him—if you look up the definition of a Fibonacci sequence it really looks like it could be perfectly solved with a recursive function.

A sequence of Fibonacci numbers, *F*, is defined with two simple rules:

- First two numbers in the sequence are both 1 ($F_1 = 1$, $F_2 = 1$),

- Every other number in the sequence is the sum of the preceding two ($F_n = F_{n-1} + F_{n-2}$).

You will also find a different definition of the Fibonacci sequence in the literature, starting with values 0 and 1, but it only differs from our definition in the initial zero. Our definition will produce the sequence 1, 1, 2, 3, 5, 8 ... while the second definition will produce 0, 1, 1, 2, 3, 5, 8.

As I've said, a naive approach to writing a Fibonacci function is to write a recursive function, as Mr. Smith did. This way, however, leads to an exceedingly slow program.

Try it yourself. A program, *Fibonacci*, from the code archive for this book implements Mr. Smith's functions in the `FibonacciRecursive` method. Enter a number up to 30 in the **Element number** edit field, click **Recursive** and you'll get your answer in a few milliseconds. Increase this value to 40 and you'll have to wait about a second!

The numbers show that if you increase the element number just by one, the calculation time goes up about 50%. That accumulates quickly. My computer needs more than 13 seconds to calculate element number 46, and 96 seconds—a minute and a half!—for element number 50. What is going on?

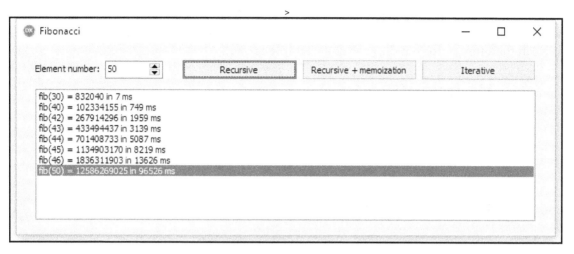

Calculating Fibonacci numbers the recursive way

The problem with the naive implementation is that it has $O(2^n)$ complexity. When you calculate a value of the function, the first call to `FibonacciRecursive` causes two new calls. These cause two more calls each ($2*2 = 4$) and these four cause two more calls each ($2*4 = 8$) and so on. We have therefore, $2^0$ (= 1) calls initially, $2^1 = 2$ on the first level of recursion, $2^2 = 4$ on the second level, $2^3 = 8$ on the third, and that goes on and on until we need to calculate elements 1 or 2.

A careful examination of these recursive calls shows us something interesting. Let's say we want to calculate the 10th element in the sequence, $F_{10}$. That causes recursive calls to calculate $F_9$ and $F_8$. $F_9$ causes recursive calls for $F_8$ and $F_7$, while $F_8$ causes recursive calls for $F_7$ and $F_6$. In the next level of recursion we have to calculate $F_7$ an $F_6$, $F_6$ and $F_5$, $F_6$ and $F_5$ again, and $F_5$ and $F_4$. We see that we are calculating the same values over and over again, and that definitely doesn't help the execution speed.

A solution to this type of problem is *caching* (sometimes also called *memoization*). Simply put, whenever we calculate a result corresponding to some inputs, we put it into a storage—a *cache*. When we have to calculate a value corresponding to the *same* inputs, we just pull it from the cache.

This is a very powerful technique that brings in its own collection of problems. We have to decide the size of the cache. Maybe we could cache every already-calculated value, but they will often be too abundant to store. We also have to create and destroy this cache somewhere.

When dealing with the Fibonacci sequence, the size of the cache is not really a problem. If we want the $n^{th}$ Fibonacci number, we will only need to store values of elements from 1 to $n$. We can therefore represent the cache by a simple array:

```
var
  FFibonacciTable: TArray<int64>;

function TfrmFibonacci.FibonacciMemoized(element: int64): int64;
var
  i: Integer;
begin
  SetLength(FFibonacciTable, element+1);
  for i := Low(FFibonacciTable) to High(FFibonacciTable) do
    FFibonacciTable[i] := -1;
  Result := FibonacciRecursiveMemoized(element);
end;
```

The main function, `FibonacciMemoized`, firstly creates the cache `FFibonacciTable`. As dynamic arrays start counting elements with 0, the code allocates one element more than needed, simply to be able to address this array with index `[element]` instead of `[element-1]`. One `int64` more for better code clarity; not a bad compromise!

Secondly, the code initializes all cache elements to -1. As the elements of the Fibonacci sequence are always a positive number, we can use -1 to represent an uninitialized cache slot.

At the end, the code calls the memoized version of the recursive function.

As dynamic arrays are managed by the compiler, we don't have to destroy the cache after the calculation.

The recursive method, `FibonacciRecursiveMemoized`, is very similar to Mr. Smith's code, except that it adds the cache management. At the beginning, it will check the cache to see if the value for the current element was already calculated. If it was, the result is simply taken from the cache. Otherwise, the value is calculated recursively and the result is added to the cache:

```
function TfrmFibonacci.FibonacciRecursiveMemoized(element: int64): int64;
begin
  if FFibonacciTable[element] >= 0 then
    Result := FFibonacciTable[element]
  else
  begin
    if element < 3 then
      Result := 1
```

```
    else
      Result := FibonacciRecursiveMemoized(element - 1) +
               FibonacciRecursiveMemoized(element - 2);
    FFibonacciTable[element] := Result;
  end;
end;
```

In the *Fibonacci* program, you can use the *Recursive + memoization* button to test this version. You'll see that it will need very little time to calculate Fibonacci sequence elements up to number 92. On my computer it always needs less than 1 millisecond.

Why 92, actually? Well, because the 93rd Fibonacci number exceeds the highest int64 value and the result turns negative. Indeed, $F_{92}$ is larger than $2^{63}$, which is a really big number by itself!

So, is this memoized solution a good way of calculating Fibonacci numbers? No, it is not! A much better way is just to start with the first two values (1 and 1), then add them to get $F_3$ (1 + 1 = 2), add $F_2$ and $F_3$ to get $F_4$ (1 + 2 = 3), and so on. This *iterative* solution is much faster than the cached recursive solution although our timing doesn't show that. The precision is simply not good enough and both versions will show a running time of 0 milliseconds:

```
function TfrmFibonacci.FibonacciIterative(element: int64): int64;
var
  a,b: int64;
begin
  a := 1;
  b := 0;
  repeat
    if element = 1 then
      Exit(a);
    b := b + a;
    if element = 2 then
      Exit(b);
    a := a + b;
    Dec(element, 2);
  until false;
end;
```

# Dynamic cache

A static cache that can only grow has only a limited use. We could, for example, use it to store RTTI properties of types, as access to the RTTI is relatively slow. In most cases, however, a limited-size cache that stores only N most recently used values is more appropriate.

Writing such a cache is quite a tricky operation. First and foremost, we need quick access to a value associated with a specific input (let's call that input a **key**). In Chapter 1, *About Performance*, we found out that the best way to do that is a hash table (or, in Delphi terms, TDictionary), which has *O(1)* lookup time.

So that's solved, our cache will store data in a dictionary. But we also have to remove the values from the dictionary (as this cache has a limited size) and there lies the big problem!

When a cache is full (when it reaches some pre-set size) we would like to remove the **oldest** element from the cache. We could, for example, replace the value part of the dictionary with a pair (date/time, value) where *date/time* would contain the last modification time of this key, but finding the oldest key in the cache then becomes an *O(n)* operation (in the worst case we have to scan all (date/time, value) pairs) which is something that we would like to avoid.

 Removing the *oldest* elements from the cache is an implementation detail, not a requirement. We could also remove the element which was not *accessed* for the longest time or which was least recently *updated*.

Another alternative would be a sorted list of all keys. When we need to update a key, we can find it with *O(log n)* steps and insert it at the beginning in *O(1)* steps (but this is an expensive step as it needs to move other elements around in memory). To get the oldest element, we can just check the last element in the list (very fast *O(1)*). However, we can do even better than that.

Let's look again at the requirements. We need a data structure that satisfies the following criteria:

- Data is kept in *modification* order. In other words, when you insert an item into the structure, that item becomes the first element in the structure.

- When you update an item, it moves to the front (it becomes the first element).

Whenever you need a data structure with these conditions, the answer is always a *doubly-linked list*. This is a list of items where each item contains some value, plus two pointers - one pointing to the previous element and one to the next one. The first element doesn't have a predecessor and the last element doesn't have a successor. These two links point to a special value (for example, nil).

A doubly-linked list

Removing an element from such a list is very fast. You just have to change a few pointers. The same goes for insertion into such a list.

Keep in mind that *pointers* in this context doesn't necessarily mean Delphi pointers. One can also build a list in an array and a *pointer* would then simply be an integer index into this array.

I have implemented a very fast cache, TDHPCache<K,V>, based around a hash table and doubly-linked list. You can find it in the DHPCache unit, together with a simple test app, CacheDemo.

TDHPCache is a generic cache class with two type parameters—the key K and value V. Its public interface implements only a few functions:

```
TDHPCache<K,V> = class
public
  constructor Create(ANumElements: Integer; AOwnsValues: boolean = false);
  destructor Destroy; override;
  function TryGetValue(const key: K; var value: V): boolean;
  procedure Update(const key: K; const value: V);
end;
```

The Create constructor creates a cache with the specified maximum size. The cache can optionally own values that you insert into the cache, which allows you to cache objects.

The TryGetValue function tries to retrieve a value associated with the specified key. Success or failure is indicated through the Boolean result.

The Update procedure stores the value in the cache and associates it with the specified key. It also makes sure that the key is now first in the list of most recently used keys.

Internally, all keys and values are stored in a doubly-linked list. As we know the maximum size of this list (ANumElements parameter passed to the constructor), we can create it as a simple array of elements of (internal) type TListElement:

```
strict private type
  TListElement = record
```

```
    Next : Integer;
    Prev : Integer;
    Key : K;
    Value: V;
  end;
var
  FCache : TDictionary<K,Integer>;
  FKeys : TArray<TListElement>;
  FFreeList : Integer;
  FHead : Integer;
  FTail : Integer;
```

This list is not using Delphi pointers to link elements. Instead, each `Next` and `Prev` field simply contains an index into the `FKeys` array or -1 if there is no next/previous item. (-1 in this case corresponds to a `nil` pointer.)

Two lists are actually stored in this array. One element is always in exactly one of those two lists, so parallel storage is not a problem.

The first list contains all unused items. The `FFreeList` field points to the first element in this list. When a `TDHPCache` class is created, the `BuildLinkedList` method (not shown here) adds all elements of `FKeys` to this list.

The second list contains all used (cached) items. The `FHead` field points to the first (most recently modified) element in this list and the `FTail` field points to the last (oldest) element in this list. At the beginning, this list is empty and both `FHead` and `FTail` contain -1.

The cache also uses a `FCache` dictionary, which maps keys into array indexes.

To retrieve a value, `TryGetValue` calls `FCache.TryGetValue` to get the array index associated with the key. If that function returns `True`, the associated value is read from the `FKeys` array. Both operations execute in *O(1)* time, which makes the whole function *O(1)*:

```
function TDHPCache<K, V>.TryGetValue(const key: K; var value: V): boolean;
var
  element: Integer;
begin
  Result := FCache.TryGetValue(key, element);
  if Result then
    value := FKeys[element].Value;
end;
```

Updating a value is a bit more complicated. The function first tries to find the key in the cache. If found, the value in the `FKeys` is updated. Both operations are *O(1)*.

The code looks a bit more complicated because it must handle destruction of the old value when the cache owns its values:

```
procedure TDHPCache<K, V>.UpdateElement(element: Integer; const key: K;
const value: V);
var
  oldValue: V;
begin
  if not FOwnsValues then
    FKeys[element].Value := value
  else
  begin
    oldValue := FKeys[element].Value;
    if PObject(@value)^ <> PObject(@oldValue)^ then
    begin
      FKeys[element].Value := value;
      PObject(@oldValue)^.DisposeOf;
    end;
  end;
  MoveToFront(element);
end;

procedure TDHPCache<K, V>.Update(const key: K; const value: V);
var
  element: Integer;
begin
  if FCache.TryGetValue(key, element) then
    UpdateElement(element, key, value)
  else
    AddElement(key, value);
end;
```

The AddElement gets executed when a new (key, value) pair is added to the cache. First it checks whether the list is full. This can be done simply by checking the FFreeList pointer—if it points to an array element, the list is not yet full. Then the code either removes the oldest element from the list (discussed in the following) or allocates a new element from the free list. The latter is done by moving a few pointers around in *O(1)* time.

Next, a new element is inserted at the beginning of the list. Again, just a few pointers are moved and the code runs in *O(1)*.

Finally, key and value are updated and (key, index) mapping is inserted into the dictionary, which is again an *O(1)* operation:

```
procedure TDHPCache<K, V>.AddElement(const key: K; const value: V);
```

```
var
  element: integer;
begin
  if IsFull then
    element := RemoveOldest
  else
    element := GetFree;
  InsertInFront(element);
  FKeys[element].Key := key;
  FKeys[element].Value := value;
  FCache.Add(key, element);
end;
```

The only unsolved part is the `RemoveOldest` function. It will firstly remove the last element from the list (`Unlink(FTail)`), which is a simple *O(1)* operation. Then it will remove the (key, index) mapping from the cache (*O(1)*) and destroy the old value if the cache owns its values:

```
function TDHPCache<K, V>.RemoveOldest: Integer;
var
  element: Integer;
begin
  if FTail < 0 then
    raise Exception.Create('TDHPCache<K, V>.RemoveOldest: List is empty!');
  Result := FTail;
  Unlink(FTail);
  FCache.Remove(FKeys[Result].Key);
  if FOwnsValues then
    PObject(@FKeys[Result].Value)^.DisposeOf;
end;
```

As you can see, we have created a data structure which can insert, update, delete (when it is full), and retrieve elements all in *O(1)*. In Chapter 1, *About Performance*, however, I stated that there is always a trade-off and that not all operations can be fast in one data structure. What is going on here?

The answer is that we are gaining speed by duplicating the data, namely the keys. Each key is stored twice—once in the doubly—linked list and once in the dictionary. If you remove one copy of this key, some operations will slow down.

# Speeding up SlowCode

For the last practical example, we can try speeding up Mr. Smith's SlowCode from Chapter 1, *About Performance*. Here, we immediately ran into a problem. To fix or change an algorithm we must understand what the code does. This happens a lot in practice, especially when you inherit some code. Reading and understanding code that you didn't write is an important skill.

Let's try to understand the first part of SlowCode. The for loop in SlowMethod starts counting with 2. Then it calls ElementInDataDivides, which does nothing as the data list is empty. Next, SlowMethod adds 2 to the list.

Next, i takes the value of 3. ElementInDataDivides checks if 3 is divisible by 2. It is not, so SlowMethod adds 3 to the list.

In the next step, $i = 4$, it is divisible by 2, and 4 is **not** added to the list. 5 is then added to the list (it is not divisible by 2 or 3), 6 is not (divisible by 2), 7 is added (not divisible by 2, 3, or 5), 8 is not (divisible by 2), 9 is not (divisible by 3), and so on:

```
function ElementInDataDivides(data: TList<Integer>; value: Integer):
boolean;
var
  i: Integer;
begin
  Result := True;
  for i in data do
    if (value <> i) and ((value mod i) = 0) then
      Exit;
  Result := False;
end;

function SlowMethod(highBound: Integer): TArray<Integer>;
var
  i: Integer;
  temp: TList<Integer>;
begin
  temp := TList<Integer>.Create;
  try
    for i := 2 to highBound do
      if not ElementInDataDivides(temp, i) then
        temp.Add(i);
    Result := Filter(temp);
  finally
    FreeAndNil(temp);
  end;
```

```
end;
```

We now understand what the first part (before calling the `Filter` method) does. It calculates prime numbers with a very simple test. It tries to divide each candidate by every already-generated prime. If the candidate number is not divisible by any known prime number, it is also a prime number and we can add it to the list.

Can we improve this algorithm? With a bit of mathematical knowledge, we can do exactly that! As it turns out (the proof is in the next information box and you can safely skip it), we don't have to test divisibility with every generated prime number. If we are testing number *value*, we only have to test divisibility with a prime number smaller or equal to *Sqrt(value)* (square root of *value*).

My assumption is this: If we have number *n*, which is not divisible by any number smaller than or equal to *Sqrt(n)*, then it is also not divisible by any number larger than *Sqrt(n)*. The simplest way to prove that is by establishing a contradiction.

Let's say that we can divide *n* by *p*. We can therefore write $n = p * k$. As *n* is not divisible by numbers smaller than or equal to *Sqrt(n)*, both *p* and *k* must be strictly larger than *Sqrt(n)*. If that is true, *p* * *k* must be strictly larger than *Sqrt(n) * Sqrt(n)*, or *n*.

On one side we have $n = p * k$, and on the other $p * k > n$. These cannot both be true at the same time so we have run into a contradiction. Therefore, the initial assumption is correct.

We can therefore rewrite `ElementInDataDivides` so that it will stop the loop when the first prime number larger than `Sqrt(value)` is encountered. You can find the following code in the `SlowCode_v2` program:

```
function ElementInDataDivides(data: TList<Integer>; value: Integer):
boolean;
var
  i: Integer;
  highBound: integer;
begin
  Result := True;
  highBound := Trunc(Sqrt(value));
  for i in data do begin
    if i > highBound then
      break;
    if (value <> i) and ((value mod i) = 0) then
      Exit;
```

```
   end;
   Result := False;
end;
```

If we compare the original version with time complexity $O(n^2)$ with this improved version with time complexity $O(n * sqrt\ n)$, we can see definite improvement. Still, we can do even better!

Try to search *prime number generation* on the internet and you'll quickly find a very simple algorithm which was invented way before computers. It is called the *sieve of Eratosthenes* and was invented by the Greek scholar who lived in the third century BC.

I will not go into details here. For the theory you can check Wikipedia and for a practical example, see the `SlowCode_Sieve` program in the code archive. Let me just say that the sieve of Eratosthenes has a time complexity of $O(n\ log\ log\ n)$, which is very close to $O(n)$. It should therefore be quite a bit faster than our *Sqrt(n)* improvement.

The following table compares `SlowCode`, `SlowCode_v2`, and `SlowCode_Sieve` for different inputs. The highest input was not tested with the original program as it would run for more than an hour. All times are in milliseconds:

| highest number tested | SlowCode | SlowCode_v2 | SlowCode_Sieve |
|---|---|---|---|
| 10,000 | 19 | 2 | 0 |
| 100,000 | 861 | 29 | 7 |
| 1,000,000 | 54.527 | 352 | 77 |
| 10,000,000 | not tested | 5769 | 1072 |

# Summary

In this chapter, I touched on two very different topics. First, I looked at responsive user interfaces and how to make them faster and then I continued with the concept of *caching*. That topic was introduced with a simple example, followed by a fully featured cache implementation that you can use in your programs.

At the end, I returned to the example `SlowCode` program from `Chapter 1`, *About Performance*. First, I used some detective work to find out what it really does, which allowed me to improve it a lot. The code now processes a million numbers in mere milliseconds and not **minutes** as the original program did.

In the next chapter, I'll focus on optimizing the code on a smaller level. We will look at various Delphi language and RTL elements and you'll learn which parts of the language and system libraries can behave slower than one would expect and what you can do to improve that.

# 3
# Fine-Tuning the Code

I have stated repeatedly that the best way to improve code speed is to change the algorithm. Sometimes, however, this is just not possible because you are already using the best possible algorithm. It may also be completely impractical as changing the algorithm may require rewriting a large part of the program.

If this is the case and the code is still not running fast enough, we have multiple available options. We can start *optimizing* the program, by which I mean that we can start changing small parts of the program and replacing them with faster code. This is the topic of the chapter that you are currently reading.

Another option would be to rewrite a part of the program in *assembler*. Delphi offers quite decent support for that and we'll look into that possibility near the end of this chapter. We can also find a *library* that solves our problem. It could be written in an assembler or created by a compiler that produces faster code than Delphi—typically we don't care. We only have to know how to *link* it into our program and that will be the topic of `Chapter 8`, *Using External Libraries.*

The last option is to somehow split our problem into multiple parts and solve them in parallel. We'll dig into this approach in Chapters 5 to 7.

But first, fine-tuning the code, or how to make the program run faster with small changes. In this chapter, you'll find:

- How Delphi compiler settings can affect the program speed
- Why it is good to use local variables to store intermediate results
- How to work with the CPU window
- What happens behind the scenes when you work with different data types

- How to speed up the code by using RTL functions
- How to use an assembler to speed up the code
- How we can make `SlowCode` run even faster

# Delphi compiler settings

First things first—before you start meddling with the code, you should check the Delphi compiler settings for your project. In some situations, they can affect the code speed quite a lot.

To check and possibly change compiler settings, open your project, then select **Project** | **Options** from the menu or press *Ctrl + Shift + F11*. Relevant options can be found in the branch **Delphi Compiler** | **Compiling**, as shown in the following screenshot here:

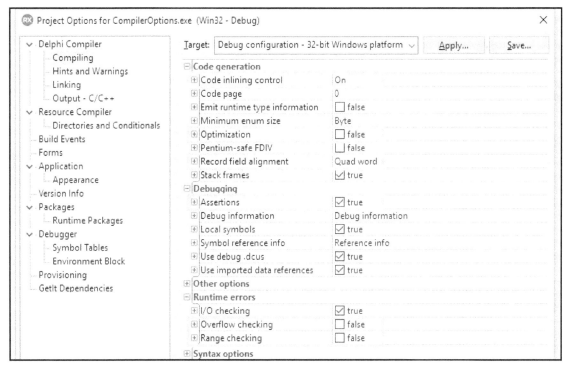

Compiler settings that influence program speed

We will look into the following options:

- Code inlining control
- Optimization
- Record field alignment
- Assertions
- Overflow checking
- Range checking

All of these settings can be enabled/disabled for the complete project and they can also be turned on/off in the code by using *compiler directives* (comments that start with {$).

# Code inlining control

We will look into the concept of **code inlining** later in this chapter, in the section, *Optimizing method calls*, so this text will serve just as an introduction.

By setting the value of **Code inlining control**, you define the default behavior for the complete project. The possible values for that setting are On, Off, and Auto. This default value can be changed in the code by inserting {$INLINE ON}, {$INLINE OFF}, or {$INLINE AUTO} into the source.

The INLINE state can be set to a different value at a place where the inlined method is defined and a place where it is used (called). This creates six possible combinations.

When we look at the method definition, INLINE has the following meaning:

- INLINE ON: If the method is marked with the inline directive (more on that later), it will be marked as *inlineable*
- INLINE AUTO: Same as INLINE ON, with the addition that any routine not marked with inline will still be marked *inlineable* if its code size is less than or equal to 32 bytes
- INLINE OFF: The routine will not be marked as *inlineable* even if it is marked with inline

At the place of use, INLINE has a different meaning:

- INLINE ON: If a called method is marked as *inlineable*, it will be expanded inline (at the place of call) if possible

- `INLINE AUTO`: Same as `INLINE ON`
- `INLINE OFF`: The routine will not be expanded inline, even if it is marked *inlineable*

# Optimization

The **Optimization** option controls code optimization. The possible values are `On` and `Off`. This setting can also be controlled with compiler directives `{$OPTIMIZATION ON}` and `{$OPTIMIZATION OFF}` or with equivalent `{$O+}` and `{$O-}`.

When optimization is enabled, the compiler optimizes generated code for speed. Optimizations are guaranteed not to change the behavior of the program. The only reason you may want to turn optimization off is to improve debugging. When optimization is turned on, debugging—especially stepping through the code and evaluating variables—may not be working correctly in all cases.

My approach is to turn optimization off during development, and on when building the release version.

The `$O` (or `$OPTIMIZATION`) directive can only turn optimization on or off for an entire method. You cannot turn optimization on or off for selected lines within a method.

To show the effect of different compiler options, I have written a `CompilerOptions` demo. When you click the **Optimization** button, the following code will be run twice—once with optimization turned on and once off.

The code initializes an array and then does some calculations on all of its elements. All of this is repeated 1,000 times because otherwise it is hard to measure differences. Modern CPUs are fast!

```
function NonOptimized: int64;
var
  arr1: array [1..50000] of Integer;
  i,j: Integer;
begin
  for j := 1 to 1000 do
  begin
    for i := Low(arr1) to High(arr1) do
      arr1[i] := i;
    for i := Low(arr1) to High(arr1)-1 do
```

```
        arr1[i] := arr1[i] + arr1[i+1];
    end;
end;
```

The results will be different depending on the CPU speed and model, but on all computers the optimized version should be significantly faster. On my test machine, the optimized version runs approximately six times faster than the non-optimized! Here are the results:

Although you can turn compilation options on and off with compiler directives, Delphi provides no direct support for switching back to the previous state. You can, however, check whether a compilation option is currently turned on or off by using the {$IFOPT} compiler directive.

Then you can define or undefine some conditional compilation symbol that will tell you later what the original state of the compilation option was:

```
{$IFOPT O+}{$DEFINE OPTIMIZATION}{$ELSE}{$UNDEF OPTIMIZATION}{$ENDIF}
  {$OPTIMIZATION ON}
```

When you want to restore the original state, use this conditional to turn the compilation option on or off:

```
{$IFDEF OPTIMIZATION}{$OPTIMIZATION ON}{$ELSE}{$OPTIMIZATION OFF}{$ENDIF}
```

This technique is used throughout the `CompilerOptions` demo with different compilation options.

# Record field alignment

The third compiler option I'd like to discuss regulates the alignment of fields in Delphi record and class types. It can be set to the following values: `Off`, `Byte`, `Word`, `Double Word`, and `Quad Word`. Settings are a bit misleading, as the first two values actually result in the same behavior.

You can use compiler directives {$ALIGN 1}, {$ALIGN 2}, {$ALIGN 4}, and {$ALIGN 8} to change record field alignment in code, or equivalent short forms {$A1}, {$A2}, {$A4}, and {$A8}. There are also two directives which exist only for backward compatibility. {$A+} means the same as {$A8} (which is also a default for new programs) and {$A-} is the same as {$A1}.

Field alignment controls exactly how fields in records and classes are laid out in memory.

Let's say that we have the following record. And let's say that the address of the first field in the record is simply 0:

```
type
  TRecord = record
    Field1: byte;
    Field2: int64;
    Field3: word;
    Field4: double;
  end;
```

With the {$A1} alignment, each field will simply follow the next one. In other words, Field2 will start at address 1, Field3 at 9, and Field4 at 11. As the size of double is 8 (as we'll see later in this chapter), the total size of the record is 19 bytes.

The Pascal language has a syntax that enforces this behavior without the use of compiler directives. You can declare a record as a packed record and its fields will be packed together as with the {$A1} alignment, regardless of the current setting of this directive. This is very useful when you have to interface with libraries written in other languages.

With the {$A2} alignment, each field will start on a word boundary. In layman's terms, the address of the field (offset from the start of the record) will be divisible by 2. Field2 will start at address 2, Field3 at 10, and Field4 at 12. The total size of the record will be 20 bytes.

With the {$A4} alignment, each field will start on a double word boundary so its address will be divisible by 4. (You can probably see where this is going.) Field2 will start at address 4, Field3 at 12, and Field4 at 16. The total size of the record will be 24 bytes.

Finally, with the {$A8} alignment, each field will start on a quad word boundary so its address will be divisible by 8. Field2 will start at address 8, Field3 at 16, and Field4 at 24. The total size of the record will be 32 bytes.

Saying all that, I have to add that $A directive doesn't function exactly as I described it. Delphi knows how simple data types should be aligned (for example, it knows that an integer should be aligned on a double word boundary) and will not move them to higher alignment, even if it is explicitly specified by a directive. For example, the following record will use only 8 bytes even though we explicitly stated that fields should be quad word aligned:

```
{$A8}
TIntegerPair = record
  a: integer;
  b: integer:
end;
```

If you need to exactly specify size and alignment of all fields (for example if you pass records to some API call), it is best to use the packed record directive and insert unused padding fields into the definition. The next example specifies a record containing two quad word aligned integers:

```
TIntegerPair = packed record
  a: integer;
  filler: integer;
  b: integer:
end;
```

The following image shows how this record is laid out in memory with different record field alignment settings. Fields are renamed F1 to F4 so that their names would fit in the available space. X marks unused memory:

Why is all this useful? Why don't we always just pack fields together so that the total size of a record or class is as small as possible? Well, that is an excellent question!

As traditional wisdom says, CPUs work faster when the data is correctly aligned. Accessing a four-byte data (an integer, for example) is faster if its address is double word aligned (is divisible by four). Similarly, two-byte data (word) should be word aligned (address divisible by two) and eight-byte data (int64) should be quad word aligned (address divisible by eight). This will significantly improve performance in your program.

Will it really? Does this traditional wisdom make any sense in the modern world?

The `CompilerOptions` demo contains sets of measurements done on differently aligned records. It is triggered with the **Record field align** button.

Running the test shows something surprising—all four tests (for A1, A2, A4, and A8) run at almost the same speed. Actually, the code operating on the best-aligned record (A8) is the slowest! I must admit that I didn't expect this while preparing the test.

A little detective work has shown that somewhere around year 2010, Intel did a great job optimizing the data access on its CPUs. If you manage to find an older machine, it will show a big difference between unaligned and aligned data. However, all Intel CPUs produced after that time will run on unaligned and aligned data at the same speed. Working on unaligned (packed) data may actually be faster as more data will fit into the processor cache.

What is the moral lesson of all that? **Guessing is nothing, hard numbers are all!** Always measure. There is no guarantee that your changes will actually speed up the program.

# Assertions

The **Assertions** compiler options enables or disables code generation for `Assert` statements. You can use compiler directives `{$ASSERTIONS ON}` and `{$ASSERTIONS OFF}` to turn this option on or off in the code. Short forms of this directive are rather cryptic `{$C+}` and `{$C-}`.

Delphi allows us to use runtime checks in the code in a form of `Assert` statements. `Assert` will check whether the first parameter evaluates to `false` and will raise an exception with the (optional) second parameter in an exception message, if that is true.

The following statement will raise an exception if variable `i` is smaller than zero:

```
Assert(i >= 0, 'Expecting a positive value here');
```

If you turn code generation for assertions off, the compiler will just skip such statements and they will not generate any code. You can for example use this to remove assertions from the release code. Even if any argument to `Assert` contains a function call, this function will not be called when assertions are turned off.

# Overflow checking

The **Overflow checking** option regulates whether the compiler checks if certain arithmetic operations (+, -, *, Abs, Sqr, Inc, Dec, Succ, and Pred) produce a number that is too large or too small to fit into the data type. You can use compiler options, `{$OVERFLOWCHECKS ON}` and `{$OVERFLOWCHECKS OFF}` (or short forms `{$Q+}` and `{$Q-}`), to turn this option on and off in a specific part of a program.

For example, the following program will silently increment `$FFFFFFFF` to 0 in the first `Inc` statement but will raise `EIntOverflow` exception in the second `Inc` statement:

```
procedure TfrmCompilerOptions.btnOverflowErrorClick(Sender: TObject);
var
  i: cardinal;
begin
  {$Q-}
  i := $FFFFFFFF;
  // Without overflow checks, Inc will work and i will be 0
  Inc(i);

  {$Q+}
  i := $FFFFFFFF;
  // With overflow checks, Inc will raise an exception
  Inc(i);
end;
```

Enabling overflow checking doesn't make a big change in the program speed, so you can freely use it whenever it is needed. I would suggest turning it on at least in debug configuration as that will help with finding errors in the code.

# Range checking

The last compiler option I want to discuss, **Range checking**, tells the compiler whether to check indexes to arrays and strings. In other words, it will check if in expression such as `s[idx+1]`, `idx+1` represents a valid index.

You can turn range checking on and off with compiler directives `{$RANGECHECKS ON}` and `{RANGECHECKS OFF}` (or `{$R+}` and `{$R-}`).

Let's take a look at an example. In the method shown here, the second `for` loop accesses element `arr[101]` without any error, although the maximum array element is `arr[100]`. The third `for` loop, however, will raise an `ERangeCheck` exception when accessing `arr[101]`:

```
procedure TfrmCompilerOptions.btnRangeErrorClick(Sender: TObject);
var
  arr: array [1..100] of Integer;
  i: Integer;
begin
  for i := Low(arr) to High(arr) do
    arr[i] := i;
  {$R-}
  for i := Low(arr) to High(arr) do
    arr[i] := arr[i] + arr[i+1];

  {$R+}
  for i := Low(arr) to High(arr) do
    arr[i] := arr[i] + arr[i+1];
end;
```

This kind of checking is so important that I always leave it in my code, even in the release version. Accessing a nonexistent array or string element may not seem so dangerous, but what if you are writing into that element? If this is not caught, your code just overwrites some other data with nonsense values. This leads to extremely hard to find problems! By default, range checking is turned off even in debug build and you really should turn it on in every program.

What about the "cost" of this checking? As the `CompilerOptions` program shows, it can be significant. In this example, turning range checking on slows down the code by a whole 50%:

Comparing the code running with or without overflow checking and range checking

In such cases, turning range checking off can speed up the program. I would still recommend that you do that just for critical parts of code, not for the whole program.

This brings us to the end of this very long, but necessary, section as understanding the developer tools is always a good thing. Let us now—finally!—switch to something more interesting, to real programming.

# Extracting common expressions

This next tip will sound obvious, but it will nicely introduce us to the next topic. Plus, it is a real problem frequently found in production code.

The `ExtractCommonExpression` demo creates a list box with a mere 1,000 entries, all in the form Author–Title. A click on the **Complicated expression** button runs a short code which reverts the order of Author and Title in the list box so that it shows entries in the form Title–Author:

```
procedure TfrmCommonExpression.Button1Click(Sender: TObject);
var
  i: Integer;
  sw: TStopwatch;
begin
  ListBox1.Items.BeginUpdate;
  try
    sw := TStopwatch.StartNew;
    for i := 0 to ListBox1.Count - 1 do
      ListBox1.Items[i] :=
        Copy(ListBox1.Items[i], Pos('-', ListBox1.Items[i]) + 1,
          Length(ListBox1.Items[i]))
        + '-'
        + Copy(ListBox1.Items[i], 1, Pos('-', ListBox1.Items[i]) - 1);
    sw.Stop;
    Button1.Caption := IntToStr(sw.ElapsedMilliseconds);
  finally ListBox1.Items.EndUpdate; end;
end;
```

The code goes over the list and for each entry finds the '-' character, extracts the first and second part of the entry and combines them back together, reversed. It does that, however, in a terrible copy-and-paste way. The code refers to `ListBox1.Items[i]` five times while calculating the result. It also calls `Pos('-', ListBox1.Items[i])` twice.

In a language with a really good compiler, you could expect that both subexpressions mentioned in the previous paragraph would be calculated only once. Not with Delphi's compiler, though. It has some optimization built in, but Delphi's optimization is far from the level required for such tricks to work. That leaves a burden of optimization on us, the programmers.

The second button in this demo executes the code shown next. This implementation of the same algorithm is not only more readable, but accesses `ListBox1.Items[i]` only once. It also calculates the position of `'-'` inside the string only once:

```
procedure TfrmCommonExpression.Button2Click(Sender: TObject);
var
  i: Integer;
  s: string;
  p: Integer;
  sw: TStopwatch;
begin
  ListBox1.Items.BeginUpdate;
  try
    sw := TStopwatch.StartNew;
    for i := 0 to ListBox1.Count - 1 do begin
      s := ListBox1.Items[i];
      p := Pos('-', s);
      ListBox1.Items[i] := Copy(s, p + 1, Length(s)) + '-' +
        Copy(s, 1, p - 1);
    end;
    sw.Stop;
    Button2.Caption := IntToStr(sw.ElapsedMilliseconds);
  finally ListBox1.Items.EndUpdate; end;
end;
```

Comparing both approaches shows a definite improvement in the second case. The first method uses around 40 ms and the second one around 30 ms, which is 25% faster. The code only times the inner `for` loop, not the updating of the list box itself, which takes the same time in both cases.

I can recap all this with a simple statement—*Calculate every subexpression only once*. Good advice but, still, don't exaggerate. Simple expressions, such as `i+1` or `2*i` are so *cheap* (in computing time) that extracting them in a subexpression won't speed up the code.

# The helpful CPU window

In situations similar to the previous example, it doesn't hurt if you can look at the generated assembler code to check what is going on behind the scenes. Luckily, Delphi IDE provides a great way to do just that.

I will be the first to admit that examining assembler code is not for everyone. You can be a great Delphi programmer and still have no idea how to read assembler instructions.

If you found yourself in the previous words, don't worry. This section is included just for people who want to know everything. You can safely skip it knowing that you'll still be able to understand everything else in the book. However, if you're still interested then, by all means, read on!

The Delphi IDE gives us a few different tools for viewing the low-level state of the code and computer. They are stowed away in the not-so-obvious submenu **View, Debug Windows, CPU Windows**. The most useful view is called **Entire CPU** and encompasses all other views in that submenu. It is displayed as an editor tab named **CPU**.

Be aware, though, that it is only useful while you are debugging the program. The best way to use it is to pause the program (either by inserting a breakpoint or clicking the *pause* icon or selecting the **Run, Program Pause** menu) and then switch to the **CPU** view.

 You can quickly access the **Entire CPU** view with the key combination *Ctrl + Alt + C*. If that doesn't work, check whether you have installed some add-on expert which overrides this key combination. For example, GExperts assigns this combination to the `Copy Raw Strings` command.

This view is composed of five parts. The **Disassembly** panel (top left) shows your code as assembler instructions intermixed with Pascal source lines for easier orientation. If you don't see Pascal lines, right-click into that view and verify if the menu item, **Mixed source** is checked.

On the right of that (top right corner) are two small panels showing **processor registers** and **flags**. Below them (bottom right corner) is the current thread's **stack**. To finish it up, a panel in the bottom left corner shows process' **memory** at some address.

If you use the *F8* key to step to the next command while the **Entire CPU** view is active, Delphi will not step to the next Pascal instruction but to the next assembler instruction. If you want to go to the next Pascal instruction, use the *Shift + F7* combination or menu **Run, Trace to Next Source Line**.

We can use the **CPU** view to verify that the first code example from the previous section really compiles to much worse code than the second example.

The image here shows part of the code from the original (on the left) and hand-optimized method (on the right). Green rectangles mark the code that accesses `ListBox1.Items[i]`. We can clearly see that the original code does that three times before calling the `Pos` function (at the very bottom of the image) while the hand-optimized method executes the same sequence of instructions only once:

```
ExtractCommonExpressionMain.pas.54: ListBox1.Items[i] :=
005D1C33 8D4DE8          lea ecx,[ebp-$18]
005D1C36 8B45FC          mov eax,[ebp-$04]
005D1C39 8B80CC030000    mov eax,[eax+$000003cc]
005D1C3F 8B80A8020000    mov eax,[eax+$000002a8]
005D1C45 8B55F8          mov edx,[ebp-$08]
005D1C48 8B18            mov ebx,[eax]
005D1C4A FF530C          call dword ptr [ebx+$0c]
005D1C4D 8D4DC4          lea ecx,[ebp-$3c]
005D1C50 8B45FC          mov eax,[ebp-$04]
005D1C53 8B80CC030000    mov eax,[eax+$000003cc]
005D1C59 8B80A8020000    mov eax,[eax+$000002a8]
005D1C5F 8B55F8          mov edx,[ebp-$08]
005D1C62 8B18            mov ebx,[eax]
005D1C64 FF530C          call dword ptr [ebx+$0c]
005D1C67 8B45C4          mov eax,[ebp-$3c]
005D1C6A 8945F0          mov [ebp-$10],eax
005D1C6D 8B45F0          mov eax,[ebp-$10]
005D1C70 8945EC          mov [ebp-$14],eax
005D1C73 837DEC00        cmp dword ptr [ebp-$14],$00
005D1C77 740B            jz $005d1c84
005D1C79 8B45EC          mov eax,[ebp-$14]
005D1C7C 83E804          sub eax,$04
005D1C7F 8B00            mov eax,[eax]
005D1C81 8945EC          mov [ebp-$14],eax
005D1C84 8D45BC          lea eax,[ebp-$44]
005D1C87 50              push eax
005D1C88 8D4DB8          lea ecx,[ebp-$48]
005D1C8B 8B45FC          mov eax,[ebp-$04]
005D1C8E 8B80CC030000    mov eax,[eax+$000003cc]
005D1C94 8B80A8020000    mov eax,[eax+$000002a8]
005D1C9A 8B55F8          mov edx,[ebp-$08]
005D1C9D 8B18            mov ebx,[eax]
005D1C9F FF530C          call dword ptr [ebx+$0c]
005D1CA2 8B55B8          mov edx,[ebp-$48]
005D1CA5 B901000000      mov ecx,$00000001
005D1CAA B8EC1D5D00      mov eax,$005d1dec
005D1CAF E8648FE3FF      call Pos
```

```
ExtractCommonExpressionMain.pas.74: s := ListBox1.Items[i];
005D1E6B 8D4DF4          lea ecx,[ebp-$0c]
005D1E6E 8B45FC          mov eax,[ebp-$04]
005D1E71 8B80CC030000    mov eax,[eax+$000003cc]
005D1E77 8B80A8020000    mov eax,[eax+$000002a8]
005D1E7D 8B55F8          mov edx,[ebp-$08]
005D1E80 8B18            mov ebx,[eax]
005D1E82 FF530C          call dword ptr [ebx+$0c]
ExtractCommonExpressionMain.pas.75: p := Pos('-', s);
005D1E85 B901000000      mov ecx,$00000001
005D1E8A 8B55F4          mov edx,[ebp-$0c]
005D1E8D B8A81F5D00      mov eax,$005d1fa8
005D1E92 E8818DE3FF      call Pos
005D1E97 8945F0          mov [ebp-$10],eax
ExtractCommonExpressionMain.pas.76: ListBox1.Items[i] := Copy(s,
005D1E9A 8B45F4          mov eax,[ebp-$0c]
005D1E9D 8945E8          mov [ebp-$18],eax
005D1EA0 837DE800        cmp dword ptr [ebp-$18],$00
005D1EA4 740B            jz $005d1eb1
005D1EA6 8B45E8          mov eax,[ebp-$18]
005D1EA9 83E804          sub eax,$04
005D1EAC 8B00            mov eax,[eax]
005D1EAE 8945E8          mov [ebp-$18],eax
005D1EB1 8D45C0          lea eax,[ebp-$40]
005D1EB4 50              push eax
005D1EB5 8B55F0          mov edx,[ebp-$10]
005D1EB8 42              inc edx
005D1EB9 8B4DE8          mov ecx,[ebp-$18]
005D1EBC 8B45F4          mov eax,[ebp-$0c]
005D1EBF E8448BE3FF      call @UStrCopy
005D1EC4 FF75C0          push dword ptr [ebp-$40]
005D1EC7 68A81F5D00      push $005d1fa8
005D1ECC 8D45BC          lea eax,[ebp-$44]
005D1ECF 50              push eax
005D1ED0 8B4DF0          mov ecx,[ebp-$10]
005D1ED3 49              dec ecx
005D1ED4 BA01000000      mov edx,$00000001
005D1ED9 8B45F4          mov eax,[ebp-$0c]
```

# Behind the scenes

A critical part of writing fast code is to understand what happens behind the scenes. Are you appending strings? You should know how that is implemented in a compiler. Passing a dynamic array into a function? Ditto. Wondering whether you should create 10,000 instances of a class or just create a large array of records? Knowing the implementation details will give you the answer.

In this section, I'll dig down into some frequently used data types and show how using them will bring in unexpected complexity. I will discuss memory and memory allocation, but I will treat them as very abstract entities. I'll say words like "A new string gets allocated" with which I'll mean that a secret part of code, called **memory manager**, gets memory from the Windows and tells the program: "You can store your string here." We'll dig deep into the bowels of memory manager in `Chapter 4`, *Memory Management*.

# A plethora of types

The Delphi language contains an immense number of built-in types. There's no chance to cover them one by one, so let us firstly establish some classification that will simplify the rest of the discussion.

The most basic of all built-in types are **simple types**. In this group belong **integer types** (Byte, ShortInt, Word, SmallInt, Integer, Cardinal, Int64, UInt64, NativeInt, NativeUInt, LongInt, and LongWord), **character types** (Char, AnsiChar, WideChar, UCS2Char, and UCS4Char), **boolean types** (Boolean, ByteBool, WordBool, LongBool), **enumerated types** (such as TScrollBarStyle = (ssRegular, ssFlat, ssHotTrack)), and **real types** (Real48, Single, Real, Double, Extended, Comp, and Currency).

Similar to them are **pointer types**, such as pointer, `PByte`, `^TObject` etc. They are, after all, just memory addresses, so we can always treat a pointer as a NativeUInt and vice versa.

Following them are **strings**, a very interesting family hiding intriguing implementation details. It contains **short strings** (such a string[42]), *ansi strings* (AnsiString, RawByteString, UTF8String), and **unicode strings** (string, UnicodeString, and WideString).

The last group is **structured types**. This group, which will be of great interest in this chapter, is composed of **sets** (such as TAlignSet = set of TAlign), **arrays** (static arrays and dynamic arrays), **records** (traditional and advanced—records with methods), **classes**, and **interfaces**. Anonymous methods can also be treated as interfaces as they are implemented in the same way.

A different classification, which I'll also occasionally use, splits all types into two groups—unmanaged and managed. Managed types are types for which the compiler automatically generates life cycle management code and unmanaged types are all the rest.

When a type's life cycle is managed, the compiler automatically initializes variables and fields of that type. The compiler also inserts the code that automatically releases memory associated with data of such type when it is no longer used anywhere in the program (goes *out of scope* are the words often used).

Managed types include strings, dynamic arrays, and interfaces. Records are managed only when they contain at least one field of these types. On platforms that support ARC (iOS, Android, and Linux), classes are also managed.

Different types (more specifically, different classes of types) are implemented differently by the Delphi compiler and as such, present a different challenge for a developer. In the rest of this section I'll describe the internal implementation of the most interesting data types.

 The best resource to really understand how all data types are implemented in Delphi is available in Embarcadero's *Docwiki* under the title *Internal Data Formats (Delphi)*. http://docwiki.embarcadero.com/RADStudio/en/Internal_Data_Formats_(Delphi).

# Simple types

Let's start with simple types, as their implementation is indeed simple. Simple types don't allocate any memory. They are either stored as part of structured types (classes, records and so on), on the stack (local variables of such types) or in the part of a process memory (global variables of such types). Because of that, all operations with them are very fast.

To initialize the variable of a simple type, the compiler just has to move a few bytes around. The same goes for modifying the variable or copying one variable into another. (Fields behave just the same as variables for all Delphi data types so in the future I'll just talk about variables.)

# Strings

String are probably the most used data type in Delphi. They also have a very interesting implementation, optimized for fast execution. To be exact, AnsiString (with all its variations) and UnicodeString (also known as string) are optimized. The WideString type is implemented in a different manner. As short strings (declarations like `string[17]`) are only used for backwards compatibility, I won't discuss them in this book.

Let's deal with the more widely used AnsiString and UnicodeString first. A data of such type is represented with a pointer to a block, allocated from the memory manager. If a string is empty, this pointer will be `nil` (which is at the CPU level represented with number zero) and if a string is not empty, it will point to some memory.

Strings are managed types and as such are always initialized to the default value, `nil`. When you set a string to a value (when you assign a constant to it, for example `s :=` `'Delphi'`), the compiler allocates a memory block to store the string and copies a new value into that block.

Something similar happens when you extend a string (`s := s + '!'`). In such cases, the compiler will reallocate the memory holding the string (more on that in the next chapter), and copy new characters to that memory.

Initializing a string and appending to a string are therefore relatively expensive operations as both allocate memory. (Memory manager performs some interesting optimizations to make string modification much cheaper—in terms of CPU cycles—than one would expect. Read more about that in the next chapter.)

Modifying part of the string without changing its length is, however, a pretty simple operation. Code just has to move the appropriate number of bytes from one place in memory to another and that's that.

Interesting things happen when you assign one non-empty string to another (`s := '42';` `s1 := s;`). To make such operations fast and efficient, the compiler just points both variables to the same memory and increments an integer-sized counter (called *reference count*) in that same memory. A reference count represents the number of variables that are currently sharing the same string data.

A reference count is initialized to 1 when a string is initialized (meaning that only one variable is using this string). After the `s1 := s`, both s and s1 are pointing to the same memory and the reference count is set to 2.

If one of these two variables is no longer accessible (for example, it was a local variable in a method which is no longer executing), the compiler will generate life cycle management code which decrements the reference count. If the new reference count is zero, nobody is using the string data anymore and that memory block is released back to the system.

After s := s1 we therefore have two strings pointing to the same memory. But what happens if one of these strings is modified? What happens, for example, if we do s1[1] := 'a'? It would be very bad if that would also modify the original string, s.

Again, the compiler comes to the rescue. Before any modification of a string, the code will check whether the string's reference count is larger than one. If so, this string is shared with another variable. To prevent any mess, the code will at that point allocate new memory for the modified string, copy the current contents into this memory, and decrement the original reference count. After that, it will change the string so it will point to the new memory and modify the content of that memory. This mechanism is called **copy-on-write**.

You can also force this behavior without actually modifying the string by calling the UniqueString function. After s1 := s; UniqueString(s1); both variables will point to separate parts of memory and both will have a reference count of 1.

 Calling the SetLength method on a string also makes the string unique.

The following code, taken from the DataTypes demo, demonstrates a part of that behavior. Firstly, the code initializes s1 and s2 so that they point to the same string. It will then log two items for each string—a pointer to the string memory and the contents of the string. After that, the code will modify one of the strings and log the same information again:

```
procedure TfrmDataTypes.btnCopyOnWriteClick(Sender: TObject);
var
  s1, s2: string;
begin
  s1 := 'Delphi';
  s2 := s1;
  ListBox1.Items.Add(Format('s1 = %p [%s], s2 = %p [%s]',
    [PPointer(@s1)^, s1, PPointer(@s2)^, s2]));

  s2[1] := 'd';
  ListBox1.Items.Add(Format('s1 = %p [%s], s2 = %p [%s]',
    [PPointer(@s1)^, s1, PPointer(@s2)^, s2]));
end;
```

If you run this program and click on the **string copy-on-write** button, you'll see that in the first log line, both pointers will be the same and in the second, the pointers will be different:

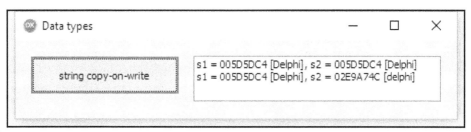

Demonstration of a copy-on-write mechanism

This wraps up the implementation behind Ansi and Unicode strings. The `WideString` type is, however, implemented completely differently. It was designed to be used in OLE applications where strings can be sent from one application to another. Because of that, all `WideStrings` are allocated with Windows' OLE memory allocator, not with standard Delphi's memory management mechanism.

There is also no copy-on-write implemented for `WideStrings`. When you assign one `WideString` to another, new memory is allocated and data is copied. Because of that, `WideStrings` are slower than Ansi and Unicode strings, and as such, should not be used needlessly.

# Arrays

Delphi supports two kinds of arrays. One is of a fixed size and has settable lower and upper bounds. We call them **static arrays**. Others have a lower bound fixed at zero, while the upper bound is variable. In other words, they can grow and shrink. Because of that, they are called **dynamic arrays.**

The following code fragment shows how static and dynamic arrays are declared in Delphi:

```
var
  sarr1: array [2..22] of integer; // static array
  sarr2: array [byte] of string;   // static array
  darr1: array of TDateTime;       // dynamic array
  darr2: TArray<string>;           // dynamic array
```

Every array stores elements of some type. The compiler will treat these elements just the same as variables of that type. In the second declaration above, for example, the element type is `string`. This is a managed type and all 256 elements of the array will be initialized to `nil` automatically.

Static arrays are pretty dull. They have a constant size and as such are created exactly the same way as simple types (except that they typically use more space). Dynamic arrays, on the other hand, are similar to strings, but with a twist.

When you declare a dynamic array, it will start as empty and the variable will contain a `nil` pointer. Only when you change an array size (by using `SetLength` or a `TArray` constructor), a memory will be allocated and a pointer to that memory will be stored in the dynamic array variable. Any change to array size will reallocate this storage memory—just like with the strings.

Modifying elements of an array is simple—again just like with the strings. An address of the element that is being modified is calculated and then item data is copied from one location to another. Of course, if array elements are not of a simple type, appropriate rules for that type will apply. Setting an element of `array of string` brings in the rules for the `string` type and so on.

When you assign one array to another, Delphi again treats them just the same as strings. It simply copies one pointer (to the array data) into another variable. At the end both variables contain the same address. A reference count in the array memory is also incremented. Again, just as strings.

The similarities with string types end here. If you now modify one element in one of the arrays, the same change will apply to the second array! There is no copy-on-write mechanism for dynamic arrays and both array variables will still point to the same array memory.

This is great from the efficiency viewpoint, but may not be exactly what you wanted. There's, luckily, a workaround that will split both arrays into two separate copies. Any time you call a `SetLength` on a shared array, the code will make this array unique, just like `UniqueString` does to strings. Even if the new length is the same as the old one, a unique copy of an array will still be made.

The following code from the `DataTypes` demo demonstrates this. Firstly, it allocates the `arr1` array by using a handy syntax introduced in Delphi XE7. Then it assigns `arr1` to `arr2`. This operation merely copies the pointers and increments the reference count. Both pointers and contents of the arrays are then shown in the log.

After that, the code modifies one element of `arr1` and logs again. To complete the test, the code calls `SetArray` to make `arr2` unique and modifies `arr1` again:

```
procedure TfrmDataTypes.btnSharedDynArraysClick(Sender: TObject);
var
  arr1, arr2: TArray<Integer>;
begin
  arr1 := [1, 2, 3, 4, 5];
  arr2 := arr1;
  ListBox1.Items.Add(Format('arr1 = %p [%s], arr2 = %p [%s]',
    [PPointer(@arr1)^, ToStringArr(arr1),
      PPointer(@arr2)^, ToStringArr(arr2)]));

  arr1[2] := 42;
  ListBox1.Items.Add(Format('arr1 = %p [%s], arr2 = %p [%s]',
    [PPointer(@arr1)^, ToStringArr(arr1),
      PPointer(@arr2)^, ToStringArr(arr2)]));

  SetLength(arr2, Length(arr2));
  arr1[2] := 17;
  ListBox1.Items.Add(Format('arr1 = %p [%s], arr2 = %p [%s]',
    [PPointer(@arr1)^, ToStringArr(arr1),
      PPointer(@arr2)^, ToStringArr(arr2)]));
end;
```

The output of the program shows that after the assignment both arrays point to the same memory and contain the same data. This doesn't change after `arr1[2] := 42`. Both arrays still point to the same memory and contain the same (changed) data.

After `SetLength`, however, arrays point to a separate memory address and changing `arr1` only changes that array:

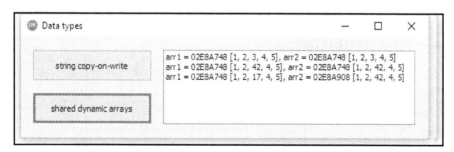

# Records

To wrap up the analysis of built-in data types, we have to discuss structured types that can store elements of different types—namely records, classes, and interfaces.

The simplest of them are records. They are actually quite similar to simple types and static arrays. As simple types, records are, as we say, statically allocated. Local variables of record type are part of a thread's stack, global variables are part of the global process memory, and records that are parts of other structured types are stored as part of the owner's memory.

The important thing that you have to remember when using records is that the compiler manages the life cycle for their fields that are themselves managed. In other words, if you declare a local variable of a record type, all its managed fields will be automatically initialized, while unmanaged types will be left at random values (at whatever value the stack at that position contains at that moment).

The following code from the `DataTypes` demo demonstrates this behavior. When you run it, it will show some random values for fields `a` and `c` while the `b` field will always be initialized to an empty string.

The code also shows the simplest way to initialize a record to default values (zero for integer and real types, empty string for strings, `nil` for classes and so on). The built-in (but mostly undocumented) function `Default` creates a record in which all fields are set to default values and you can then assign it to a variable:

```
type
  TRecord = record
    a: integer;
    b: string;
    c: integer;
  end;

procedure TfrmDataTypes.ShowRecord(const rec: TRecord);
begin
  ListBox1.Items.Add(Format('a = %d, b = ''%s'', c = %d',
    [rec.a, rec.b, rec.c]));
end;

procedure TfrmDataTypes.btnRecordInitClick(Sender: TObject);
var
  rec: TRecord;
```

```
begin
  ShowRecord(rec);
  rec := Default(TRecord);
  ShowRecord(rec);
end;
```

When you run this code, you'll get some random numbers for a and c in the first log, but they will always be zero in the second log:

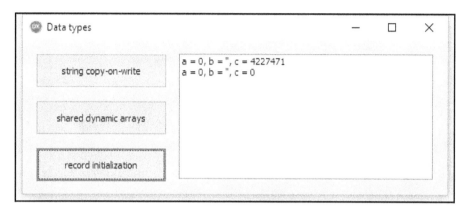

The initialization of managed fields affects the execution speed. The compiler doesn't create an optimized initialization code for each record type, but does the initialization by calling generic and relatively slow code.

This also happens when you assign one record to another. If all fields are unmanaged, the code can just copy data from one memory location to another. However, when at least one of the fields is of a managed type, the compiler will again call a generic copying method which is not optimized for the specific record.

The following example from the DataTypes demo shows the difference. It copies two different records a million times. Both records are of the same size, except that TUnmanaged contains only fields of unmanaged type NativeUInt and TManaged contains only fields of managed type IInterface:

```
type
  TUnmanaged = record
    a, b, c, d: NativeUInt;
  end;

  TManaged = record
    a, b, c, d: IInterface;
  end;
```

```
procedure TfrmDataTypes.btnCopyRecClick(Sender: TObject);
var
  u1, u2: TUnmanaged;
  m1, m2: TManaged;
  i: Integer;
  sw: TStopwatch;
begin
  u1 := Default(TUnmanaged);
  sw := TStopwatch.StartNew;
  for i := 1 to 1000000 do
    u2 := u1;
  sw.Stop;
  ListBox1.Items.Add(Format('TUnmanaged: %d ms',
[sw.ElapsedMilliseconds]));

  m1 := Default(TManaged);
  sw := TStopwatch.StartNew;
  for i := 1 to 1000000 do
    m2 := m1;
  sw.Stop;
  ListBox1.Items.Add(Format('TManaged: %d ms', [sw.ElapsedMilliseconds]));
end;
```

The following image shows the measured difference in execution time. Granted, 31 ms to copy a million records is not a lot, but still the *unmanaged* version is five times faster. In some situations, that can mean a lot:

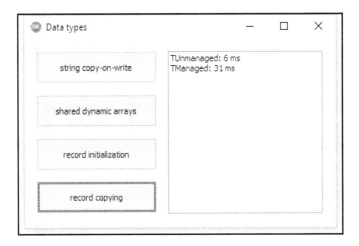

# Classes

While classes look superficially similar to records, they are in fact implemented in a completely different manner.

When you create an object of a class by calling the constructor for that class, the code allocates memory from the memory manager and fills it with zeroes. That, in effect, initializes all fields, managed and unmanaged, to default values. A pointer to this memory is stored in the variable which receives the result of a constructor.

When an object is destroyed, its memory is returned to the system (again, through the memory manager).

The rest of this section applies only to *standard* compilers (Window 32- and 64-bit and OS/X). If you are using an ARC-enabled compiler (Android, iOS, and Linux) then classes behave the same as interfaces. See the next section for more details.

Copying one variable of a class type to another just copies the pointer. In effect you then have two variables pointing to the same object. There is no reference counting associating with objects and if you now destroy one variable (by calling the Free method), the other will still point to the same part of memory. Actually, both variables will point to that unused memory and if it gets allocated later (and it will), both variables will point to memory belonging to another object:

```
var
  o1, o2: TObject;
begin
  o1 := TObject.Create;
  o2 := o1;
  // o1 and o2 now point to the same object
  o1.Free;
  // o1 and o2 now point to unowned memory
  o1 := nil;
  // o2 still points to unowned memory
end;
```

If you have a long-living variable or field containing an object of some class and you destroy the object, make sure that you also set the value/field to nil.

# Interfaces

From the viewpoint of memory management, interfaces in Delphi are implemented as classes with added reference counting. To create an interface, you actually have to create an object of a class, which will get a reference count of 1. If you then assign this interface to another variable, both will point to the same memory and the reference count will be incremented to 2.

There is no equivalent to `SetLength` or `UniqueString` that would make a unique copy of an interface. That would require duplicating the underlying object and Delphi has no built-in support for that.

The object implementing the interface is destroyed when its reference count falls to 0:

```
var
  i1, i2: IInterface;
begin
  i1 := TInterfacedObject.Create;
  // i1 points to an object with reference count 1
  i2 := i1;
  // both i1 and i2 point to a same object with reference count 2
  i1 := nil;
  // i2 now points to an object with reference count 1
  i2 := nil;
  // reference count dropped to 0 and object is destroyed
end;
```

Although interfaces are very similar to classes, all this reference count management takes its cost. It is implemented with something called *interlocked* instructions which are a bit slower than normal increment/decrement instructions. I'll discuss this in more detail in Chapter 5, *Getting Started with the Parallel World*.

This only makes a measurable difference when you are assigning interfaces a lot, but sometimes this is exactly what happens. I'll show an example in the next section.

# Optimizing method calls

I know you are eagerly waiting to optimize some real code, but please let me stay for a little bit more on the theoretical side of the equation. I spent all that time talking about the behavior of built-in data types but I didn't say anything about how data is passed to methods. This, much shorter and more surprising section (you'll see!) will fix this. As I'll be talking about speeding up method calls, I'll also throw in a short discussion of method inlining, just for a good measure. But first, parameters!

# Parameter passing

In essence, Delphi knows two ways of passing parameters to a method (or procedure, or function, or anonymous method, it's all the same). Parameters can be passed by value or by reference.

The former makes a copy of the original value and passes that copy to a method. The code inside the method can then modify its copy however it wants and this won't change the original value.

The latter approach doesn't pass the value to the method but just an address of that value (a pointer to it). This can be faster than passing by value as a pointer will generally be smaller than an array or a record. In this case, the method can then use this address to access (and modify) the original value; something that is not possible if we pass a parameter by value.

Passing by reference is indicated by prefixing a parameter name with var, out, or const. A parameter is passed by value when no such prefix is used.

The difference between var and out is mostly semantic (although small changes in generated code are possible). Prefixing a parameter by out tells the compiler that we are not passing anything into the method (it may even be an uninitialized value) and we are only interested in the result. The var prefix, on the other hand, declares that we will be passing some value in and that we expect to get something out.

In practice, var is usually used even when a parameter is not used to provide any data to the method; just to return something.

The const prefix is a bit different. When it is used, the compiler will prevent us from making any changes to the parameter. (With some exceptions, as we'll soon see.) In essence, const is an optimization prefix used when we want to pass a larger amount of data (a record, for example). It will ensure that the parameter is passed by reference while the compiler will make sure that the data is not changed.

The const prefix is also useful when the parameter is a managed type (for example a string or interface). When you pass such type by value, the code increments the reference count at the beginning of the method and decrements it at the end. If the parameter is marked as const, the reference count is not incremented/decremented and this can make a difference in the long run.

The `ParameterPassing` demo passes array, string, record, and interface parameters to a method multiple times and measures the time. I will skip most of the code here as it is fairly dull and looks all the same. I'll just focus on a few interesting details first and then give an overview of measured results.

The most uninteresting of all are static arrays and records. Passing by value makes a copy while passing by reference just passes a pointer to the data. That is all.

When you pass a string by using `const`, just an address is passed to the method and a reference count is not touched. That makes such calls very fast.

Passing by value, however, uses the copy-on-write mechanism. When a string is passed by value, a reference count is incremented and a pointer to string data is passed to the method. Only when the method modifies the string parameter, is a real copy of the string data made.

As an example, the following code in the demo is called 10 million times when you click the **string** button:

```
procedure TfrmParamPassing.ProcString(s: string);
begin
  // Enable next line and code will suddenly become much slower!
  // s[1] := 'a';
end;
```

This executes in a few hundred milliseconds. Uncomment the assignment and the code will suddenly run for 20 seconds (give or take) as a copy of quite large string will be made each time the method is called.

Interfaces behave similarly to strings, except that there is no copy-on-write mechanism. The only difference in execution speed comes from incrementing and decrementing the reference count.

At the beginning of this section, I promised some interesting results, so here they are! When a parameter is a dynamic array, strange things happen. But let's start with the code.

To measure parameter passing, the code creates an array of 100,000 elements, sets the element `[1]` to 1 and calls `ScanDynArray` 10,000 times. `ScanDynArray` sets `arr[1]` to 42 and exits.

Another method, `btnConstDynArrayClick` (not shown) works exactly the same except that it calls `ScanDynArrayConst` instead of `ScanDynArray`:

```
const
  CArraySize = 100000;

procedure TfrmParamPassing.ScanDynArray(arr: TArray<Integer>);
begin
  arr[1] := 42;
end;

procedure TfrmParamPassing.ScanDynArrayConst(const arr: TArray<Integer>);
begin
  // strangely, compiler allows that
  arr[1] := 42;
end;

procedure TfrmParamPassing.btnDynArrayClick(Sender: TObject);
var
  arr: TArray<Integer>;
  sw: TStopwatch;
  i: Integer;
begin
  SetLength(arr, CArraySize);
  arr[1] := 1;
  sw := TStopwatch.StartNew;
  for i := 1 to 10000 do
    ScanDynArray(arr);
  sw.Stop;
  ListBox1.Items.Add(Format('TArray<Integer>: %d ms, arr[1] = %d',
    [sw.ElapsedMilliseconds, arr[1]]));
end;
```

Can you spot the weird code in this example? It is the assignment in the `ScanDynArrayConst` method. I said that the `const` prefix will prevent such modifications of parameters, and in most cases it does. Dynamic array are, however different.

When you pass a dynamic array to a method, Delphi treats it just like a pointer. If you mark it as `const`, nothing changes as only this pointer is treated as a constant, not the data it points to. That's why you can modify the original array even through the `const` parameter.

That's the first level of weirdness. Let's crank it up!

If you check the System unit, you'll see that `TArray<T>` is defined like this:

```
type
  TArray<T> = array of T;
```

So, in theory, the code will work the same if we replace `TArray<Integer>` with `array of Integer`? Not at all!

```
procedure TfrmParamPassing.ScanDynArray2(arr: array of integer);
begin
  arr[1] := 42;
end;

procedure TfrmParamPassing.ScanDynArrayConst2(const arr: array of integer);
begin
  // in this case following line doesn't compile
  // arr[1] := 42;
end;
```

In this case, the compiler won't allow us to modify `arr[1]` when the parameter is marked `const`! Even more, in the `ScanDynArray2` method the code makes a full copy of the array, just as if we were passing a normal static array!

This is a legacy from the versions before Delphi 2009, when we didn't have generics yet but we already got dynamic arrays through the `array of T` syntax. The compiler has special handling for this syntax built in and this handling is still in effect in the modern day.

Is this weird enough for you? No? No problem, I can go one better.

If we declare `type TIntArray = array of Integer` and then rewrite the code to use this array, we get the original `TArray<T>` behavior back. The array is always passed by reference and the code can modify the original array through the `const` parameter:

```
type
  TIntArray = array of Integer;

procedure TfrmParamPassing.ScanDynArray3(arr: TIntArray);
begin
  arr[1] := 42;
end;

procedure TfrmParamPassing.ScanDynArrayConst3(const arr: TIntArray);
begin
  // it compiles!
  arr[1] := 42;
end;
```

Let's now analyze the results of the `ParameterPassing` demo program.

Static arrays are passed as a copy (by value) or as a pointer (by reference). The difference in speed clearly proves that (174 vs. 0 ms). In both cases, the original value of the array element is not modified (it is 1).

The same happens when the array is declared as `array of Integer` (lines starting with `array of Integer` and `const array of Integer`) in the image.

`TArray<Integer>` and `TIntArray` behave exactly the same. An array is always passed by reference and the original value can be modified (it shows as `42` in the log).

Records are either copied (by value) or passed as a pointer (by reference) which brings the difference of 157 vs. 51 ms.

Strings are always passed as a pointer. When they are passed as a normal parameter, the reference count is incremented/decremented. When they are passed as a `const` parameter, the reference count is not modified. This brings a difference of 257 vs. 47 ms. A similar effect shows with the interface type parameters:

I have to point out that demos for different types cannot be compared directly with one another. For example, the loop for testing array types repeats 10,000 times while the loop for testing strings and interfaces repeats 10,000,000 times.

# Method inlining

Previously in this chapter, I spent quite some time describing the mechanics of enabling and disabling method inlining, but I never said what that actually means. To put it simply, method inlining allows one method to be compiled as if its code would be a part of another.

When you call a method that is not marked as inlineable (doesn't have the `inline` suffix), the compiler prepares method parameters in an appropriate way (in registers and on stack, but I'm not going there) and then executes a `CALL` assembler instruction.

If the called method is marked as inlineable, then compiler basically just inserts the body of the inlineable method inside the code of the caller. This speeds up the code, but also makes it larger as this happens in every place that calls the inlineable method.

Let me give you an example. The following code from the `Inlining` demo increments a value 10 million times:

```
function IncrementInline(value: integer): integer; inline;
begin
  Result := value + 1;
end;

procedure TfrmInlining.Button2Click(Sender: TObject);
var
  value: Integer;
  i: Integer;
begin
  value := 0;
  for i := 1 to 10000000 do
    value := IncrementInline(value);
end;
```

As the `IncrementInline` is marked as `inline` (and is therefore inlineable if the compiler settings are not preventing it), the code generated by the compiler doesn't actually `CALL` into that method 10 million times. The code actually looks more like a code generated by the next example:

```
procedure TfrmInlining.Button2Click(Sender: TObject);
var
  value: Integer;
```

```
    i: Integer;
begin
  value := 0;
  for i := 1 to 10000000 do
    value := value + 1;
end;
```

If you run the demo, you'll see that the inlined version executes much faster than the non-inlined code. On my test computer, the non-inlined version needed 53 ms while the inline version executed in 26 ms.

When you call the `inline` method from the same unit, make sure that the `inline` method is implemented **before** it is called. Otherwise, the compiler will just silently use the method as if it was a normal method and won't generate even a hint. In the next example, the method is actually not inlined, although we may expect it to be:

```
type
  TfrmInlining = class(TForm)
    // some unimportant stuff ...
    procedure Button3Click(Sender: TObject);
  private
    function IncrementShouldBeInline(value: integer): integer; inline;
  public
  end;

procedure TfrmInlining.Button3Click(Sender: TObject);
var
  value: Integer;
  i: Integer;
begin
  value := 0;
  for i := 1 to 10000000 do
    value := IncrementShouldBeInline(value);
end;

function TfrmInlining.IncrementShouldBeInline(value: integer): integer;
begin
  Result := value + 1;
end;
```

Another problem that inline code can cause, is that in some situations the result may even be slower than the non-inlined version. Sometimes the compiler just doesn't do a good enough job. Remember, always measure!

For a long time, the compiler had another problem. When the inlined function returned an interface, it made another, hidden copy of the returned value which was only released at the end of the method that called the inlined function. That could cause the interface to not be destroyed as the programmer expected.

This problem, for example, caused threads in Delphi's `TThreadPool` object not to be released at the correct time. It was only fixed in the 10.2 Tokyo release where Embarcadero introduced an improved compiler which generates better code.

And now I'm really finished with theory. Let's do some code!

# The magic of pointers

Our friend, Mr. Smith, has progressed a lot from his first steps in Delphi. Now he is playing with graphics. He wants to build a virtual reality app that would allow you to walk through the Antarctica forests. While he's getting some success, he has problems displaying the correct colors on the screen.

A part of his code is producing textures in **Blue-Green-Red** (**BGR**) byte order, while the graphics driver needs them in the more standard **Red-Green-Blue** (**RGB**) order. He already wrote some code to fix this problem, but his solution is a bit too slow. He'd like to push a frame or two more from the system and so I promised that I'd help him optimize the converter. I'd be glad to do it, as his problem neatly fits into the story of *pointers*.

A pointer is a variable that stores an *address* of some data (other variables, dynamically allocated memory, specific character in the string ...). It is always of the same size, 4 bytes on 32-bit systems and 8 bytes on 64-bit systems—just the same as `NativeInt` and `NativeUInt`. This is not a coincidence as converting a pointer into an integer or back is sometimes quite practical.

Let's say, for example, that we have a `TPoint3` record containing a three-dimensional point. We can then declare a pointer to this type with the syntax `^TPoint3` and we can give this type a name, `PPoint3`. While the size of `TPoint3` is 24 bytes, the size of `PPoint3` is 4 or 8 bytes, depending on the compiler target (32- or 64-bit):

```
type
  TPoint3 = record
    X,Y,Z: double;
  end;
  PPoint3 = ^TPoint3;
```

If we now declare a variable P3 of type TPoint3 and variable PP3 of type PPoint3, we can then change the contents of PP3 to the address of P3 by executing `PP3 := @P3`. After that, we can use the `PP3^` notation to refer to the data that PP3 is *pointing to* (that is P3).

Delphi also allows a shorter form to access fields via a pointer variable. We don't have to write `PP3^.X`; a simpler `PP3.X` is enough:

```
var
  P3: TPoint3;
  PP3: PPoint3;
begin
  PP3 := @P3;
  PP3^.X := 1;
  // P3.X is now 1
  PP3.Y := 2;
  // P3.Y is now 2
  P3.Z := 3;
  // PP3^.Z is now 3
end;
```

Unlike the original Pascal, Delphi allows some arithmetical operations on the pointer. For example, you can always do `Inc(ptr)` and that will increment the address stored in `ptr`. It will not increment it by 1, though, but by the size of the type that the `ptr` is pointing to.

Some types, such as `PChar`, `PAnsiChar`, and `PByte`, will also allow you to use them in some basic arithmetic expressions. In reality, all pointer types support that, but only pointer types that were defined when the compiler directive `{$POINTERMATH ON}` was in effect will allow you to do that by default. For other types, you have to enable `{$POINTERMATH ON}` in the place where you do the calculation.

In the following example, the code `pi := pi + 1` wouldn't compile without explicit `{$POINTERMATH ON}` as this directive is not present in the System unit where `PInteger` is defined:

```
procedure TfrmPointers.btnPointerMathClick(Sender: TObject);
var
  pb: PByte;
  pi: PInteger;
  pa: PAnsiChar;
  pc: PChar;
begin
  pb := pointer(0);
  pb := pb + 1;
  ListBox1.Items.Add(Format('PByte increment = %d', [NativeUInt(pb)]));
```

```
pi := pointer(0);
{$POINTERMATH ON}
pi := pi + 1;
{$POINTERMATH OFF}
ListBox1.Items.Add(Format('PInteger increment = %d', [NativeUInt(pi)]));

pa := pointer(0);
pa := pa + 1;
ListBox1.Items.Add(Format('PAnsiChar increment = %d', [NativeUInt(pa)]));

pc := pointer(0);
pc := pc + 1;
ListBox1.Items.Add(Format('PChar increment = %d', [NativeUInt(pc)]));
end;
```

Pointers are very useful when you are creating dynamic data structures, such as trees and linked lists, but that is a bit beyond the scope of this book. They are also important when you want to dynamically allocate records. We'll cover that in the next chapter. And they are very handy—as you'll see immediately—when we are processing data buffers.

Let us return to Mr. Smith's problem. He has a graphic texture, organized as an array of pixels. Each pixel is stored as a cardinal value. The highest byte of a pixel contains the Transparency component (also known as **Alpha**), the next byte contains the Blue component, the byte after that the Green component, and the lowest byte contains the Red component:

Pixel storage. Above—original format. Below—desired format.

Mr. Smith has already created a small test code which you can find in the demo `Pointers`. The code creates an array with 10 million elements and fills it with the value $0055AACC. The Blue color is set to $55, Green to $AA, and Red to $CC for all pixels.

The code then walks over the array and processes each element. Firstly, it extracts the Blue component by masking only one byte (AND $00FF0000) and moving it 16 bits to the right (SHR 16). Then it extracts the Red component (AND $000000FF). At the end, it clears both Blue and Red out of the original data (AND $FF00FF00) and ORs the Red and Blue components back in. Red is now shifted left by 16 places (SHL 16) so that it will be stored in the second highest byte:

```
function TfrmPointers.PrepareData: TArray<Cardinal>;
var
  i: Integer;
begin
  SetLength(Result, 100000000);
  for i := Low(Result) to High(Result) do
    Result[i] := $0055AACC;
end;

procedure TfrmPointers.btnArrayClick(Sender: TObject);
var
  rgbData: TArray<Cardinal>;
  i: Integer;
  r,b: Byte;
begin
  rgbData := PrepareData;

  for i := Low(rgbData) to High(rgbData) do
  begin
    b := rgbData[i] AND $00FF0000 SHR 16;
    r := rgbData[i] AND $000000FF;
    rgbData[i] := rgbData[i] AND $FF00FF00 OR (r SHL 16) OR b;
  end;
end;
```

This code runs quite fast, but all that bit operations take some time. How can we speed it up?

The best approach is just to ignore the concept that *a pixel is a Cardinal* and treat each color component as an individual byte. We can then point one pointer to the Red component of the first pixel and another to the Blue component and just swap the values. Then we can advance each pointer to the next pixel and repeat the process.

To do that, we have to know at least a few things about how Delphi stores integer values in memory. The simple answer to that is—as the CPU expects them. Intel processors are using a *little-endian* format (yes, that is a technical term) which defines that the least important byte is stored in memory first (*little end* first).

If we put three pixels into memory so that the first starts at address 0, they would look just as in the image here:

Memory layout of three consecutive pixels

Our improved code uses that knowledge. It uses two pointers, both of type `PByte` (a pointer to a `byte` value). The `pBlue` pointer points to the current Blue byte and the `pRed` pointer points to the current Red byte. To initialize them, the code sets both to the address of the first pixel (which is the same as the address of its lowest byte) and then increments `pBlue` by 2 bytes.

In the loop, the code simply stores current the Red pixel into a temporary value (`r := pRed^`), copies the Blue pixel into the Red pixel (`pRed^ := pBlue^`) and stores the temporary Red pixel into the Blue location (`pBlue^ := r`). It then increments both pointers to the next pixel:

```
procedure TfrmPointers.btnPointerClick(Sender: TObject);
var
  rgbData: TArray<cardinal>;
  i: Integer;
  r: Byte;
  pRed: PByte;
  pBlue: PByte;
begin
  rgbData := PrepareData;

  pRed := @rgbData[0];
  pBlue := pRed;
  Inc(pBlue,2);
  for i := Low(rgbData) to High(rgbData) do
  begin
    r := pRed^;
    pRed^ := pBlue^;
    pBlue^ := r;
    Inc(pRed, SizeOf(rgbData[0]));
    Inc(pBlue, SizeOf(rgbData[0]));
  end;
end;
```

The code is a bit more convoluted but not that harder to understand, as all that pixel operations (AND, SHR ...) in the original code weren't easy to read either. It is also much faster. On my test computer, the original code needs 159 ms, while the new code finishes in 72 ms, which is more than twice the speed!

To make a long story short—pointers are incredibly useful. They also make the code harder to understand, so use them sparingly and document the code.

# Going the assembler way

Sometimes, when you definitely have to squeeze everything from the code, there is only one solution—rewrite it in assembler. My response to any such idea is always the same—don't do it! Rewriting code in an assembler is almost always much more trouble than it is worth.

I do admit that there are legitimate reasons for writing an assembler code. I looked around and quickly found five areas where an assembler is still significantly present. They are: memory managers, graphical code, cryptography routines (encryption, hashing), compression, and interfacing with hardware.

Even in these areas,  situations change quickly. I tested some small assembler routines from the graphical library, *GraphicEx*, and was quite surprised to find out that they are not significantly faster than equivalent Delphi code.

The biggest gain that you'll get from using an assembler is when you want to process a large buffer of data (such as a bitmap) and then do the same operation on all elements. In such cases, you can maybe use the SSE2 instructions which runs circles around the slow 386 instruction set that Delphi compiler uses.

As assembler is not my game, (I can read it but I can't write good, optimized assembler code), my example is extremely simple. The code in the demo program, AsmCode implements a four-dimensional vector (a record with four floating point fields) and a method that multiplies two such fields:

```
type
  TVec4 = packed record
    X, Y, Z, W: Single;
  end;

function Multiply_PAS(const A, B: TVec4): TVec4;
begin
  Result.X := A.X * B.X;
```

```
    Result.Y := A.Y * B.Y;
    Result.Z := A.Z * B.Z;
    Result.W := A.W * B.W;
  end;
```

As it turns out, this is exactly an operation that can be implemented using SSE2 instructions. In the code shown next, first `movups` moves vector *A* into register `xmm0`. Next, `movups` does the same for the other vector. Then, the magical instruction `mulps` multiplies four single-precision values in register `xmm0` with four single-precision values in register `xmm1`. At the end, `movups` is used to copy the result of the multiplication into the function result:

```
function Multiply_ASM(const A, B: TVec4): TVec4;
asm
  movups xmm0, [A]
  movups xmm1, [B]
  mulps xmm0, xmm1
  movups [Result], xmm0
end;
```

Running the test shows a clear winner. While `Multiply_PAS` needs 53 ms to multiply 10 million vectors, `Multiply_ASM` does that in half the time—24 ms.

As you can see in the previous example, assembler instructions are introduced with the `asm` statement and ended with `end`. In the Win32 compiler, you can mix Pascal and assembler code inside one method. This is not allowed with the Win64 compiler. In 64-bit mode, a method can only be written in pure Pascal or in pure assembler.

The `asm` instruction is only supported by Windows and OS/X compilers. In older sources, you'll also find an `assembler` instruction which is only supported for backwards compatibility and does nothing.

I'll end this short excursion into the assembler world with some advice. Whenever you are implementing a part of your program in assembler, please also create a Pascal version. The best practice is to use a conditional symbol, `PUREPASCAL` as a switch. With this approach, we could rewrite the multiplication code as follows:

```
function Multiply(const A, B: TVec4): TVec4;
{$IFDEF PUREPASCAL}
begin
  Result.X := A.X * B.X;
  Result.Y := A.Y * B.Y;
  Result.Z := A.Z * B.Z;
  Result.W := A.W * B.W;
end;
{$ELSE}
```

```
asm
  movups xmm0, [A]
  movups xmm1, [B]
  mulps xmm0, xmm1
  movups [Result], xmm0
end;
{$ENDIF}
```

# Returning to SlowCode

At the end of this chapter, I'll return to the now well-known `SlowCode` example. At the end of the previous chapter, we significantly adapted the code and ended with a version that calculates prime numbers with the Sieve of Eratosthenes (`SlowCode_Sieve`). That version processed 10 million numbers in 1,072 milliseconds. Let's see if we can improve that.

The obvious target for optimization is the `Reverse` function which creates the result by appending characters one at a time. We've seen in this chapter that modifying a string can cause frequent memory allocations:

```
function Reverse(s: string): string;
var
  ch: char;
begin
  Result := '';
  for ch in s do
    Result := ch + Result;
end;
```

Instead of optimizing this function, let's look at how it is used. The `Filter` method uses it to reverse a number:

```
reversed := StrToInt(Reverse(IntToStr(i)));
```

This statement brings in another memory allocation (in function `IntToStr` which creates a new string), and executes some code that has to parse a string and return a number (`StrToInt`). Quite some work for an operation that doesn't really need strings at all.

It turns out that it is very simple to reverse a decimal number without using strings. You just have to repeatedly divide it by 10 and multiply remainders back into a new number:

```
function ReverseInt(value: Integer): Integer;
begin
  Result := 0;
  while value <> 0 do
```

```
    begin
      Result := Result * 10 + (value mod 10);
      value := value div 10;
    end;
end;
```

The new `Filter` method can then use this method to reverse a number:

```
function Filter(list: TList<Integer>): TArray<Integer>;
var
  i: Integer;
  reversed: Integer;
begin
  SetLength(Result, 0);
  for i in list do
  begin
    reversed := ReverseInt(i);
    if not ElementInDataDivides(list, reversed) then
    begin
      SetLength(Result, Length(Result) + 1);
      Result[High(Result)] := i;
    end;
  end;
end;
```

The new code in the demo program, `SlowCode_Sieve_v2` indeed runs a bit faster. It processes 10 million elements in 851 milliseconds, which is roughly a 20% improvement.

Is there something more that we learned in this chapter and can be applied to that program? Sure—turn on the optimization! Just add one line—`{$OPTIMIZATION ON}`—and you'll get a significantly faster version. `SlowCode_Sieve_v2_opt` processes 10 million elements in a mere 529 ms!

There is still room for improvement in that program. It will, however, have to wait until the next chapter.

# Summary

The topic of this chapter was fine-tuning the code. We started with Delphi compiler settings which can, in some cases, significantly change the code execution speed, and we learned what those situations are.

Then I introduced a simple but effective optimization—extracting common expressions. This optimization served as an introduction to the *CPU Window*, which can help us analyze compiled Delphi code.

After that I returned to basics. Creating a fast program means knowing how Delphi works and so I looked into built-in data types. We saw what is fast and what is not.

As a logical follow-up to data types we looked into methods—what happens when you pass parameters to a method and how to speed that up. We also reviewed a few surprising implementation details which can create problems in your code.

I ended the chapter with three practical examples. Firstly, we used pointers to speed up bitmap processing. Next, a short section on assembler code has shown how to write a fast assembler replacement for Pascal code. At the end, we revisited the `SlowCode` program (which isn't so slow anymore) and made it even faster.

In the next chapter, we'll go even deeper. I'll explore the topic of *memory managers*—what and how they are and why it is important to know how the built-in memory manager in Delphi is implemented. As usual, we'll also optimize some code. So stay tuned!

# 4

# Memory Management

In the previous chapter, I explained a few things with a lot of hand-waving. I was talking about memory being *allocated* but I never told what that actually means. Now is the time to fill in the missing pieces.

Memory management is part of practically every computing system. Multiple programs must coexist inside a limited memory space, and that can only be possible if the operating system is taking care of it. When a program needs some memory, for example, to create an object, it can ask the operating system and it will give it a slice of shared memory. When an object is not needed anymore, that memory can be returned to the loving care of the operating system.

Slicing and dicing memory straight from the operating system is a relatively slow operation. In lots of cases, a memory system also doesn't know how to return small chunks of memory. For example, if you call Windows' `VirtualAlloc` function to get 20 bytes of memory, it will actually reserve 4 KB (or 4,096 bytes) for you. In other words, 4,076 bytes would be wasted.

To fix these and other problems, programming languages typically implement their own internal memory management algorithms. When you request 20 bytes of memory, the request goes to that internal memory manager. It still requests memory from the operating system but then splits it internally into multiple parts.

In a hypothetical scenario, the internal memory manager would request 4,096 bytes from the operating system and give 20 bytes of that to the application. The next time the application would request some memory (30 bytes for example), the internal memory manager would get that memory from the same 4,096-byte block.

To move from hypothetical to specific, Delphi also includes such a memory manager. From Delphi 2006, this memory manager is called *FastMM*. It was written as an open source memory manager by Pierre LeRiche with help from other Delphi programmers, and was later licensed by Borland. FastMM was a great improvement over the previous Delphi memory manager and, although it does not perform perfectly in the parallel programming world, it still functions very well after more than ten years.

Delphi exposes a public interface to replace the internal memory manager, so you can easily replace FastMM with a different memory manager. As we'll see later in this chapter, this can sometimes be helpful.

We will cover the following topics in this chapter:

- What happens when strings and arrays are reallocated and how can we speed this up?
- Which functions can an application use to allocate memory?
- How can we use memory manager to dynamically create a record?
- How is FastMM internally implemented and why does it matter to a programmer?
- How can we replace FastMM with a different memory manager?
- What can we do to improve SlowCode even more?

# Optimizing strings and array allocations

When you create a string, the code allocates memory for its content, copies the content into that memory, and stores the address of this memory in the string variable. Of course, you all know that by now as this was the topic of the previous chapter.

If you append a character to this string, it must be stored somewhere in that memory. However, there is no place to store the string. The original memory block was just big enough to store the original content. The code must therefore enlarge that memory block, and only then can the appended character be stored in the newly acquired space.

As we'll see further on in the chapter, FastMM tries to make sure that the memory can be expanded *in place*, that is, without copying the original data into a new, larger block of memory. Still, this is not always possible and sometimes data must be copied around.

A very similar scenario plays out when you extend a dynamic array. Memory that contains the array data can sometimes be extended in place (without moving), but often this cannot be done.

If you do a lot of appending, these constant reallocations will start to slow down the code. The Reallocation demo shows a few examples of such behavior and possible workarounds.

The first example, activated by the **Append String** button, simply appends the `'*'` character to a string 10 million times. The code looks simple, but the `s := s + '*'` assignment hides a potentially slow string reallocation:

```
procedure TfrmReallocation.btnAppendStringClick(Sender: TObject);
var
  s: String;
  i: Integer;
begin
  s := '';
  for i := 1 to CNumChars do
    s := s + '*';
end;
```

By now, you probably know that I don't like to present problems that I don't have solutions for and this is not an exception. In this case, the solution is called SetLength. This function sets a string to a specified size. You can make it shorter, or you can make it longer. You can even set it to the same length as before.

In case you are enlarging the string, you have to keep in mind that SetLength will allocate enough memory to store the new string, but it will not initialize it. In other words, the newly allocated string space will contain random data.

A click on the **SetLength String** button activates the optimized version of the string appending code. As we know that the resulting string will be CNumChars long, the code can call SetLength(s, CNumChars) to preallocate all the memory in one step. After that, we should not *append* characters to the string as that would add new characters at the end of the preallocated string. Rather, we have to store characters directly into the string by writing to s[i]:

```
procedure TfrmReallocation.btnSetLengthClick(Sender: TObject);
var
  s: String;
  i: Integer;
begin
  SetLength(s, CNumChars);
  for i := 1 to CNumChars do
```

```
      s[i] := '*';
  end;
```

Comparing the speed shows that the second approach is significantly faster. It runs in 33 ms instead of the original 142 ms.

 This code still calls some string management functions internally, namely `UniqueString`. It returns fairly quickly, but still represents some overhead. If you are pushing for the fastest possible execution, you can initialize the string by using a *sliding pointer*, just as in the example from the previous chapter.

A similar situation happens when you are extending a dynamic array. The code triggered by the **Append array** button shows how an array may be extended by one element at a time in a loop. Admittedly, the code looks very weird as nobody in their right mind would write a loop like this. In reality, however, similar code would be split into multiple longer functions and may be hard to spot:

```
procedure TfrmReallocation.btnAppendArrayClick(Sender: TObject);
var
  arr: TArray<char>;
  i: Integer;
begin
  SetLength(arr, 0);
  for i := 1 to CNumChars do begin
    SetLength(arr, Length(arr) + 1);
    arr[High(arr)] := '*';
  end;
end;
```

The solution is similar to the string case. We can preallocate the whole array by calling the `SetLength` function and then write the data into the array elements. We just have to keep in mind that the first array element always has index 0:

```
procedure TfrmReallocation.btnSetLengthArrayClick(Sender: TObject);
var
  arr: TArray<char>;
  i: Integer;
begin
  SetLength(arr, CNumChars);
  for i := 1 to CNumChars do
    arr[i-1] := '*';
end;
```

Improvements in speed are similar to the string demo. The original code needs 230 ms to append ten million elements, while the improved code executes in 26 ms.

The third case when you may want to preallocate storage space is when you are appending to a list. As an example, I'll look into a TList<T> class. Internally, it stores the data in a TArray<T>, so it again suffers from constant memory reallocation when you are adding data to the list.

The short demo code appends 10 million elements to a list. As opposed to the previous array demo, this is a completely normal looking code, found many times in many applications:

```
procedure TfrmReallocation.btnAppendTListClick(Sender: TObject);
var
  list: TList<Char>;
  i: Integer;
begin
  list := TList<Char>.Create;
  try
    for i := 1 to CNumChars do
      list.Add('*');
  finally
    FreeAndNil(list);
  end;
end;
```

To preallocate memory inside a list, you can set the Capacity property to an expected number of elements in the list. This doesn't prevent the list from growing at a later time; it just creates an initial estimate. You can also use Capacity to reduce memory space used for the list after deleting lots of elements from it.

The difference between a list and a string or an array is that, after setting Capacity, you still cannot access list[i] elements directly. Firstly you have to Add them, just as if Capacity was not assigned:

```
procedure TfrmReallocation.btnSetCapacityTListClick(Sender: TObject);
var
  list: TList<Char>;
  i: Integer;
begin
  list := TList<Char>.Create;
  try
    list.Capacity := CNumChars;
    for i := 1 to CNumChars do
      list.Add('*');
```

```
   finally
     FreeAndNil(list);
   end;
 end;
```

Comparing the execution speed shows only a small improvement. The original code executed in 167 ms, while the new version needed 145 ms. The reason for that relatively small change is that `TList<T>` already manages its storage array. When it runs out of space, it will always at least double the previous size. Internal storage therefore grows from 1 to 2, 4, 8, 16, 32, 64, ... elements.

This can, however, waste a lot of memory. In our example, the final size of the internal array is 16,777,216 elements, which is about 60% elements too many. By setting the capacity to the exact required size, we have therefore saved 6,777,216 * *SizeOf(Char)* bytes or almost 13 megabytes.

Other data structures also support the `Capacity` property. We can find it in `TList`, `TObjectList`, `TInterfaceList`, `TStrings`, `TStringList`, `TDictionary`, `TObjectDictionary` and others.

# Memory management functions

Besides the various internal functions that the Delphi runtime library (RTL) uses to manage strings, arrays and other built-in data types, RTL also implements various functions that you can use in your program to allocate and release memory blocks. In the next few paragraphs, I'll tell you a little bit about them.

Memory management functions can be best described if we split them into a few groups, each including functions that were designed to work together.

The first group includes `GetMem`, `AllocMem`, `ReallocMem`, and `FreeMem`.

The procedure `GetMem(var P: Pointer; Size: Integer)` allocates a memory block of size `Size` and stores an address of this block in a pointer variable `P`. This pointer variable is not limited to `pointer` type, but can be of any pointer type (for example `PByte`).

The new memory block is not initialized and will contain whatever is stored in the memory at that time. Alternatively, you can allocate a memory block with a call to the function `AllocMem(Size: Integer): Pointer` which allocates a memory block, fills it with zeroes, and then returns its address.

To change the size of a memory block, call the procedure `ReallocMem(var P: Pointer; Size: Integer)`. Variable `P` must contain a pointer to a memory block and `Size` can be either smaller or larger than the original block size. FastMM will try to resize the block in place. If that fails, it will allocate a new memory block, copy the original data into the new block and return an address of the new block in the `P`. Just as with the `GetMem`, newly allocated bytes will not be initialized.

To release memory allocated in this way, you should call the `FreeMem(var P: Pointer)` procedure.

The second group includes `GetMemory`, `ReallocMemory`, and `FreeMemory`. These three work just the same as functions from the first group, except that they can be used from C++ Builder.

The third group contains just two functions, `New` and `Dispose`.

These two functions can be used to dynamically create and destroy variables of any type. To allocate such a variable, call `New(var X: Pointer)` where `P` is again of any pointer type. The compiler will automatically provide the correct size for the memory block and it will also initialize all *managed* fields to zero. Unmanaged fields will not be initialized.

To release such variables, don't use `FreeMem` but `Dispose(var X: Pointer)`. In the next section, I'll give a short example of using `New` and `Dispose` to dynamically create and destroy variables of a record type.

 You must **never** use `Dispose` to release memory allocated with `GetMem` or `AllocateMem`. You must also **never** use `FreeMem` to release memory allocated with `New`.

The fourth and last group also contains just two functions, `Initialize` and `Finalize`. Strictly speaking, they are not memory management functions. Still, they are used almost exclusively when dynamically allocating memory and that's why they belong in this chapter.

If you create a variable containing managed fields (for example, a record) with a function other than `New` or `AllocMem`, it will not be correctly initialized. Managed fields will contain random data and that will completely break the execution of the program. To fix that, you should call `Initialize(var V)` passing in the variable (and not the pointer to this variable!). An example in the next section will clarify that.

Before you return such a variable to the memory manager, you should clean up all references to managed fields by calling `Finalize(var V)`. It is better to use `Dispose`, which will do that automatically, but sometimes that is not an option and you have to do it manually.

Both functions also exist in a form that accepts a number of variables to initialize. This form can be used to initialize or finalize an array of data:

```
procedure Initialize(var V; Count: NativeUInt);
procedure Finalize(var V; Count: NativeUInt);
```

In the next section, I'll dig deeper into the dynamic allocation of record variables. I'll also show how most of the memory allocation functions are used in practice.

# Dynamic record allocation

While it is very simple to dynamically create new objects—you just call the `Create` constructor—dynamic allocation of records and other data types (arrays, strings ...) is a bit more complicated.

In the previous section, we saw that the preferred way of allocating such variables is with the `New` method. The `InitializeFinalize` demo shows how this is done in practice.

The code will dynamically allocate a variable of type `TRecord`. To do that, we need a pointer variable, pointing to `TRecord`. The cleanest way to do that is to declare a new type `PRecord = ^TRecord`:

```
type
  TRecord = record
    s1, s2, s3, s4: string;
  end;
  PRecord = ^TRecord;
```

Now, we can just declare a variable of type `PRecord` and call `New` on that variable. After that, we can use the `rec` variable as if it was a normal record and not a pointer. Technically, we would have to always write `rec^.s1`, `rec^.s4` and so on, but the Delphi compiler is friendly enough and allows us to drop the `^` character:

```
procedure TfrmInitFin.btnNewDispClick(Sender: TObject);
var
  rec: PRecord;
begin
  New(rec);
```

```
  try
    rec.s1 := '4';
    rec.s2 := '2';
    rec.s4 := rec.s1 + rec.s2 + rec.s4;
    ListBox1.Items.Add('New: ' + rec.s4);
  finally
    Dispose(rec);
  end;
end;
```

 Technically, you could just use `rec: ^TRecord` instead of `rec: PRecord`, but it is customary to use explicitly declared pointer types, such as `PRecord`.

Another option is to use `GetMem` instead of `New`, and `FreeMem` instead of `Dispose`. In this case, however, we have to manually prepare allocated memory for use with a call to `Initialize`. We must also prepare it to be released with a call to `Finalize` before we call `FreeMem`.

If we use `GetMem` for initialization, we must manually provide the correct size of allocated block. In this case, we can simply use `SizeOf(TRecord)`.

We must also be careful with parameters passed to `GetMem` and `Initialize`. You pass a pointer (`rec`) to `GetMem` and `FreeMem` and the actual record data (`rec^`) to `Initialize` and `Finalize`:

```
procedure TfrmInitFin.btnInitFinClick(Sender: TObject);
var
  rec: PRecord;
begin
  GetMem(rec, SizeOf(TRecord));
  try
    Initialize(rec^);
    rec.s1 := '4';
    rec.s2 := '2';
    rec.s4 := rec.s1 + rec.s2 + rec.s4;
    ListBox1.Items.Add('GetMem+Initialize: ' + rec.s4);
  finally
    Finalize(rec^);
    FreeMem (rec);
  end;
end;
```

This demo also shows how the code doesn't work correctly if you allocate a record with `GetMem`, but then don't call `Initialize`. To test this, click the third button (**GetMem**). While in actual code the program may sometimes work and sometimes not, I have taken some care so that `GetMem` will always return a memory block which will not be initialized to zero and the program will certainly fail:

It is certainly possible to create records dynamically and use them instead of classes, but one question still remains—why? Why would we want to use records instead of objects when working with objects is simpler? The answer, in one word, is **speed**.

The demo program, `Allocate`, shows the difference in execution speed. A click on the **Allocate objects** button will create ten million objects of type `TNodeObj`, which is a typical object that you would find in an implementation of a *binary tree*. Of course, the code then cleans up after itself by destroying all those objects:

```
type
  TNodeObj = class
    Left, Right: TNodeObj;
    Data: NativeUInt;
  end;

procedure TfrmAllocate.btnAllocClassClick(Sender: TObject);
var
  i: Integer;
  nodes: TArray<TNodeObj>;
begin
  SetLength(nodes, CNumNodes);
  for i := 0 to CNumNodes-1 do
    nodes[i] := TNodeObj.Create;
  for i := 0 to CNumNodes-1 do
```

```
        nodes[i].Free;
    end;
```

A similar code, activated by the **Allocate records** button creates ten million records of type TNodeRec, which contains the same fields as TNodeObj:

```
type
  PNodeRec = ^TNodeRec;
  TNodeRec = record
    Left, Right: PNodeRec;
    Data: NativeUInt;
  end;

procedure TfrmAllocate.btnAllocRecordClick(Sender: TObject);
var
  i: Integer;
  nodes: TArray<PNodeRec>;
begin
  SetLength(nodes, CNumNodes);
  for i := 0 to CNumNodes-1 do
    New(nodes[i]);
  for i := 0 to CNumNodes-1 do
    Dispose(nodes[i]);
end;
```

Running both methods shows a big difference. While the class-based approach needs 366 ms to initialize objects and 76 ms to free them, the record-based approach needs only 76 ms to initialize records and 56 to free them. Where does that big difference come from?

When you create an object of a class, lots of things happen. Firstly, TObject.NewInstance is called to allocate an object. That method calls TObject.InstanceSize to get the size of the object, then GetMem to allocate the memory and in the end, InitInstance which fills the allocated memory with zeros. Secondly, a chain of constructors is called. After all that, a chain of AfterConstruction methods is called (if such methods exist). All in all, that is quite a process which takes some time.

Much less is going on when you create a record. If it contains only unmanaged fields, as in our example, a GetMem is called and that's all. If the record contains managed fields, this GetMem is followed by a call to the _Initialize method in the *System* unit which initializes managed fields.

The problem with records is that we cannot declare generic pointers. When we are building trees, for example, we would like to store some data of type T in each node. The initial attempt at that, however, fails. The following code does not compile with the current Delphi compiler:

```
type
  PNodeRec<T> = ^TNodeRec<T>;
  TNodeRec<T> = record
    Left, Right: PNodeRec<T>;
    Data: T;
  end;
```

We can circumvent this by moving the TNodeRec<T> declaration inside the generic class that implements a tree. The following code from the Allocate demo shows how we could declare such internal type as a generic object and as a generic record:

```
type
  TTree<T> = class
  strict private type
    TNodeObj<T1> = class
      Left, Right: TNodeObj<T1>;
      Data: T1;
    end;

    PNodeRec = ^TNodeRec;
    TNodeRec<T1> = record
      Left, Right: PNodeRec;
      Data: T1;
    end;
    TNodeRec = TNodeRec<T>;
  end;
```

If you click the **Allocate node<string>** button, the code will create a TTree<string> object and then create 10 million class-based nodes and the same amount of record-based nodes. This time, New must initialize the managed field Data: string but the difference in speed is still big. The code needs 669 ms to create and destroy class-based nodes and 133 ms to create and destroy record-based nodes.

Another big difference between classes and records is that each object contains two hidden pointer-sized fields. Because of that, each object is 8 bytes larger than you would expect (16 bytes in 64-bit mode). That amounts to 8 * 10,000,000 bytes or a bit over 76 megabytes. Records are therefore not only faster but also save space!

# FastMM internals

To get a full speed out of anything, you have to understand how it works and memory managers are no exception to this rule. To write very fast Delphi applications, you should therefore understand how Delphi's default memory manager works.

FastMM is not just a memory manager—it is three memory managers in one! It contains three significantly different subsystems—*small block allocator*, *medium block allocator*, and *large block allocator*.

The first one, the allocator for *small blocks*, handles all memory blocks smaller than 2,5 KB. This boundary was determined by observing existing applications. As it turned out, in most Delphi applications, this covers 99% of all memory allocations. This is not surprising, as in most Delphi applications most memory is allocated when an application creates and destroys objects and works with arrays and strings, and those are rarely larger than a few hundred characters.

Next comes the allocator for *medium blocks*, which are memory blocks with a size between 2,5 KB and 160 KB. The last one, allocator for *large blocks*, handles all other requests.

The difference between allocators lies not just in the size of memory that they serve, but in the strategy they use to manage memory.

The *large* block allocator implements the simplest strategy. Whenever it needs some memory, it gets it directly from Windows by calling `VirtualAlloc`. This function allocates memory in 4 KB blocks so this allocator could waste up to 4,095 bytes per request. As it is used only for blocks larger than 160 KB, this wasted memory doesn't significantly affect the program, though.

The *medium* block allocator gets its memory from the large block allocator. It then carves this larger block into smaller blocks, as they are requested by the application. It also keeps all unused parts of the memory in a linked list so that it can quickly find a memory block that is still free.

The *small* block allocator is where the real smarts of FastMM lies. There are actually 56 small memory allocators, each serving only one size of memory block. The first one serves 8-byte blocks, the next one 16-byte blocks, followed by the allocator for 24, 32, 40, ... 256, 272, 288, ... 960, 1056, ... 2384, and 2608-byte blocks. They all get memory from the medium block allocator.

 If you want to see block sizes for all 56 allocators, open `FastMM4.pas` and search for `SmallBlockTypes`.

What that actually means is that each memory allocation request will waste some memory. If you allocate 28 bytes, they'll be allocated from the 32-byte allocator, so 4 bytes will be wasted. If you allocate 250 bytes, they'll come from the 256-byte allocator and so on. The sizes of memory allocators were carefully chosen so that the amount of wasted memory is typically below 10%, so this doesn't represent a big problem in most applications.

Each allocator is basically just an array of equally sized elements (memory blocks). When you allocate a small amount of memory, you'll get back one element of an array. All unused elements are connected into a linked list so that the memory manager can quickly find a free element of an array when it needs one.

The following image shows a very simplified representation of FastMM allocators. Only two small block allocators are shown. Boxes with thick borders represent allocated memory. Boxes with thin borders represent unused (free) memory. Free memory blocks are connected into linked lists. Block sizes in different allocators are not to scale:

Simplified representation of FastMM memory manager

FastMM implements a neat trick which helps a lot when you resize strings or arrays by a small amount. In the beginning of this chapter, I talked about that (*Optimizing strings and array allocations*), and have shown a small program that demonstrated how appending characters one by one works much slower than preallocating a whole string. There was a 4x speed difference (142 vs 33 ms) between these approaches.

Well, the truth be told, I had to append lots and lots of characters—ten million of them—for this difference to show. If I were appending only a few characters, both versions would run at nearly the same speed. If you can, on the other hand, get your hands on a pre-2006 Delphi and run the demo program there, you'll see that the *one-by-one* approach runs terribly slow. The difference in speed will be of a few more orders of magnitude larger than in my example.

The trick I'm talking about assumes that if you had resized memory once, you'll probably want to do it again, soon. If you are enlarging the memory, it will limit the smallest size of the new memory block to be at least twice the size of the original block plus 32 bytes. Next time you'll want to resize, FastMM will (hopefully) just update the internal information about the allocated memory and return the same block, knowing that there's enough space at the end.

All that trickery is hard to understand without an example, so here's one. Let's say we have a string of 5 characters which neatly fits into a 24-byte block. Sorry, what am I hearing? "What? Why!? 5 unicode characters need only 10 bytes!" Oh, yes, strings are more complicated than I told you before.

In reality, each Delphi `UnicodeString` and `AnsiString` contains some additional data besides the actual characters that make up the string. Parts of the string are also: 4-byte length of string, 4-byte reference count, 2-byte field storing the size of each string character (either 1 for `AnsiString` or 2 for `UnicodeString`), and 2-byte field storing the character code page. In addition to that, each string includes a terminating `Chr(0)` character. For a 5-character `string` this gives us *4 (length) + 4 (reference count) + 2 (character size) + 2 (codepage) + 5 (characters) * 2 (size of a character) + 2 (terminating Chr(0)) = 24* bytes.

When you add one character to this string, the code will ask the memory manager to enlarge a 24-byte block to 26 bytes. Instead of returning a 26-byte block, FastMM will round that up to *2 * 24 + 32 = 80* bytes. Then it will look for an appropriate allocator, find one that serves 80-byte blocks (great, no memory loss!) and return a block from that allocator. It will, of course, also have to copy data from the original block to the new block.

 This formula, *2 * size + 32*, is used only in small block allocators. A medium block allocator only overallocates by 25%, and a large block allocator doesn't implement this behavior at all.

Next time you add one character to this string, FastMM will just look at the memory block, determine that there's still enough space inside this 80-byte memory block and return the same memory. This will continue for quite some time while the block grows to 80 bytes in two-byte increments. After that, the block will be resized to *2 * 80 + 32 = 192* bytes (yes, there **is** an allocator for this size), data will be copied and the game will continue.

This behavior indeed wastes some memory but, under most circumstances, significantly boosts the speed of code that was not written with speed in mind.

# Memory allocation in a parallel world

We've seen how FastMM boosts the reallocation speed. Let's take a look at another optimization which helps a lot when you write a multithreaded code—as we will in the next three chapters.

The life of a memory manager is simple when there is only one thread of execution inside a program. When the memory manager is dealing out the memory, it can be perfectly safe in the knowledge that nothing can interrupt it in this work.

When we deal with parallel processing, however, multiple paths of execution simultaneously execute the same program and work on the same data. (We call them *threads* and I'll explain them in the next chapter.) Because of that, life from the memory manager's perspective suddenly becomes very dangerous.

For example, let's assume that one thread wants some memory. The memory manager finds a free memory block on a free list and prepares to return it. At that moment, however, another thread also needs some memory from the same allocator. This second execution thread (running in parallel with the first one) would also find a free memory block on the free list. If the first thread didn't yet update the free list, that may even be the same memory block! That can only result in one thing—complete confusion and crashing programs.

It is extremely hard to write a code that manipulates some data structures (such as a free list) in a manner that functions correctly in a multithreaded world. So hard that FastMM doesn't even try it. Instead of that, it regulates access to each allocator with a lock. Each of the 56 small block allocators get their own lock, as do medium and large block allocators.

When a program needs some memory from, say, a 16-byte allocator, FastMM will lock this allocator until the memory is returned to the program. If, during this time, another thread requests a memory from the same 16-byte allocator, it will have to wait until the first thread finishes.

This indeed fixes all problems but introduces a *bottleneck*—a part of the code where threads must wait to be processed in a serial fashion. If threads do lots of memory allocation, this serialization will completely negate the speed-up that we expected to get from the parallel approach. Such a memory manager would be useless in a parallel world.

To fix that, FastMM introduces memory allocation optimization which only affects small blocks.

When accessing a small block allocator, FastMM will try to lock it. If that fails, it will not wait for the allocator to become unlocked, but will try to lock the allocator for the next block size. If that succeeds, it will return memory from the second allocator. That will indeed waste more memory, but will help with the execution speed. If the second allocator also cannot be locked, FastMM will try to lock the allocator for yet the next block size. If the third allocator can be locked, you'll get back memory from it. Otherwise, FastMM will repeat the process from the beginning.

This process can be somehow described with the following pseudo-code:

```
allocIdx := find best allocator for the memory block
repeat
  if can lock allocIdx then
    break;
  Inc(allocIdx);
  if can lock allocIdx then
    break;
  Inc(allocIdx);
  if can lock allocIdx then
    break;
  Dec(allocIdx, 2)
until false

allocate memory from allocIdx allocator

unlock allocIdx
```

A careful reader would notice that this code fails when the first line finds the last allocator in the table, or the one before that. Instead of adding some conditional code to work around the problem, FastMM rather repeats the last allocator in the list three times. The table of small allocators actually ends with the following sizes: 1,984; 2,176; 2,384; 2,608; 2,608; 2,608. When requesting a block size above 2,384 the first line in the pseudo-code above will always find the first 2,608 allocator, so there will always be two more after it.

This approach works great when memory is allocated but hides another problem. And how can I better explain a problem than with a demonstration ...?

An example of this problem can be found in the program, `ParallelAllocations`. If you run it and click the **Run** button, the code will compare the serial version of some algorithm with a parallel one. I'm aware that I did not explain parallel programming at all, but the code is so simple that even somebody without any understanding of the topic will guess what it does.

The core of a test runs a loop with the `Execute` method on all objects in a list. If a `parallelTest` flag is set, the loop is executed in parallel, otherwise it is executed serially. The only mystery part in the code, `TParallel.For` does exactly what it says—executes a `for` loop in parallel.

```
if parallelTest then
  TParallel.For(0, fList.Count - 1,
    procedure(i: integer)
    begin
      fList[i].Execute;
    end)
else
  for i := 0 to fList.Count - 1 do
    fList[i].Execute;
```

If you'll be running the program, make sure that you execute it without the debugger (*Ctrl + Shift + F9* will do that). Running with the debugger slows down parallel execution and can skew the measurements.

On my test machine I got the following results:

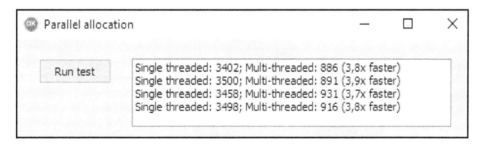

In essence, parallelizing the program made it almost 4 times faster. Great result!

Well, no. Not a great result. You see, the machine I was testing on has 12 cores. If all would be running in parallel, I would expect an almost 12x speed-up, not a mere 4-times improvement!

If you take a look at the code, you'll see that each `Execute` allocates a ton of objects. It is obvious (even more given the topic of the current chapter) that a problem lies in the memory manager. The question remains though, where exactly lies this problem and how can we find it?

I ran into exactly the same problem a few years ago. A highly parallel application which processes gigabytes and gigabytes of data was not running fast enough. There were no obvious problematic points and I suspected that the culprit was FastMM. I tried swapping the memory manager for a more multithreading-friendly one and, indeed, the problem was somehow reduced but I still wanted to know where the original sin lied in my code. I also wanted to continue using FastMM as it offers great debugging tools.

In the end, I found no other solution than to dig in the FastMM internals, find out how it works, and add some logging there. More specifically, I wanted to know when a thread is waiting for a memory manager to become unlocked. I also wanted to know at which locations in my program this happens the most.

To cut a (very) long story short, I extended FastMM with support for this kind of logging. This extension was later integrated into the main FastMM branch. As these changes are not included in Delphi, you have to take some steps to use this code.

Firstly, you have to download FastMM from the official repository at `https://github.com/pleriche/FastMM4`. Then you have to unpack it somewhere on the disk and add `FastMM4` as a first unit in the project file (`.dpr`). For example, the `ParallelAllocation` program starts like this:

```
program ParallelAllocation;
uses
  FastMM4 in 'FastMM\FastMM4.pas',
  Vcl.Forms,
  ParallelAllocationMain in 'ParallelAllocationMain.pas'
{frmParallelAllocation};
```

When you have done that, you should firstly rebuild your program and test if everything is still working. (It should but you never know ...)

To enable the memory manager logging, you have to define a conditional symbol `LogLockContention`, rebuild (as `FastMM4` has to be recompiled) and, of course, run the program without the debugger.

If you do that, you'll see that the program runs quite a bit slower than before. On my test machine, the parallel version was only 1.6x faster than the serial one. The logging takes its toll, but that is not important. The important part will appear when you close the program.

At that point, the logger will collect all results and sort them by frequency. The 10 most frequent sources of locking in the program will be saved to a file called `<programname>_MemoryManager_EventLog.txt`. You will find it in the folder with the `<programname>.exe`. The three most frequent sources of locking will also be displayed on the screen.

The following screenshot shows a cropped version of this log. Some important parts are marked out:

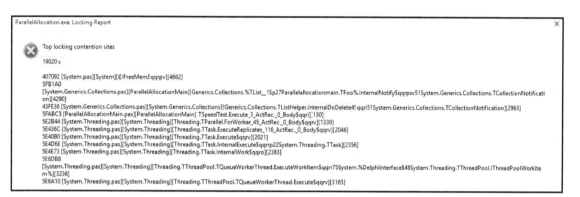

For starters, we can see that at this location the program waited **19,020** times for a memory manager to become unlocked. Next, we can see that the memory function that caused the problem was `FreeMem`. Furthermore, we can see that somebody tried to delete from a list (`InternalDoDelete`) and that this deletion was called from `TSpeedTest.Execute`, line 130. `FreeMem` was called because the list in question is actually a `TObjectList` and deleting elements from the list caused it to be destroyed.

The most important part here is the memory function causing the problem—`FreeMem`. Of course! Allocations are optimized. If an allocator is locked, the next one will be used and so on. Releasing memory, however, is not optimized! When we release a memory block, it **must** be returned to the same allocator that it came from. If two threads want to release memory to the same allocator at the same time, one will have to wait.

I had an idea on how to improve this situation by adding a small stack (called **release stack**) to each allocator. When `FreeMem` is called and it cannot lock the allocator, the address of the memory block that is to be released will be stored on that stack. `FreeMem` will then quickly exit.

When a `FreeMem` successfully locks an allocator, it firstly releases its own memory block. Then it checks if anything is waiting on the release stack and releases these memory blocks too (if there are any).

This change is also included in the main FastMM branch, but it is not activated by default as it increases the overall memory consumption of the program. However, in some situations it can do miracles and if you are developing multithreaded programs you certainly should test it out.

To enable release stacks, open the project settings for the program, remove the conditional define `LogLockContention` (as that slows the program down) and add the conditional define `UseReleaseStack`. Rebuild, as `FastMM4.pas` has to be recompiled.

On my test machine, I got much better results with this option enabled. Instead of a 3,9x speed-up, the parallel version was 6,3x faster than the serial one. The factor is not even close to 12x, as the threads do too much fighting for the memory, but the improvement is still significant:

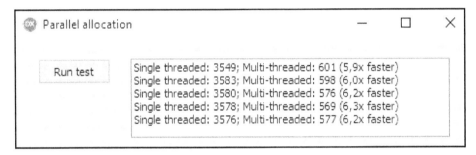

That is as far as FastMM will take us. For a faster execution, we need a more multithreading-friendly memory manager.

# Replacing the default memory manager

While writing a new memory manager is a hard job, installing it in Delphi—once it is completed—is very simple. The *System* unit implements functions `GetMemoryManager` and `SetMemoryManager` that help with that:

```
type
  TMemoryManagerEx = record
    {The basic (required) memory manager functionality}
    GetMem: function(Size: NativeInt): Pointer;
    FreeMem: function(P: Pointer): Integer;
    ReallocMem: function(P: Pointer; Size: NativeInt): Pointer;
    {Extended (optional) functionality.}
    AllocMem: function(Size: NativeInt): Pointer;
    RegisterExpectedMemoryLeak: function(P: Pointer): Boolean;
```

```
    UnregisterExpectedMemoryLeak: function(P: Pointer): Boolean;
  end;

  procedure GetMemoryManager(var MemMgrEx: TMemoryManagerEx); overload;
  procedure SetMemoryManager(const MemMgrEx: TMemoryManagerEx); overload;
```

A proper way to install a new memory manager is to call `GetMemoryManager` and store the result in some global variable. Then, the code should populate the new `TMemoryManagerEx` record with pointers to its own replacement methods and call `SetMemoryManager`. Typically, you would do this in the `initialization` block of the unit implementing the memory manager.

The new memory manager **must** implement functions `GetMem`, `FreeMem`, and `ReallocMem`. It **may** implement the other three functions (or only some of them). Delphi is smart enough to implement `AllocMem` internally, if it is not implemented by the memory manager, and the other two will just be ignored if you call them from the code.

When memory manager is uninstalled (usually from the `finalization` block of the memory manager unit), it has to call `SetMemoryManager` and pass to it the original memory manager configuration stored in the global variable.

The nice thing with memory managers is that you can call functions from the previous memory manager in your code. That allows you to just add some small part of functionality which may be useful when you are debugging some hard problem or researching how Delphi works.

To demonstrate this approach, I have written a small logging memory manager. After it is installed, it will log all memory calls (except the two related to memory leaks) to a file. It has no idea how to handle memory allocation, though, so it forwards all calls to the existing memory manager.

The demonstration program, `LoggingMemoryManager`, shows how to use this logging functionality. When you click the **Test** button, the code installs it by calling the `InstallMM` function. In the current implementation, it logs information info the file, `<projectName>_memory.log` which is saved to the `<projectName>.exe` folder.

Then the code creates a `TList<integer>` object, writes 1,024 integers into it and destroys the list.

At the end, the memory manager is uninstalled by calling `UninstallMM` and the contents of the log file are loaded into the listbox:

```
  procedure TfrmLoggingMM.Button1Click(Sender: TObject);
  var
```

```
  list: TList<integer>;
  i: Integer;
  mmLog: String;
begin
  mmLog := ChangeFileExt(ParamStr(0), '_memory.log');
  if not InstallMM(mmLog) then
    ListBox1.Items.Add('Failed to install memory manager');

  list := TList<integer>.Create;
  for i := 1 to 1024 do
    list.Add(i);
  FreeAndNil(list);

  if not UninstallMM then
    ListBox1.Items.Add('Failed to uninstall memory manager');

  LoadLog(mmLog);
end;
```

The memory manager itself is implemented in the unit *LoggingMM*. It uses three global variables. MMIsInstalled contains the current installed/not installed status, OldMM stores the configuration of the existing state, and LoggingFile stores a handle of the logging file:

```
var
  MMIsInstalled: boolean;
  OldMM: TMemoryManagerEx;
  LoggingFile: THandle;
```

The installation function firstly opens a logging file with a call to the Windows API CreateFile. After that, it retrieves the existing memory manager state, sets a new configuration with pointers to the logging code, and exits. Memory leak functions are not used so corresponding pointers are set to nil:

```
function InstallMM(const fileName: string): boolean;
var
  myMM: TMemoryManagerEx;
begin
  if MMIsInstalled then
    Exit(False);

  LoggingFile := CreateFile(PChar(fileName), GENERIC_WRITE, 0, nil,
    CREATE_ALWAYS, FILE_ATTRIBUTE_NORMAL, 0);
  if LoggingFile = INVALID_HANDLE_VALUE then
    Exit(False);

  GetMemoryManager(OldMM);
```

```
  myMM.GetMem := @LoggingGetMem;
  myMM.FreeMem := @LoggingFreeMem;
  myMM.ReallocMem := @LoggingReallocMem;
  myMM.AllocMem := @LoggingAllocMem;
  myMM.RegisterExpectedMemoryLeak := nil;
  myMM.UnregisterExpectedMemoryLeak := nil;
  SetMemoryManager(myMM);

  MMIsInstalled := True;
  Result := True;
end;
```

Using Windows API makes my logging memory manager bound to the operating system so why don't I simply use a `TStream` for logging?

Well, you have to remember that the purpose of this exercise is to log all memory requests. Using any built-in Delphi functionality may cause hidden memory manager operations. If I'm not careful, an object may get created somewhere or a string could get allocated. That's why the code stays on the safe side and uses Windows API to work with the logging file.

Uninstalling memory manager is simpler. We just have to close the logging file and restore the original configuration:

```
function UninstallMM: boolean;
begin
  if not MMIsInstalled then
    Exit(False);

  SetMemoryManager(OldMM);

  if LoggingFile <> INVALID_HANDLE_VALUE then begin
    CloseHandle(LoggingFile);
    LoggingFile := INVALID_HANDLE_VALUE;
  end;

  MMIsInstalled := False;
  Result := True;
end;
```

Logging itself is again tricky. The logging code is called from the memory manager itself, so it can't use any functionality that would use the memory manager. Most important of all, we cannot use any `UnicodeString` or `AnsiString` variable. The logging code therefore pieces the log output together from small parts:

```
function LoggingGetMem(Size: NativeInt): Pointer;
begin
  Result := OldMM.GetMem(Size);
  Write('GetMem(');
  Write(Size);
  Write(') = ');
  Write(NativeUInt(Result));
  Writeln;
end;
```

Logging a string is actually pretty easy as Delphi already provides a terminating `Chr(0)` character at the end of a string. A `Write` method just passes correct parameters to the `WriteFile` Windows API:

```
procedure Write(const s: PAnsiChar); overload;
var
  written: DWORD;
begin
  WriteFile(LoggingFile, s^, StrLen(s), written, nil);
end;

procedure Writeln;
begin
  Write(#13#10);
end;
```

Logging a number is tricky, as we can't call `IntToStr` or `Format`. Both are using dynamic strings which means that memory manager would be used to manage strings, but as we are already inside the memory manager we cannot use memory management functions.

The logging function for numbers therefore implements its own conversion from `NativeUInt` to a buffer containing a hexadecimal representation of that unit. It uses the knowledge that `NativeUInt` is never more than 8 bytes long, which generates, at max, 16 hexadecimal numbers:

```
procedure Write(n: NativeUInt); overload;
var
  buf: array [1..18] of AnsiChar;
  i: Integer;
  digit: Integer;
begin
```

```
  buf[18] := #0;
  for i := 17 downto 2 do
  begin
    digit := n mod 16;
    n := n div 16;
    if digit < 10 then
      buf[i] := AnsiChar(digit + Ord('0'))
    else
      buf[i] := AnsiChar(digit - 10 + Ord('A'));
  end;
  buf[1] := '$';
  Write(@buf);
end;
```

Even with these complications, the code is far from perfect. The big problem with the current implementation is that it won't work correctly in a multithreaded code. A real-life implementation would need to add locking around all the `Logging*` methods.

Another problem with the code is that logging is really slow because of the frequent `WriteFile` calls. A better implementation would collect log data in a larger buffer and only write it out when the buffer becomes full. An improvement in that direction is left as an exercise for the reader.

The following image shows the demonstration program, `LoggingMemoryManager` in action. The first `GetMem` call creates the `TList<Integer>` object. The second creates a `TArray<Integer>` used internally inside the `TList<Integer>` to store the list data. After that, `ReallocMem` is called from time to time to enlarge this `TArray`. We can see that it is not called for every element that the code adds to the list, but in larger and larger steps. Memory is firstly enlarged to $10 bytes, then to $18, $28, $48, and so on to $1,008 bytes. This is a result of the optimization inside the `TList<T>` that I mentioned at the beginning of this chapter.

Furthermore, we can see that the built-in memory manager doesn't always move the memory around. When a memory is enlarged to $10 bytes, the memory manager returns a new pointer (original value was $2E98B20, new value is $2ED3990). After the next two allocations, this pointer stays the same.

Only when the memory is enlarged to $48 bytes, does the memory manager have to allocate a new block and move the data:

An interesting call happens after all the reallocations. Another copy of the list data is allocated with a call to `GetMem($1008)`. A little digging shows that this happens when list capacity is set to 0 inside the destructor:

```
destructor TList<T>.Destroy;
begin
  Capacity := 0;
  inherited;
end;
```

This allocation is caused by the notification mechanism which allows `TObjectList<T>` to destroy owned objects. Data needs to be stored temporary before it is passed to the notification event and that is done with a temporary array.

I'm pretty sure you will not be writing a new memory manager just to improve speed of multithreaded programs. I'm sure I won't do it. Luckily, there are crazier and smarter people out there who put their work out as open source.

# ScaleMM

First such memory manager is *ScaleMM*. It is the work of André Mussche and can be downloaded from `https://github.com/andremussche/scalemm`. You can use it in practically any application, as it is released under a tri-license MPL 1.1/GPL 2.0/LGPL 2.1. It only supports the Windows platform.

ScaleMM is written in Delphi and assembler. To use ScaleMM, you just have to download it, store it somewhere on the disk and add the *ScaleMM2* unit as a first unit in the program.

ScaleMM was created as a faster replacement for FastMM. It is not as loaded with debugging features as FastMM but implements just a base memory manager functionality. Because of that, it makes sense to run FastMM while debugging, and ScaleMM while testing and in production.

The older version of Delphi didn't like it if you put the `{$IFDEF}` directive inside the main program's uses list. Delphi will remove this directive when you add a new form to the program. The easiest way to fix this is to create a new unit and add it as a first unit in the main program's uses list. In this new unit, you can then put `{$IFDEF}` in the used memory manager however you wish.

An example of the uses list in such a main program is shown here:

```
program ParallelAllocation;

uses
  ParallelAllocationMM,
  Vcl.Forms,
  ParallelAllocationMain in 'ParallelAllocationMain.pas'
  {frmParallelAllocation};
```

Unit `ParallelAllocationMM` can then be implemented as shown here:

```
unit ParallelAllocationMM;

interface

uses
  {$IFDEF DEBUG}
  FastMM4 in 'FastMM\FastMM4.pas';
  {$ELSE}
  ScaleMM2 in 'ScaleMM\ScaleMM2.pas';
  {$ENDIF}

implementation
```

```
end.
```

Replacing FastMM with ScaleMM in the test program, `ParallelAllocation` shows a noticeable improvement. With FastMM and `{$DEFINE UseReleaseStack}`, the parallel version is at best 6.3x faster than the serial one. With ScaleMM it is up to 6.7x faster:

# TBBMalloc

Another good alternative for a memory manager is Intel's *TBBMalloc*, part of their *Thread Building Blocks* library. It is released under the Apache 2.0 license which allows usage in open source and commercial applications. You can also buy a commercial license, if the Apache 2.0 license doesn't suite you. As ScaleMM, this memory manager only supports the Windows platform.

Intel's library was designed for C and C++ users. While you can go and download it from `https://www.threadingbuildingblocks.org`, you will still need a Delphi unit that will connect Delphi's memory management interface with the functions exported from Intel's *tbbmalloc* DLL.

Alternatively, you can download the *Intel TBBMalloc Interfaces* project from `https://sites.google.com/site/aminer68/intel-tbbmalloc-interfaces-for-delphi-and-delphi-xe-versions-and-freepascal`. The package you'll get there contains both compiled `tbbmalloc.dll` and a unit *cmem* which links this DLL into your application.

In order to be able to run the application, you'll have to make sure that it will find `tbbmalloc.dll`. The simplest way to do that is to put the DLL in the `exe` folder. For 32-bit applications, you should use the DLL from the `tbbmalloc32` subfolder and for 64-bit applications, you should use the DLL from the `tbbmalloc64` subfolder.

*Intel TBBMalloc Interfaces* actually implements three different interface units, all named *cmem*. A version in subfolder cmem_delphi can be used with Delphis up to 2010, subfolder cmem_xe contains a version designed for Delphi XE and newer, and there's also a version for FreePascal in subfolder cmem_fps.

Creating an interface unit to a DLL is actually pretty simple. The *cmem* unit firstly imports functions from the tbbmalloc.dll:

```
function scalable_getmem(Size: nativeUInt): Pointer; cdecl;
  external 'tbbmalloc' name 'scalable_malloc';

procedure scalable_freemem(P: Pointer); cdecl;
  external 'tbbmalloc' name 'scalable_free';

function scalable_realloc(P: Pointer; Size: nativeUInt): Pointer; cdecl;
  external 'tbbmalloc' name 'scalable_realloc';
```

After that, writing memory management functions is a breeze. You just have to redirect calls to the DLL functions:

```
function CGetMem(Size: NativeInt): Pointer;
begin
  Result := scalable_getmem(Size);
end;

function CFreeMem(P: Pointer): integer;
begin
  scalable_freemem(P);
  Result := 0;
end;

function CReAllocMem(P: Pointer; Size: NativeInt): Pointer;
begin
  Result := scalable_realloc(P, Size);
end;
```

The AllocMem function is implemented by calling the scallable_getmem DLL function and filling the memory with zeroes afterwards:

```
function CAllocMem(Size : NativeInt) : Pointer;
begin
  Result := scalable_getmem(Size);
  if Assigned(Result) then
    FillChar(Result^, Size, 0);
end;
```

The `ParallelAllocation` demo is all set for testing with *TBBMalloc*. You only have to copy `tbbmalloc.dll` from the `tbbmalloc32` folder to `Win32\Debug` and change the `ParallelAllocation.dpr` so that it will load *cmem* instead of *FastMM* or *ScaleMM*:

```
program ParallelAllocation;

uses
  cmem in 'tbbmalloc\cmem_xe\cmem.pas',
  Vcl.Forms,
  ParallelAllocationMain in 'ParallelAllocationMain.pas'
{frmParallelAllocation};
```

What about the speed? Unbeatable! Running the `ParallelAllocation` demo with *TBBMalloc* shows parallel code being up to 8.6x faster than the serial code:

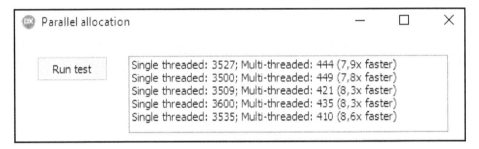

# Fine-tuning SlowCode

We are near the end of the chapter. Let's step back a little and take a breath.

This chapter is packed with information, but if I would have to pick the most important lesson, it would be: don't enlarge strings (arrays, lists) element by element. If you know how much space some data will take, allocate the space at the beginning.

As all recommendations go, this too must be taken with a grain of salt. Most of the time such optimizations will not matter. You should always have the following checklist in mind:

1. Measure. Find where the problem actually is.
2. See if you can improve the algorithm. This will give the best results.
3. Fine-tune the code.

In the previous chapter, we have optimized the heart out of our old friend, `SlowCode`. Just to remind you, the latest version `SlowCode_Sieve_v2_opt` processes 10 million elements in a mere 529 ms. Still, there is a little room for improvement that I've neglected so far.

The problem lies in the function, `Filter` which expands the `Result` array, element by element:

```
function Filter(list: TList<Integer>): TArray<Integer>;
var
  i: Integer;
  reversed: Integer;
begin
  SetLength(Result, 0);
  for i in list do
  begin
    reversed := ReverseInt(i);
    if not ElementInDataDivides(list, reversed) then
    begin
      SetLength(Result, Length(Result) + 1);
      Result[High(Result)] := i;
    end;
  end;
end;
```

A much better approach would be to create a "just right" result array at the beginning. But how big is "just right"? We don't know how many elements the resulting array will have to store.

That's true, but we know one thing—it will not be larger than the `list`. All elements that are inserted into `Result` come from this list so `Result` can only contain the same amount or less elements, not more.

If we don't know how big the resulting array will be, we'll do the next best thing. At the beginning, we'll set it to the maximum possible value. Then we'll add elements to it. At the end, we'll truncate it to the correct size.

This method is implemented in the function `Filter` in the program, `SlowCode_Sieve_v3`:

```
function Filter(list: TList<Integer>): TArray<Integer>;
var
  i: Integer;
  reversed: Integer;
  outIdx: Integer;
begin
  SetLength(Result, list.Count);
  outIdx := 0;
```

```
for i in list do
begin
  reversed := ReverseInt(i);
  if not ElementInDataDivides(list, reversed) then
  begin
    Result[outIdx] := i;
    Inc(outIdx);
  end;
end;
SetLength(Result, outIdx);
end;
```

How fast is this "improved and optimized" version? Sadly, not very much. The time to process 10 million numbers went from 529 to 512 ms.

So, what does this prove? Exactly what I was telling you before. Most of the time you don't gain much by fiddling with small details. That, and—oh my, is FastMM fast!

Don't forget though that in a multithreaded world the overhead from the memory manager is automatically higher (as I have shown earlier). When you write multithreaded programs such small optimizations can give you a bigger improvement than in the single-threaded world.

Just to be sure I'm not missing something, I've enlarged the test set from 10 to 100 million numbers. `SlowCode_Sieve_v2_opt` needed 7,524 ms and `SlowCode_Sieve_v3` needed 7,512 ms. The difference is miniscule. It is quite obvious that the biggest problem is not memory reallocations but other processing. Maybe a parallel approach will be able to help? We'll see.

# Summary

This chapter dove deep into the murky waters of memory managers. We started on the light side with a discussion of strings, arrays and how memory for them is managed.

After that, I enumerated all memory management functions exposed by Delphi. We saw how we can allocate memory blocks, change their size, and free them again. We also learned about memory management functions designed to allocate and release managed data—strings, interfaces, dynamic arrays, and so on.

The next part of the chapter was dedicated to records. We saw how to allocate them, how to initialize them, and even how to make dynamically allocated records function together with generic types. We also saw that records are not just faster to create than objects, but also uses less memory.

Then we went really deep into the complicated world of memory manager implementation. I explained—from a very distant viewpoint—how FastMM is organized internally and what tricks it uses to speed up frequently encountered situations.

After that, I proved that even FastMM is not perfect. It offers great performance in single-threaded applications but can cause slowdowns in a multithreaded scenario. I have shown a way to detect such bottlenecks in a multithreaded program and also how to improve the FastMM speed in such situations.

Sometimes, this is still not enough but Delphi offers a solution. You can swap the memory manager for another. To show this approach, I developed a small memory manager wrapper which logs all memory manager calls to a file. After that, I showed how you can replace FastMM with two alternative memory managers, ScaleMM and TBBMalloc.

The question may arise whether to always replace FastMM with an alternative. After all, alternatives are faster. The answer to that question is a resounding - **no**! I believe that the program should be—if at all possible—deployed with the same memory manager that it was tested with. FastMM offers such great capabilities for debugging (which I sadly didn't have space to discuss here) that I simply refuse to use anything else during development. I would create a release version of a program with a non-default memory manager only under very specific circumstances and only after extensive testing.

At the end, we have returned to the `SlowCode` program. Although it contained excessive memory reallocations, it turned out that they didn't slow down the program in a significant way. Still, fixing that was an interesting exercise.

In the next chapter, I'll return to the bigger picture. We'll forget all about the optimizations at the level of memory allocations and object creation, and we'll again start fiddling with the algorithms. This time we'll look in a completely new direction. We'll force our programs to do multiple things at once! In other words, we'll learn to multithread.

# 5
# Getting Started with the Parallel World

If you are reading this book from start to finish, without skipping chapters, you've been through quite a lot. I've discussed algorithms, optimization techniques, memory management, and more, but I've quite pointedly stayed away from parallel programming (or *multithreading*, as it is also called).

I had a very good reason for that. Parallel programming is hard. It doesn't matter if you are an excellent programmer. It doesn't matter how good the supporting tools are. Parallel programming gives you plenty of opportunities to introduce weird errors into the program: errors that are hard to repeat and even harder to find. That's why I wanted you to explore other options first.

If you can make your program fast enough without going the parallel way, then make it so! Classical non-parallel (*single-threaded*) code will always contain less bugs and hidden traps than parallel code.

Sometimes this is not possible, and you have to introduce parallel programming techniques into the code. To do it successfully, it's not enough to know how to **do** parallel programming. Much more important is that you know what you should absolutely **never** do in parallel code.

To set you in the right mood, this chapter will cover the following topics:

- What is parallel programming and multithreading?
- What are the most common causes of program errors in parallel code?
- How should we handle the user interface in a parallel world?

- What is synchronization, and why is it both good and bad?
- What is interlocking, and when is it better than synchronization?
- How can we remove the synchronization from the picture?
- What communication tools does Delphi offer to a programmer?
- What other libraries are there to help you?

# Processes and threads

As a programmer, you probably have already some understanding about what a process is. As operating systems look at it, a process is a rough equivalent of an application. When a user starts an application, an operating system creates and starts a new process. The process owns the application code and all the resources that this code uses—memory, file handles, device handles, sockets, windows, and so on.

When the program is executing, the system must also keep track of the current execution address, state of the CPU registers, and state of the program's stack. This information, however, is not part of the process, but of a **thread** belonging to this process. Even the simplest program uses one thread.

In other words, the process represents the program's *static* data while the thread represents the *dynamic* part. During the program's lifetime, the thread describes its line of execution. If we know the state of the thread at every moment, we can fully reconstruct the execution in all its details.

All operating systems support one thread per process (the main thread) but some go further and support multiple threads in one process. Actually, most modern operating systems support **multithreading,** as this approach is called. With multithreading, the operating system manages multiple execution paths through the same code. Those paths may execute at the same time (and then again, they may not—but more on that later).

 The default thread created when the program starts is called the *main thread*. Other threads that come afterwards are called **worker** or **background** threads.

In most operating systems (including Windows, OS X, iOS, and Android), processes are **heavy**. It takes a long time (at least at the operating system level where everything is measured in microseconds) to create and load a new process. In contrast to that, threads are **light**. New threads can be created almost immediately—all that the operating system has to do is to allocate some memory for the stack and set up some control structures used by the kernel.

Another important point is that processes are **isolated**. The operating system does its best to separate one process from another so that buggy (or malicious) code in one process cannot crash another process (or read private data from it). Threads, however, don't benefit from this protection.

If you're old enough to remember Windows 3, where this was not the case, you can surely appreciate the stability this isolation is bringing to the user. In contrast to that, multiple threads inside a process **share** all process resources—memory, file handles, and so on. Because of that, threading is inherently fragile—it is very simple to bring down one thread with a bug in another.

In the beginning, operating systems were single-tasking. In other words, only one task (that is, a process) could be executing at one time, and only when it completed the job (when the task terminated) could a new task be scheduled (started).

As soon as the hardware was fast enough, **multitasking** was invented. Most computers still had only one processor, but through the operating system magic it looked like this processor was executing multiple programs at the same time.

Each program was given a small amount of time to do its job. After that it was paused and another program took its place. After some indeterminate time (depending on the system load, the number of higher priority tasks, and so on), the program could execute again and the operating system would run it from the position in which it was paused, again only for a small amount of time.

Two very different approaches to multitasking were in use through history. In **cooperative** multitasking, the process itself tells the operating system when it is ready to be paused. This simplifies the operating system but gives a badly written program an opportunity to bring down the whole computer. Remember Windows 3? That was cooperative multitasking at its worst.

A better approach is **pre-emptive** multitasking, where each process is given its allotted time (typically about a few tens of milliseconds in Windows) and is then *pre-empted*; that is, the hardware timer fires and takes control from the process and gives it back to the operating system, which can then schedule next process.

This approach is used in current Windows, OS X, and all other modern desktop and mobile operating systems. That way, a multitasking system can appear to execute multiple processes at once even if it has only one processor core. Things get even better if there are multiple cores inside the computer, as multiple processes can then really execute at the same time.

The same goes for threads. Single-tasking systems were limited to one thread per process by default. Some multitasking systems were single-threaded (that is, they could only execute one thread per process), but all modern operating systems support multithreading—they can execute multiple threads inside one process. Everything I said about multitasking applies to threads too. Actually, it is the threads that are scheduled, not the processes.

# When to parallelize the code?

Before you start parallelizing the code, you should understand whether the particular code is a good candidate for parallelization or not. There are some typical examples where parallelization is particularly simple, and there are some where it is really hard to implement.

One of the most common examples is executing long parts of code in the *main thread*. In Delphi, the main thread is the only one responsible for managing the user interface. If it is running some long task and not processing user interface events, then the user interface is blocked. We can solve this problem by moving the long task into a background thread, which will allow the main thread to manage the user interface. A responsive program makes for a happy user, as I like to say.

Another problem that is usually relatively simple to solve is enabling a server application to handle multiple clients at once. Instead of processing client requests one by one, we can create a separate thread for each client (up to some reasonable limit) and process requests from that client in that thread.

As requests from different clients really should not interact directly with one another, we don't have to take care of data sharing or inter-thread communications which are, as you'll see, the biggest source of problems in multithreaded programming. The biggest problem which we usually have is to determine the upper limit for concurrent running threads, as that is affected both by the problem we are solving and the number of processors in the user's computer.

The last class of problems, which is also hardest to implement, is speeding up some algorithm. We must find a way to split an algorithm into parts, and that way will be different in each application. Sometimes we can just process part of the input data in each thread and aggregate partial results later, but that will not always be possible. We'll return to this advanced topic in `Chapter 7`, *Exploring Parallel Practices*.

# Most common problems

Before we start writing multithreaded code, I'd like to point out some typical situations that represent the most common sources of problems in multithreaded programs. After that, I'll look into the possible ways of solving such situations.

The biggest problem with the situations I'm about to describe is that they are all completely valid programming approaches if you are writing a single-threaded code. Because of that, they sometimes slip even into (multithreaded) code written by the best programmers.

As we'll see later in the chapter, the best way to work around them is just to stay away from problematic situations. Instead of data sharing, for example, we can use data duplication and communication channels. But I'm getting ahead of myself ...

All of the situations I'm going to describe have something in common. They are a source of problems that can stay well hidden. Lots of times, parallel programs seem to be working during the testing but then randomly fail only at some customers.

 The examples in this chapter are carefully chosen so they **always** cause problems in multithreaded code. In real life, sadly, the situation is quite different.

The only way to detect such problems in multithreaded code is to put a lot of effort into testing. Only automated unit tests running for a long time have any chance of finding them.

You'll notice that I'm skipping ahead a bit here. I did not tell you how to write multithreaded code at all, but I'm already using it in examples. For now, you can just believe me that the code in the examples does what I'm saying. In the next chapter, you'll learn all you need to know to really understand what I'm doing here, and then you can return to the examples from this chapter and re-examine them.

# Never access UI from a background thread

Let's start with the biggest source of hidden problems—manipulating a user interface from a background thread. This is, surprisingly, quite a common problem—even more so as all Delphi resources on multithreaded programming will simply say to never do that. Still, it doesn't seem to touch some programmers, and they will always try to find an excuse to manipulate a user interface from a background thread.

Indeed, there *may* be a situation where VCL or FireMonkey may be manipulated from a background thread, but you'll be treading on thin ice if you do that. Even if your code works with the current Delphi, nobody can guarantee that changes in graphical libraries introduced in future Delphis won't break your code. It is **always** best to cleanly decouple background processing from a user interface.

Let's look at an example which nicely demonstrates the problem. The ParallelPaint demo has a simple form, with eight TPaintBox components and eight threads. Each thread runs the same drawing code and draws a pattern into its own TPaintBox. As every thread accesses only its own Canvas, and no other user interface components, a naive programmer would therefore assume that drawing into paintboxes directly from background threads would not cause problems. A naive programmer would be very much mistaken.

If you run the program, you will notice that although the code paints constantly into some of the paint boxes, others stop to be updated after some time. You may even get a *Canvas does not allow drawing* exception. It is impossible to tell in advance which threads will continue painting and which will not.

The following image shows an example of an output. The first two paint boxes in the first row, and the last one in the last row, were not updated anymore when I grabbed the image:

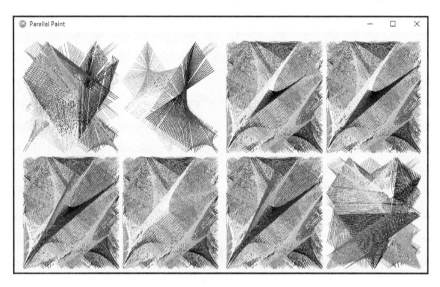

The lines are drawn in the DrawLine method. It does nothing special, just sets the color for that line and draws it. Still, that is enough to break the user interface when this is called from multiple threads at once, even though each thread uses its own Canvas:

```
procedure TfrmParallelPaint.DrawLine(canvas: TCanvas; p1, p2: TPoint;
color: TColor);
begin
  Canvas.Pen.Color := color;
  Canvas.MoveTo(p1.X, p1.Y);
  Canvas.LineTo(p2.X, p2.Y);
end;
```

Is there a way around this problem? Indeed there is. Delphi's TThread class implements a method, Queue, which executes some code in the main thread. (Actually, TThread has multiple methods that can do that; I'll return to this topic later in the chapter.)

Queue takes a procedure or anonymous method as a parameter and sends it to the main thread. After some short time, the code is then executed *in the main thread*. It is impossible to tell how much time will pass before the code is executed, but that delay will typically be very short, in the order of milliseconds. As it accepts an anonymous method, we can use the magic of *variable capturing* and write the corrected code, as shown here:

```
procedure TfrmParallelPaint.QueueDrawLine(canvas: TCanvas; p1, p2: TPoint;
color: TColor);
begin
  TThread.Queue(nil,
    procedure
    begin
      Canvas.Pen.Color := color;
      Canvas.MoveTo(p1.X, p1.Y);
      Canvas.LineTo(p2.X, p2.Y);
    end);
end;
```

In older Delphis you don't have such a nice Queue method but only a version of Synchronize that accepts a normal method. If you have to use this method, you cannot count on anonymous method mechanisms to handle parameters. Rather, you have to copy them to fields and then Synchronize a parameterless method operating on these fields. The following code fragment shows how to do that:

```
procedure TfrmParallelPaint.SynchronizedDraw;
begin
  FCanvas.Pen.Color := FColor;
  FCanvas.MoveTo(FP1.X, FP1.Y);
  FCanvas.LineTo(FP2.X, FP2.Y);
end;

procedure TfrmParallelPaint.SyncDrawLine(canvas: TCanvas; p1, p2: TPoint;
color: TColor);
begin
  FCanvas := canvas;
  FP1 := p1;
  FP2 := p2;
  FColor := color;
  TThread.Synchronize(nil, SynchronizedDraw);
end;
```

If you run the corrected program, the final result should always be similar to the following image, with all eight `TPaintBox` components showing a nicely animated image:

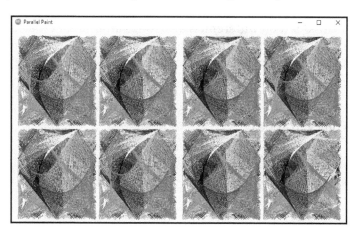

# Simultaneous reading and writing

The next situation which I'm regularly seeing while looking at a badly-written parallel code is simultaneous reading and writing from/to a shared data structure, such as a list. The `SharedList` program demonstrates how things can go wrong when you share a data structure between threads. Actually, scrap that, it shows how things **will** go wrong if you do that.

This program creates a shared list, `FList: TList<Integer>`. Then it creates one background thread which runs the method `ListWriter` and multiple background threads, each running the `ListReader` method. Indeed, you can run the same code in multiple threads. This is a perfectly normal behavior and is sometimes extremely useful.

The `ListReader` method is incredibly simple. It just reads all the elements in a list and does that over and over again. As I've mentioned before, the code in my examples makes sure that problems in multithreaded code really **do** occur, but because of that, my demo code most of the time also looks terribly stupid. In this case, the reader just reads and reads the data because that's the best way to expose the problem:

```
procedure TfrmSharedList.ListReader;
var
  i, j, a: Integer;
begin
  for i := 1 to CNumReads do
```

```
      for j := 0 to FList.Count - 1 do
        a := FList[j];
  end;
```

The `ListWriter` method is a bit different. It also loops around, but it also sleeps a little inside each loop iteration. It would actually be easier to repeat the problem without this extra `Sleep(1)`, but I'll need it to demonstrate something else later in the chapter. Just ignore it for now.

After the `Sleep`, the code either adds to the list or deletes from it. Again, this is designed so that the problem is quick to appear:

```
  procedure TfrmSharedList.ListWriter;
  var
    i: Integer;
  begin
    for i := 1 to CNumWrites do
    begin
      Sleep(1);
      if FList.Count > 10 then
        FList.Delete(Random(10))
      else
        FList.Add(Random(100));
    end;
  end;
```

If you start the program in a debugger, and click on the **Shared lists** button, you'll quickly get an `EArgumentOutOfRangeException` exception. A look at the stack trace will show that it appears in the line `a := FList[j];`.

In retrospect, this is quite obvious. The code in `ListReader` starts the inner `for` loop and reads the `FListCount`. At that time, `FList` has 11 elements so `Count` is 11. At the end of the loop, the code tries to read `FList[10]`, but in the meantime `ListWriter` has deleted one element and the list now only has 10 elements. Accessing element `[10]` therefore raises an exception.

We'll return to this topic later, in the section about *Locking*. For now you should just keep in mind that sharing data structures between threads causes problems.

# Sharing a variable

OK, so rule number two is "Shared structures *bad*". What about sharing a simple variable? Nothing can go wrong there, right? Wrong! There are actually multiple ways something can go wrong.

The program `IncDec` demonstrates one of the bad things that can happen. The code contains two methods: `IncValue` and `DecValue`. The former increments a shared `FValue: integer;` some number of times, and the latter decrements it by the same number of times:

```
procedure TfrmIncDec.IncValue;
var
  i: integer;
  value: integer;
begin
  for i := 1 to CNumRepeat do begin
    value := FValue;
    FValue := value + 1;
  end;
end;

procedure TfrmIncDec.DecValue;
var
  i: integer;
  value: integer;
begin
  for i := 1 to CNumRepeat do begin
    value := FValue;
    FValue := value - 1;
  end;
end;
```

A click on the **Inc/Dec** button sets the shared value to *0*, runs `IncValue`, then `DecValue`, and logs the result:

```
procedure TfrmIncDec.btnIncDec1Click(Sender: TObject);
begin
  FValue := 0;
  IncValue;
  DecValue;
  LogValue;
end;
```

I know you can all tell what `FValue` will hold at the end of this program. Zero, of course. But what will happen if we run `IncValue` and `DecValue` in parallel? That is, actually, hard to predict!

A click on the **Multithreaded** button does almost the same, except that it runs `IncValue` and `DecValue` in parallel. How exactly that is done is not important at the moment (but feel free to peek into the code if you're interested):

```
procedure TfrmIncDec.btnIncDec2Click(Sender: TObject);
begin
  FValue := 0;
  RunInParallel(IncValue, DecValue);
  LogValue;
end;
```

Running this version of the code may still sometimes put zero in `FValue`, but that will be extremely rare. You most probably won't be able to see that result unless you are very lucky. Most of the time, you'll just get a seemingly random number from the range *-10,000,000* to *10,000,000* (which is the value of the `CNumRepeat` constant).

In the following image, the first number is a result of the single-threaded code, while all the rest were calculated by the parallel version of the algorithm:

To understand what's going on, you should know that Windows (and all other operating systems) does many things at once. At any given time, there are hundreds of threads running in different programs and they are all fighting for the limited number of CPU cores. As our program is the active one (has focus), its threads will get most of the CPU time, but still they'll sometimes be paused for some amount of time so that other threads can run.

Because of that, it can easily happen that `IncValue` reads the current value of `FValue` into `value` (let's say that the value is *100*) and is then paused. `DecValue` reads the same value and then runs for some time, decrementing `FValue`. Let's say that it gets it down to *-20,000*. (That is just a number without any special meaning.)

After that, the `IncValue` thread is awakened. It should increment the value to *-19,999*, but instead of that it adds *1* to *100* (stored in `value`), gets *101*, and stores **that** into `FValue`. Kaboom! In each repetition of the program, this will happen at different times and will cause a different result to be calculated.

You may complain that the problem is caused by the two-stage increment and decrement, but you'd be wrong. I dare you—go ahead, change the code so that it will modify `FValue` with `Inc(FValue)` and `Dec(FValue)` and it still won't work correctly.

Well, I hear you say, so I shouldn't even modify one variable from two threads at the same time? I can live with that. But surely, it is OK to write into a variable from one thread and read from another?

The answer, as you can probably guess given the general tendency of this section, is again—no, you may not. There are some situations where this is OK (for example, when a variable is only one byte long) but, in general, even simultaneous reading and writing can be a source of weird problems.

The `ReadWrite` program demonstrates this problem. It has a shared buffer, `FBuf: Int64`, and a pointer variable used to read and modify the data, `FPValue: PInt64`. At the beginning, the buffer is initialized to an easily recognized number and a pointer variable is set to point to the buffer:

```
FPValue := @FBuf;
FPValue^ := $7777777700000000;
```

The program runs two threads. One just reads from the location and stores all the read values into a list. This value is created with `Sorted` and `Duplicates` properties, set in a way that prevents it from storing duplicate values:

```
procedure TfrmReadWrite.Reader;
var
  i: integer;
begin
  for i := 1 to CNumRepeat do
    FValueList.Add(FPValue^);
end;
```

The second thread repeatedly writes two values into the shared location:

```
procedure TfrmReadWrite.Writer;
var
  i: integer;
begin
  for i := 1 to CNumRepeat do begin
    FPValue^ := $7777777700000000;
    FPValue^ := $0000000077777777;
  end;
end;
```

At the end, the contents of the `FValueList` list are logged on the screen. We would expect to see only two values—*$7777777700000000* and *$0000000077777777*. In reality, we see four, as the following screenshot demonstrates:

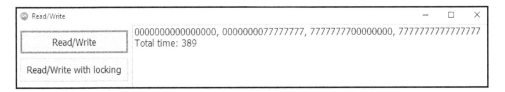

The reason for that strange result is that Intel processors in 32-bit mode can't write a 64-bit number (as `int64` is) in one step. In other words, reading and writing 64-bit numbers in 32-bit code is not *atomic*.

 When multithreading programmers talk about something being *atomic*, they want to say that an operation will execute in one indivisible step. Any other thread will either see a state before the operation or a state after the operation, but never some undefined intermediate state.

How do values *$7777777777777777* and *$0000000000000000* appear in the test application? Let's say that `FValue^` contains *$7777777700000000*. The code then starts writing *$0000000077777777* into `FValue` by firstly storing a *$77777777* into the bottom four bytes. After that it starts writing *$00000000* into the upper four bytes of `FValue^`, but in the meantime `Reader` reads the value and gets *$7777777777777777*.

In a similar way, `Reader` will sometimes see *$0000000000000000* in the `FValue^`.

We'll look into a way to solve this situation immediately, but in the meantime, you may wonder—when is it okay to read/write from/to a variable at the same time? Sadly, the answer is—it depends. Not even just on the CPU family (Intel and ARM processors behave completely differently), but also on a specific architecture used in a processor. For example, older and newer Intel processors may not behave the same in that respect.

You can always depend on access to byte-sized data being atomic, but that is that. Access (reads and writes) to larger quantities of data (words, integers) is atomic only if the data is correctly *aligned*. You can access *word* sized data atomically if it is word aligned, and integer data if it is double-word aligned. If the code was compiled in 64-bit mode, you can also atomically access int64 data if it is quad-word aligned.

When you are not using data packing (such as packed records) the compiler will take care of alignment and data access should automatically be atomic. You should, however, still check the alignment in code, if nothing else to prevent stupid programming errors.

If you want to write and read larger amounts of data, modify the data, or if you want to work on shared data structures, correct alignment will not be enough. You will need to introduce *synchronization* into your program.

# Synchronization

Whenever you need to access the same data from multiple threads, and at least one thread is modifying the data, you have to *synchronize* access to the data. As we've just seen, this holds for shared data structures and for simple variables.

Synchronization will make sure that one thread cannot see invalid intermediate states that another thread creates temporarily while updating the shared data. In a way this is similar to database transactions at the *read committed* level, when other users cannot see changes applied to the database while a transaction is in progress.

The simplest way to synchronize two (or more) threads is to use *locking*. With locking you can protect a part of the program so that only one thread will be able to access it at any time. If one thread has successfully *acquired* but not yet *released* the lock (we also say that the thread now *owns* the lock), no other threads will be able to acquire that same lock. If any thread tries to acquire a lock, it will be paused until the lock is available (after the original lock owner releases the lock).

We could compare such a lock with a real-world lock. When somebody wants to access a critical resource that must not be shared (for example, a toilet), he will lock the door behind him. Any other potential users of the critical resource will queue in a line. When the first user is finished using the critical resource, he will unlock it and leave, allowing the next user the access.

Synchronization mechanisms are almost always implemented directly by the operating system. It is possible to implement them directly in the code, but that should only be used to solve very specific circumstances. As a general rule, you should not attempt to write your own synchronization mechanism.

If you are writing a multi-platform application, accessing operating system synchronization mechanisms can be a pain. Luckily, Delphi's runtime library provides a very nice platform-independent way to work with them.

The simplest way to implement locking is to use a *critical section*. In Delphi, you should use the `TCriticalSection` wrapper implemented in the `System.SyncObjs` unit instead of accessing the operating system directly.

# Critical sections

The easiest way to explain the use of critical sections is with an example. As the `ReadWrite` example is still fresh in your mind, I'll return to it. This program implements—in addition to the unsafe reading/writing approach—a code that reads and writes data with additional protection from a critical section lock.

This critical section is created when a form is created, and destroyed when the form is destroyed. There is only one critical section object shared by both threads:

```
procedure TfrmReadWrite.FormCreate(Sender: TObject);
begin
  FLock := TCriticalSection.Create;
end;

procedure TfrmReadWrite.FormDestroy(Sender: TObject);
begin
  FreeAndNil(FLock);
end;
```

When a reader wants to read from `FPValue^`, it will firstly acquire the critical section by calling `FLock.Acquire`. At that point, the thread will either successfully acquire the ownership of the lock and continue execution or it will block until the lock becomes unowned.

After some finite time, the thread will manage to acquire the lock and continue with the next line, `value := FPValue^`. This will safely read the value into a temporary variable, knowing that nobody can be writing to the value at the same time. After that the critical section is immediately released by calling `FLock.Release`, which also makes the lock unowned:

```
procedure TfrmReadWrite.LockedReader;
var
  i: integer;
  value: int64;
begin
  for i := 1 to CNumRepeat do begin
    FLock.Acquire;
    value := FPValue^;
    FLock.Release;
    FValueList.Add(value);
  end;
end;
```

TCriticalSection also implements the aliases `Enter` and `Leave`, which function exactly the same as `Acquire` and `Release`. Which you use is entirely up to you.

The writer does something similar. Before a `FPValue^` is written to, the lock is acquired and after that the lock is released:

```
procedure TfrmReadWrite.LockedWriter;
var
  i: integer;
begin
  for i := 1 to CNumRepeat do begin
    FLock.Acquire;
    FPValue^ := $7777777700000000;
    FLock.Release;
    FLock.Acquire;
    FPValue^ := $0000000077777777;
    FLock.Release;
  end;
end;
```

Before we look into the result of that change, I'd like to point out something very important. Introducing a lock doesn't automatically solve problems. You also have to use it in the right place (in this example, when reading and writing the shared value), and you have to use it in **all** places where shared data is accessed.

For example, if `LockedReader` would be using a critical section, as it is now, but `LockedWriter` would not, access to the shared value would still be unsynchronized and we would be getting wrong results from the program.

Let's see how introducing a critical section affects our program. The following screenshot shows the result of both versions of the code—unprotected and synchronized:

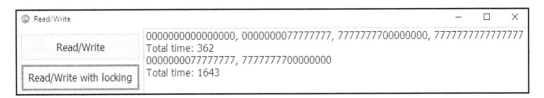

We can see two important consequences of locking here. One, the output from the code is now correct. Two, the program runs much longer with locking.

That is a typical result of synchronizing access with locks. They are slow—at least if you are trying to acquire them many thousand times per second, as my test program does. If you are using them sparingly, they will not affect the program that much.

An interesting thing about critical sections is that they will happily let through a thread that already owns a lock. A thread that already owns a lock can therefore call `Acquire` for the second time and be sure that it will not be blocked. It must then also call `Release` two times to release the critical section.

For example, the following code is perfectly valid:

```
FLock.Acquire;
FLock.Acquire;
value := FPValue^;
FLock.Release;
FLock.Release;
```

This situation sometimes comes up when procedure A locks a critical section and calls procedure B, which also locks a critical section. Instead of refactoring the code so that the critical section is only the acquired one, we can rely on this fact and acquire the critical section in both places. Acquiring an already acquired critical section is very fast.

This behavior is called *re-entrancy*, and a locking mechanism that allows such coding is deemed *re-entrant*.

There are two big problems that critical sections can introduce into your code. One we've already seen—the program runs slower with locking. The second is even worse—if such synchronization is not implemented correctly, it may cause the program to endlessly wait for a lock that will never become free. We call that **deadlocking**.

Deadlocking happens when thread 1 acquires critical section A and then tries to acquire critical section B while in the meantime thread 2 acquires critical section B and then tries to acquire critical section A. Both threads will be blocked as they will wait for a critical section that will never be released.

 Deadlocking is not specific to critical sections. It can appear regardless of the locking mechanism used in the code.

This situation is demonstrated in program *Deadlocking*. It contains two threads, both accessing the shared variable, `Counter`, stored in the shared object, `Shared`. To synchronize access to this shared variable, they both acquire and release the critical section, `shared.LockCounter`.

To demonstrate the problem, both threads also acquire the additional critical section, `shared.LockOther`. In this demo, the second critical section is meaningless, but, in a badly designed real-life code, such situations occur a lot. A code may acquire a critical section, then do some processing, and in the middle of the processing access different data, protected with a different critical section.

When multiple critical sections are always acquired in the same order, everything works just fine. But if—because of a programming error or a weird system design—one thread acquires critical sections in a different order than another thread, a deadlock may occur.

The same situation is programmed into the `Deadlocking` program. The `TaskProc1` method acquires `LockCounter` first and `LockOther` second, while the `TaskProc2` method (running in a different thread) acquires `LockOther` first and `LockCounter` second. Both methods are shown here:

```
procedure TaskProc1(const task: ITask; const shared: TSharedData);
begin
  while frmDeadlock.FTask1.Status <> TTaskStatus.Canceled do begin
    shared.LockCounter.Acquire;
    shared.LockOther.Acquire;
    shared.Counter := shared.Counter + 1;
    shared.LockOther.Release;
    shared.LockCounter.Release;
  end;
end;

procedure TaskProc2(const task: ITask; const shared: TSharedData);
begin
  while frmDeadlock.FTask1.Status <> TTaskStatus.Canceled do begin
    shared.LockOther.Acquire;
    shared.LockCounter.Acquire;
    shared.Counter := shared.Counter + 1;
    shared.LockCounter.Release;
    shared.LockOther.Release;
  end;
end;
```

If you start only one thread, everything will work just fine. Thread will continue to acquire both critical sections, increment the shared resource, and release both critical sections. If you start both threads, however, the program will quickly deadlock. `TaskProc1` will acquire `LockCounter` and block on waiting for `LockOther`, while at the same time `TaskProc2` will acquire `LockOther` and block on waiting for `LockCounter`.

Luckily, sources of deadlocking are easy to find if you can repeat the problem in a debugger. When the program blocks, just click the *Pause* icon and go through the threads in the *Thread status* window. Double-click each thread and check if the *Call stack* for the thread is currently inside an *Acquire* call. Any such thread should then be carefully investigated to see if it is part of the problem.

The following screenshot shows the `TaskProc1` method paused during a deadlock:

The best solution for such problems is good program design. The part of the code where the critical section is acquired should always be very short and should—if at all possible—never call other code that acquires critical sections. If that could not be prevented, you should design the code so that it always acquires all the needed critical sections first (and always in the same order), and only then call the protected code.

If that is also not possible, the last solution is to not use `Acquire` (or its namesake `Enter`), but the `TryEnter` function. That one tries to acquire the critical section, returns `False` if the critical section is already locked, or acquires the critical section and returns `True`. It will never block. An adapted version of the code is shown here:

```
procedure TryTaskProc1(const task: ITask; const shared: TSharedData);
begin
  while frmDeadlock.FTask1.Status <> TTaskStatus.Canceled do begin
    shared.LockCounter.Acquire;
    if shared.LockOther.TryEnter then
    begin
      shared.Counter := shared.Counter + 1;
      shared.LockOther.Leave;
    end;
    shared.LockCounter.Release;
  end;
end;

procedure TryTaskProc2(const task: ITask; const shared: TSharedData);
```

```
begin
  while frmDeadlock.FTask1.Status <> TTaskStatus.Canceled do begin
    shared.LockOther.Acquire;
    if shared.LockCounter.TryEnter then
    begin
      shared.Counter := shared.Counter + 1;
      shared.LockCounter.Leave;
    end;
    shared.LockOther.Release;
  end;
end;
```

If you enter a critical section with `TryEnter`, you should leave it with a call to `Leave`, just for readability reasons.

If you run the demo and use the `TryTask1` and `TryTask2` buttons to start the `TryTaskProc1` and `TryTaskProc2` methods, you'll notice that the program continues to work but also that it increments the counter much slower than with only one thread running. This happens because both threads are constantly fighting for the second critical section. Most of the time, each thread acquires the first critical section, then tries to acquire the second one, fails, and does nothing.

To learn more about deadlocks and ways to fix them, go to the beautiful *The Deadlock Empire* web site (`http://deadlockempire.4delphi.com/delphi/`), where you can explore this topic through a game.

# Other locking mechanisms

Critical sections are not the only mechanism that operating systems expose to applications. There are also other approaches that may be preferable in different situations. In Delphi, most of them are nicely wrapped into system-independent wrappers, implemented in the `System.SyncObjs` unit.

The first such object is a *mutex*. It is very similar to a critical section, as you can use it to protect access to a critical resource. The big difference between a mutex and a critical section is that a critical section can only be shared between the threads of one program. A mutex, on other hand, can have a *name*. Two (or more) programs can create mutexes with the same name and use them to access some shared resource (for example, a file) that may only safely be used by one program at a time.

A mutex is implemented in a `TMutex` class which exposes the same API as a `TCriticalSection`. After you `Create` a mutex, you can call `Acquire` to access and lock the mutex and `Release` to unlock it.

If you create a mutex without a name, it can only be used inside one program and functions exactly as a critical section. Locking with mutexes, however, is *significantly* slower than locking with critical sections. As the `IncDec` demo shows, locking with mutexes (activated with the **MT with mutex** button) can be more than 50 times slower than locking with critical sections (**MT with locking** button). An image with a comparison of the timing for different locking approaches is shown later in this chapter.

Mutexes do provide one advantage over a critical section. You can acquire a mutex by calling a `WaitFor` function, which accepts a timeout value in milliseconds. If the code fails to lock a mutex in that amount of time, it will return `wrTimeout` and continue. This works just the same as `TCriticalSection.TryEnter`, except with an additional timeout. Nevertheless, if you need such functionality, you'll probably be better off by using the `TSpinlock` mechanism described later in this chapter.

The next standard synchronization mechanism is a *semaphore*. A **semaphore** is used to synchronize access to resources which can be used by more than one user (more than one code path) at the same time, but have an upper limit on the number of concurrent users.

For example, if you want to protect a resource which supports up to three concurrent users, you can create a semaphore with a count of *three*. When you *acquire* such a semaphore, you decrement the number of available resources (the semaphore's internal counter) by one. If you try to acquire a semaphore when its internal counter is at zero, you'll be blocked. `Release`, on the other hand, increments the internal counter and allows another thread to enter the critical path.

Semaphores, as mutexes, can have names and can be used to synchronize multiple programs. They are also equally slow, so I won't peruse them in this book. Still, semaphores are an interesting topic as they can be used to solve many difficult problems. For more information on the topic, I'd like to recommend a beautiful (free) book, *The Little Book of Semaphores,* which you can read or download, at `http://greenteapress.com/wp/semaphores/`.

One of the problems with critical sections is that you have to create and manage them in parallel to the data being protected. To solve that, in Delphi 2009, the developers have extended the `TObject` class with an additional pointer field used by the new `TMonitor` record, which was added to the *System* unit.

As the `TObject` is the base parent of each and every class type in Delphi programs, this caused the size of every object created in your program to increment by 4 bytes (8 if you're compiling for a 64-bit processor). This and the abysmally bad `TMonitor` implementation have caused some programmers to call this the worst abuse of space in the entire history of Delphi. I must say that I mostly agree with this assessment.

The idea behind `TMonitor` was completely solid. It was designed to provide a per-object locking capability together with some additional functionality that allowed for the creation of a fast in-process event and fast in-process semaphore (more on that in a moment). In reality, the implementation was so flawed that the only part that you could safely use was the basic locking, implemented with the `Enter`, `TryEnter`, and `Exit` functions. All other implementation was broken for many Delphi versions and was only fixed a few years later.

As far as I know, in recent releases (Tokyo and a few before), `TMonitor` doesn't have any known bugs. Still, most of programmers who make a living by writing multithreaded code have developed such a deep distrust of it that we simply don't want to use it.

Regardless of my preconceptions, `TMonitor` can safely be used to function as a critical section. It is faster and simpler (you don't have to create a separate object) than a critical section. It is also sometimes inconvenient, as it can only be used to lock some existing object, and appropriate object may not exist in the code.

The `IncDec` demo works around that by locking the form object itself. This doesn't affect the normal VCL operations in any way, as VCL doesn't use `TMonitor` to lock `TForm` objects. In a larger program, however, that would be frowned upon, as the meaning of the code is hard to grasp. You should use `TMonitor` only when you really work with a shared **object** so you can put a lock directly on it.

Another small problem with `TMonitor` is a naming conflict. Delphi VCL already defines a `TMonitor` class in the `Vcl.Forms` unit. If your unit includes `Vcl.Forms` (and every form unit does that), you'll have to type `System.TMonitor` instead of `TMonitor` to make the code compile. Alternatively, you can call `MonitorEnter` and `MonitorExit` procedures which do the same.

Let's look at the code that protects access to a shared counter with `TMonitor`. It was taken from the `IncDec` demo. To synchronize access to the counter, it firstly locks the form object by calling `System.TMonitor.Enter(Self)`. After that it can safely operate on the counter. At the end, it unlocks the form object by calling `System.TMonitor.Exit(Self)`. The other part of the demo, `MonitorLockedIncValue` (not shown here) does the same:

```
procedure TfrmIncDec.MonitorLockedDecValue;
var
```

```
    value: integer;
    i: Integer;
begin
    for i := 1 to CNumRepeat do begin
        System.TMonitor.Enter(Self);
        value := FValue;
        FValue := value + 1;
        System.TMonitor.Exit(Self);
    end;
end;
```

To acquire and release a TMonitor you can also call helper methods MonitorEnter and MonitorExit.

If you run the demo, you'll notice that the TMonitor approach is much faster than working with TCriticalSection. On my test computer, it is about four times faster. This is a result of the internal implementation of TMonitor, which doesn't use a critical section, but an improved idea called **spinlock**.

The difference between a critical section and a spinlock lies in the implementation of the Acquire call. When a thread cannot access a critical section because it is already locked, Windows puts this thread to sleep. (Other operating systems behave mostly the same.) When a critical section becomes available, Windows selects one of the threads waiting for it and wakes it up.

A spinlock, on the other hand, assumes that the code protected with it is very short and that the spinlock will be released quickly. If a spinlock is already acquired from another thread, the code firstly tries to *actively wait* or *spin*. Instead of going to sleep, the code runs in a tight loop and constantly checks if the spinlock has become available. Only if that doesn't happen after some time, the thread goes to sleep.

Delphi implements a spinlock object which you can use directly in your code. It is called TSpinLock and can be found in the System.SyncObjs unit.

A TSpinLock is a record, not an object, so there's no need to free it. You still have to create it though, as some data is initialized in the constructor. The code in the IncDec demo does that by calling FSpinlock := TSpinLock.Create(false).

The code then uses `FSpinlock.Enter` to acquire a spinlock and `FSpinlock.Exit` to release it. `TSpinLock` also implements a `TryEnter` method which accepts a *timeout* parameter. If the spinlock cannot be acquired in *timeout* milliseconds, `TryEnter` returns `False`:

```
procedure TfrmIncDec.SpinlockDecValue;
var
  i: integer;
  value: integer;
begin
  for i := 1 to CNumRepeat do begin
    FSpinlock.Enter;
    value := FValue;
    FValue := value - 1;
    FSpinlock.Exit;
  end;
end;
```

The only problem with `TSpinLock` is that it is not *re-entrant*. If a thread which has already acquired a spinlock calls `Enter` for a second time, a code will either raise an exception (if you have passed `True` to the constructor) or block. The implementation, however, provides the `IsLocked` and `IsLockedByCurrentThread` functions, which you can use to write a re-entrant spinlock, using `TSpinLock` as a base.

The `System.SyncObjs` unit also implements a faster implementation of an event, `TLightweightEvent`, and a faster implementation of a semaphore, `TLightweightSemaphore`. They are both based around an idea of actively spinning in a loop (for some short time) if the object cannot be immediately acquired.

The following screenshot shows the execution time comparison for all the locking mechanisms that I've discussed so far. Well, all and one more. The last approach, *Interlocking*, will be discussed in the *Interlocked operations* section later in this chapter.

All the mechanisms I've discussed so far are completely symmetrical. They treat all the threads the same. Sometimes, though, this is not what we would like.

Lots of the time, threads in a program have to share access to data that is mostly read from and almost never changed. In this case, it is inefficient if the reader threads block one another. The only time the access must be protected is when a thread has to modify the shared data.

In such cases, we can use a synchronization mechanism that allows multiple simultaneous readers to access a shared resource, but at the same time allows only one writer. In addition, a writer must block out all the readers, as they should not read from a shared resource while it is being modified. We've seen before in the SharedList example that this is not going to work.

In Delphi, such a mechanism is called TMultiReadExclusiveWriteSynchronizer, and is defined in System.SysUtils unit. As this name is terribly impractical to type, Delphi also provides a shorter alias, TMREWSync.

> In the literature and in alternative implementations, you'll also see such a mechanism called *single writer, multiple readers,* or *SWMR.*

With a `TMREWSync` and similar mechanisms that provide multiple levels of access to a resource, we cannot just call `Acquire` or `Enter` to lock the resource. We also have to state our intentions in advance. With `TMREWSync`, we have to call `BeginRead` if we want to read from a resource and `BeginWrite` if we will write to it. Similarly, we have to call `EndRead` or `EndWrite` to release a resource.

Keep in mind that the compiler cannot tell what you are doing—reading or writing—with a shared resource. Actually, the compiler cannot event tell what the shared resource is. It is entirely your responsibility as a programmer to use the correct locking methods in appropriate places of the code.

The Delphi implementation of a single writer, multiple readers mechanism is quite complicated and that shows with the speed. I actually had to fine-tune a demo program a bit to make it perform faster than a simple critical section. In real-life programs, you should always test whether a `TCriticalSection` or `TMREWSync` make for a better performance.

# A short note on coding style

In all the examples so far, I used a simple coding style:

```
// acquire access
// work with shared resource
// release access
```

For example, the `IncDec` demo from this chapter contains the following code:

```
FSpinlock.Enter;
value := FValue;
FValue := value - 1;
FSpinlock.Exit;
```

In reality, I don't code resource locking in that way. I'm a strong proponent of the thought that all resource management pairs, such as create/destroy, acquire/release, beginupdate/endupdate, and so on should, if at all possible, be written in a `try..finally` block. I would therefore write the previous example as follows:

```
FSpinlock.Enter;
try
  value := FValue;
  FValue := value - 1;
finally
  FSpinlock.Exit;
end;
```

This approach has two big advantages. One is that acquiring and releasing a resource are now visibly connected with a `try..finally` construct. When you browse through the code, this pair of operations will immediately jump out at you.

The other advantage is that the resource will be released if your code crashes while the resource is allocated. This is important when the code that reacts to the exception also tries to access the shared resource. Or maybe the program tries to shut down cleanly and during the cleanup accesses the shared resource. Without a `try..finally`, the resource would stay acquired forever and that second part of code would just deadlock.

Saying all that, it may seem weird that I didn't insert `try..finally` blocks everywhere in the test code. Well, I had a reason for that. Two, actually.

Firstly, I wanted to keep code examples short. I don't like to read books that have long code examples spanning multiple pages and so I kept all code examples in this book very short.

Secondly, I wanted to write this note on coding style and that was a good excuse for it.

# Shared data with built-in locking

Sometimes you don't need to implement an additional locking mechanism because Delphi already does that for you. The runtime library contains three such data structures—`TThreadList`, `TThreadList<T>`, and `TThreadedQueue<T>`. The first one can be found in the `System.Classes` unit, while the other two live in `System.Generics.Collections`.

Both variants of `TThreadList` work the same. They don't expose the normal list-management functions (such as `Add`, `Remove`, `Items[]`, and so on). Instead of that, they implement the `LockList` function, which uses `TMonitor` to acquire access to an internal `TList` (or `TList<T>`) object and returns that object. To release access to this list, the program has to call the `UnlockList` function.

The following example from the `SharedList` demo shows how to use `TThreadList<Integer>` to represent the shared storage. To access the shared list, the code calls `FThreadList.LockList`. This function returns a `TList<Integer>` object, which can be then used in the code. To release the shared list, the code calls `FThreadList.UnlockList`:

```
procedure TfrmSharedList.ThreadListReader;
var
  i, j, a: Integer;
  list: TList<Integer>;
```

```
begin
  for i := 1 to CNumReads do
  begin
    list := FThreadList.LockList;
    for j := 0 to FList.Count - 1 do
      a := FList[j];
    FThreadList.UnlockList;
  end;
end;
```

> Using the list returned from the `LockList` after `UnlockList` was called is a programming error that cannot be caught by the compiler. Be careful!

Comparing the various approaches in the `SharedList` demo gives interesting results. As expected, the critical section-based locking is the slowest. More interestingly, the `TMonitor` locking used in the `TThreadList` is faster than the `TMREWSync` implementation. The following screenshot shows a comparison of execution times measured on the test computer:

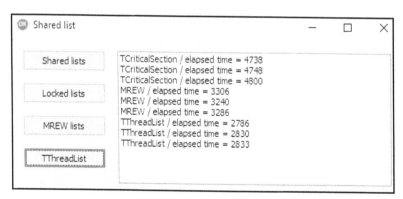

I've said it before and I'll say it again—Delphi's multiple readers, exclusive writer implementation is really not very fast. You should always compare it to a normal locking, implemented with either a `TMonitor` or a `TSpinLock`.

The third data structure, `TThreadedQueue<T>`, implements a standard first in, first out fixed-size queue. All operations on the queue are protected with a `TMonitor`. I will use this data structure in practical examples near the end of this chapter and all through Chapter 6, *Working with Parallel Tools*.

# Interlocked operations

When a shared data is small enough and you only need to increment it or swap two values, there's an option to do that without locking. All modern processors implement instructions that can do simple operations on memory locations in such a way that another processor can not interrupt the operation in progress.

Such instructions are sometimes called *interlocked operations,* while the whole idea of programming with them is called *lock-free* programming or, sometimes, *microlocking*. The latter term is actually more appropriate, as the CPU indeed does some locking. This locking happens on an assembler instruction level, and is therefore much faster than the operating system-based locking, such as critical sections.

As these operations are implemented on an assembler level, you have to adapt the code to the specific CPU target. Or, and this is very much advised, you just use the `TInterlocked` class from the `System.SyncObjs` unit.

Functions in the `TInterlocked` class are mostly just simple wrappers for the `Atomic*` family of the CPU-dependent function from the *System* unit. For example, `TInterlocked.Add` is implemented as a simple call to `AtomicIncrement`:

```
class function TInterlocked.Add(var Target: Integer; Increment: Integer):
Integer;
begin
  Result := AtomicIncrement(Target, Increment);
end;
```

Interlocked functions are declared as `inline`, so you won't lose any cycles if you call `TInterlocked.Add` instead of `AtomicIncrement` directly.

 Windows implements more interlocked functions than are exposed in the `TInterlocked` class. If you want to call them directly, you can find them in the `Winapi.Windows` unit. All their names start with `Interlocked`.

We can split interlocked functions into two big families. One set of functions modifies a shared value. You can use them to increment or decrement a shared value by some amount. Typical representatives of this family are `Increment`, `Decrement`, and `Add`.

The other set of functions is designed to exchange two values. It contains only two functions with multiple overloads that support different types of data, `Exchange` and `CompareExchange`.

The functions from the first family are easy to use. They take a value, increment or decrement it by some amount, and return the new value. All that is done *atomically,* so any other thread in the system will always see the old value or the new value but not some intermediate value.

The only exception to that pattern are the BitTestAndSet and BitTestAndClear functions. They both test if some bit in a value is set and return that as a boolean function result. After that they either set or clear the same bit, depending on the function. Of course, all that is again done atomically.

We can use TInterlocked.Increment and TInterlocked.Decrement to manipulate the shared value in the IncDec demo. Although TInterlocked is a class, it is composed purely from class functions. As such, we never create an instance of the TInterlocked class, but just use its class methods directly on our code, as shown in the following example:

```
procedure TfrmIncDec.InterlockedIncValue;
var
  i: integer;
begin
  for i := 1 to CNumRepeat do
    TInterlocked.Increment(FValue);
end;

procedure TfrmIncDec.InterlockedDecValue;
var
  i: integer;
begin
  for i := 1 to CNumRepeat do
    TInterlocked.Decrement(FValue);
end;
```

As we've seen in the previous section, this approach beats even the spinlocks, which were the fastest locking mechanism so far.

Functions in the second family are a bit harder to use. Exchange takes two parameters: shared data and a new value. It returns the original value of the shared data and sets it to the new value.

In essence, the Exchange function implements the steps outlined in the following function, except that they are done in a safe, atomic way:

```
class function TInterlocked.Exchange(var Target: Integer; Value: Integer):
Integer;
begin
  Result := Target;
```

```
    Target := Value;
  end;
```

The second set of data exchanging functions, CompareExchange, are a bit more complicated. CompareExchange takes three parameters—shared data, new value, and test value. It compares shared data to the test value and, if the values are equal, sets the shared data to the new value. In all cases, the function returns the original value of the shared data.

he following code exactly represents the CompareExchange behavior, except that the real function implements all the steps as one atomic operation:

```
class function CompareExchange(var Target: Integer; Value: Integer;
Comparand: Integer): Integer;
begin
  Result := Target;
  if Target = Comparand then
    Target := Value;
end;
```

How can we know whether the shared data was replaced with the new value? We can check the function result. If it is equal to the test value, Comparand, then the value was replaced, otherwise it was not.

A helper function, TInterlocked.Read, can be used to atomically read from the shared data. It is implemented as such:

```
class function TInterlocked.Read(var Target: Int64): Int64;
begin
  Result := CompareExchange(Target, 0, 0);
end;
```

If the original value is equal to 0, it will be replaced with 0. In other words, it will not be changed. If it is not equal to 0, it also won't be changed because CompareExchange guarantees that. In both cases, CompareExchange will return the original value, which is exactly what the function needs.

We can use TInterlocked.Read and TInterlocked.Exchange to re-implement the ReadWrite demo without locking:

```
procedure TfrmReadWrite.InterlockedReader;
var
  i: integer;
  value: int64;
begin
  for i := 1 to CNumRepeat do begin
    value := TInterlocked.Read(FPValue^);
```

```
      FValueList.Add(value);
   end;
end;

procedure TfrmReadWrite.InterlockedWriter;
var
   i: integer;
begin
   for i := 1 to CNumRepeat do begin
      TInterlocked.Exchange(FPValue^, $7777777700000000);
      TInterlocked.Exchange(FPValue^, $0000000077777777);
   end;
end;
```

If you run the code, you'll see that it is indeed faster than the locking approach. On the test computer it executes about 20% faster, as you can verify in the following screenshot:

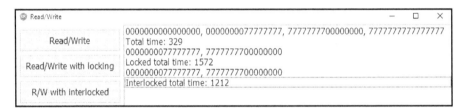

Similar to locking, interlocking is not a magic bullet. You have to use it correctly and you have to use it in all the relevant places. If you modify shared data with interlocked instructions but read that same data with a normal read, the code will not work correctly.

You can verify that by changing the `value := TInterlocked.Read(FPValue^);` line in the `InterlockedReader` method to `value := FPValue^;`. If you rerun the test, it will give the same (wrong) results as the original, fully unsafe version.

# Object life cycle

Special care should be given to the way objects are created and destroyed in a multithreaded environment. Not every approach is safe, and it is quite simple to make a mistake that would cause occasional crashes.

The simplest way is to lock all access to an object. If you create it from a critical section, use it from a critical section and destroy it in a critical section, everything will work. This way, however, is very slow and error-prone, as it is quite simple to forget to lock something.

If you create the object before the background tasks are created, and destroy it after the background tasks are destroyed, everything would work, too. If this is a normal object on a non-ARC platform, you are just sharing a pointer and that is never a problem. If you are sharing an interface-implementing object or if you are compiling for an ARC platform, the reference counting mechanism kicks into action. As the reference counting is threadsafe, that is again not a problem. Of course, all methods of that object that are called from the parallel code must work correctly if they are called from two or more threads at the same time.

Problems appear if you would like to create or destroy the shared object when the parallel tasks using that object are already running. Creation is possible—with some care. Destruction, you should stay away from.

Let's discuss the latter first. If you have a normal object in non-ARC environment, then it is obvious that you cannot destroy it in one thread while another thread is using it. With interfaces or ARC that is not very obvious. You may think that it is safe to assign nil to a shared interface in one thread (`FShared := nil;`) while another thread copies it into a different interface and uses that copy (`tmp := FShared; tmp.DoSomething;`). Trust me, that will not work. One thread will try to clear the object by calling `_IntfClear` while another will try to copy the object by calling `_IntfCopy`. Depending on luck, this will either work or the second thread will own invalid reference to a destroyed object and will crash when trying to use it.

Contrary to that, creating an object from a thread is indeed possible. (As you dig deeper and deeper into parallel code, you'll start to notice that the biggest problem in the parallel world is not how to set up parallel computation, but how to clean it up when the task is done.) Let's assume that we have a shared object of type `TSharedObject`, which for some reason cannot be initialized before the worker threads are started. At some time, a thread will need this object and will try to create it. But, hey, we're living in a parallel world, so it's entirely possible that some other thread will try to do that at the same time too!

One way to approach the problem is with locking. We have to establish a shared lock that will be used just for the purpose of initializing an object and use it to synchronize access to the object creation. The following code fragment shows an idea of how that could be implemented:

```
//In main thread
FInitializationLock := TCriticalSection.Create;

//In a thread
FInitializationLock.Acquire;
if not assigned(FSharedObject) then
  FSharedObject := TSharedObject.Create;
```

```
FInitializationLock.Release;
```

The important part of this approach is that we need to test whether the shared object is assigned from within the acquired critical section (or a spinlock or `TMonitor`). If we do the test before acquiring the critical section, the code would sometimes fail. It would be entirely possible for two threads to test whether the object is assigned, then both acquire the critical section (one after another, of course) and both store a newly created `TSharedObject` into the shared variable. After that, one instance of the shared object would be lost forever.

Instead of locking, we can use interlocked operation to create an object. The following example code shows how:

```
procedure CreateSharedObject;
var
  value: TSharedObject;
begin
  if not assigned(FSharedObject) then
  begin
    value := TSharedObject.Create;
    if TInterlocked.CompareExchange(pointer(FSharedObject), pointer(value),
nil) <> nil then
      value.Free;
  end;
end;
```

The code firstly checks whether the `FSharedObject` is already created. If not, it will create a new instance of `TSharedObject` and store it in a temporary value. After that, it will use `CompareExchange` to store the temporary value in the shared variable, but only if `FSharedObject` still contains `nil`.

`CompareExchange` can return a value that is not `nil`. That will happen if another thread has tested whether `FSharedObject` is assigned at the same time as the first thread. It also created a new `TSharedObject` but managed to execute `CompareExchange` just before the first thread. If that happens, the code keeps the value in `FSharedObject` and throws the `TSharedObject` stored in a temporary variable away.

This approach is also called *optimistic* initialization, because the thread optimistically creates an object and expects that it will be able to store it in the shared value. As in most cases a conflict between threads rarely occurs; this is, in general, a fast and useful way to create shared objects. It also doesn't require a separate synchronization primitive, which may in some occasions be a big advantage.

# Communication

Seeing all that, you may now agree with me when I say that data sharing is hard. It is hard to do it safely as there are so many opportunities to make a mistake in the code. It is also hard to do it fast, because locking approaches don't *scale* well. In other words, locking will prevent the code from working two times faster when you run the code on twice the CPU cores.

Luckily, there's a better way. Better, but way harder. Instead of sharing, we can do what I've been advocating since the beginning of this book, and change the algorithm. And to do that, we'll need some *communication* techniques. In my parallel projects, I always prefer communication to synchronization, and I strongly suggest that you try to do the same.

You may find it strange that I've dedicated that much space to data sharing and synchronization techniques if I don't recommend using them. Well, sometimes you just have to bite the bullet and share data because nothing else makes sense. In such cases, you also have to intimately know everything that can go wrong and ways to fix it.

The best way to remove data sharing from the equation is to replace it with *data duplication* and *aggregation*. Before creating the threads, we make a copy of the original data, one for each thread. A thread can then do its work in peace as it is not sharing data with anybody. At the end, the thread sends its result back to the main thread (here the *communication* comes in to play) so that the main thread can then combine (aggregate) partial results together.

Sending data from one thread to another is simpler if you don't have to care about the object ownership. It is best to always use just simple data types (such as integers) and managed data types (strings and interfaces). As this data is never simultaneously used in two threads, the rules from the section *Object life cycle* don't apply. We can create and destroy such objects in completely normal ways.

Sending data from main thread to the worker thread and sending data in the opposite direction are two completely different problems, and we have to approach them in a different way. The way we choose to send data always depends on the implementation of the receiving thread. Before we learn how to send data to worker threads, we have to learn how to create and manage them. I'll therefore cover this in the latter chapters.

Sending data from worker threads to the main thread depends only on the implementation of the main thread, and that is something we are familiar with. In the rest of the chapter, we'll look into four techniques for communicating with the main thread—sending Windows messages, `Synchronize`, `Queue`, and polling.

To demonstrate the technique, I have re-implemented the code from the `IncDemo` in new program, `IncDecComm`. All background tasks in that program are started in the same way. A click on a button calls the `RunInParallel` method and passes, as parameters, names of two methods, one to increment and one to decrement the initial value.

`RunInParallel` creates a new background task for each worker method and passes to it the initial value, 0. In this program, passing the same value to both worker methods represents the most basic implementation of *data copying*:

```
procedure TfrmIncDecComm.RunInParallel(task1, task2: TProc<integer>);
begin
  FNumDone := 0;
  FTasks[0] := TTask.Run(procedure begin task1(0); end);
  FTasks[1] := TTask.Run(procedure begin task2(0); end);
end;
```

Result *aggregation* depends on the communication method and will be evaluated separately for each approach.

# Windows messages

The first method works by sending Windows messages to the main thread. As the name suggests, it is limited to the Windows operating system. I'll show two ways to achieve the same result. The first works only in VCL applications, while the second also works with FireMonkey.

Before the tasks are started, the code initializes the result `FValue` to zero so that partial results can be aggregated correctly. It also sets the variable `FNumDone` to zero. This variable counts the tasks that have completed their work:

```
procedure TfrmIncDecComm.btnMessageClick(Sender: TObject);
begin
  FValue := 0;
  FNumDone := 0;
  RunInParallel(IncMessage, DecMessage);
end;
```

Both tasks are implemented in the same way, so I'll only show one method here. `IncMessage` increments the starting value `CNumRepeat` times. At the end, it posts a `MSG_TASK_DONE` message back to the main form and passes the resulting `value` as a parameter. `DecMessage` looks the same except that the value is decremented inside the `for` loop:

```
procedure TfrmIncDecComm.IncMessage(startValue: integer);
var
  i: integer;
  value: integer;
begin
  value := startValue;
  for i := 1 to CNumRepeat do
    value := value + 1;
  PostMessage(Handle, MSG_TASK_DONE, value, 0);
end;
```

 Message parameters wParam and lParam can be used to pass data alongside the message. They have the same size as a pointer, which allows us to use an object or an interface as data storage. I'll show an example of such code near the end of this section.

To process this message in the main form, we have to declare the MSG_TASK_DONE variable (WM_USER indicates the start of the message range reserved for custom use) and add a message-handling method MsgTaskDone to the form:

```
const
  MSG_TASK_DONE = WM_USER;

procedure MsgTaskDone(var msg: TMessage); message MSG_TASK_DONE;
```

This method is called every time the main form receives the message, MSG_TASK_DONE. Inside, we firstly increment the FValue value by the partial result, passed in the msg.WParam field (*aggregation* step). After that, we increment the FNumDone counter. We know that we will receive exactly two messages, so we can call the cleanup method, Done, when FNumDone is equal to 2:

```
procedure TfrmIncDecComm.MsgTaskDone(var msg: TMessage);
begin
  Inc(FValue, msg.WParam);
  Inc(FNumDone);
  if FNumDone = 2 then
    Done('Windows message');
end;
```

In the Done method, we only have to clean the worker task interfaces:

```
procedure TfrmIncDecComm.Done(const name: string);
begin
  FTasks[0] := nil;
  FTasks[1] := nil;
end;
```

This seems like a lot of work, but it is worth it. I'll show the actual results after I finish discussing all four methods, but I can already tell you that this approach is finally faster than the single-threaded code.

This method of declaring a message handler is specific to VCL. On FireMonkey, you have to invest a bit more work and create a hidden window which will receive and process messages.

When you click on a **Message** + **AllocateHwnd** button, the following code executes. It initializes `FValue` and `FNumDone`, as in the previous example, and then creates a hidden window by calling `AllocateHwnd`:

```
procedure TfrmIncDecComm.btnAllocateHwndClick(Sender: TObject);
begin
  FValue := 0;
  FNumDone := 0;
  FMsgWnd := AllocateHwnd(MsgWndProc);
  Assert(FMsgWnd <> 0);
  RunInParallel(IncMsgHwnd, DecMsgHwnd);
end;
```

The task method, `IncMsgHwnd`, looks the same as `IncMethod`, except the last line which must now post the message to the handle `FMsgWnd`:

```
PostMessage(FMsgWnd, MSG_TASK_DONE, value, 0);
```

The `MsgWndProc` method processes all messages sent to this hidden window. We are only interested in `MSG_TASK_DONE`. Any other messages are passed to the Windows function, `DefWindowProc`. The code that handles `MSG_TASK_DONE` is identical to code in the `MsgTaskDone` method:

```
procedure TfrmIncDecComm.MsgWndProc(var msg: TMessage);
begin
  if Msg.Msg = MSG_TASK_DONE then
  begin
    Inc(FValue, msg.WParam);
    Inc(FNumDone);
    if FNumDone = 2 then
      Done('Windows message');
  end
  else
    DefWindowProc(FMsgWnd, msg.Msg, msg.wParam, msg.lParam);
end;
```

To clean up this hidden window, we have to call the `DeallocateHwnd` method:

```
if FMsgWnd <> 0 then
begin
  DeallocateHwnd(FMsgWnd);
  FMsgWnd := 0;
end;
```

I promised before to show how you can send an object or an interface as message parameters, so here's a short example. To send an object, we simply have to cast it to the appropriate type. In Delphi 10.2 Tokyo that is `NativeUInt` for `wParam` and `NativeInt` for `lParam`.

If we did the same with an interface, it would be destroyed on exit from `btnObjIntClick`. To prevent that, we have to increase its reference count by calling `_AddRef`:

```
procedure TfrmIncDecComm.btnObjIntClick(Sender: TObject);
var
  tobj: TObject;
  iint: IInterface;
begin
  tobj := TObject.Create;
  iint := TInterfacedObject.Create;
  iint._AddRef;
  PostMessage(Handle, MSG_OBJ_INT, NativeUInt(tobj), NativeInt(iint));
end;
```

On the receiving side, we can simply cast the object back to the appropriate object type (`TObject` in this example). We also have to remember to destroy it when we're done with it.

An interface can also be cast to the appropriate interface type (`IInterface` in this example) but then we also have to remove the reference added in `btnObjIntClick` by calling `_Release`. We can then use this interface as we need, and it will be destroyed once it is no longer in use and its reference count drops to zero. The following code demonstrates this:

```
procedure TfrmIncDecComm.MsgObjInt(var msg: TMessage);
var
  tobj: TObject;
  iint: IInterface;
begin
  tobj := TObject(msg.WParam);
  tobj.Free;
  iint := IInterface(msg.LParam);
  iint._Release;
end;
```

# Synchronize and Queue

The second and third approaches are so similar that I've condensed them into one section.

The setup for this approach is the same as with the first shown in the Windows message method—we only have to initialize FValue and FNumTasks. The code in increment and decrement tasks also starts the same, with a for loop that increments or decrements the value but then uses a different approach to pass the value back to the main thread.

The following code uses TThread.Synchronize to execute an anonymous method in the target thread. Synchronize accepts a TThread object as a first parameter and an anonymous method in the second. It will execute the second parameter in the main thread. In the first parameter, we can pass either the current TThread object or, as the following code does, a nil value. In the next chapter, I will discuss this parameter in more detail.

```
procedure TfrmIncDecComm.IncSynchronize(startValue: integer);
var
  i: integer;
  value: integer;
begin
  value := startValue;
  for i := 1 to CNumRepeat do
    value := value + 1;

  TThread.Synchronize(nil,
    procedure
    begin
      PartialResult(value);
    end);
end;
```

Synchronize **pauses** the execution in the worker thread, then somehow (the implementation depends on the graphical library in use) passes the second parameter to the main thread, waits for the main thread to execute that code, and only then resumes the worker thread. Let me explain this again as it is important. While the TThread.Synchronize call executes in the **worker** thread, the anonymous method passed as the second parameter—and by extension the PartialResult method—executes in the **main** thread.

The fast that Synchronize pauses the execution of a worker thread is not important in our case, as the worker had already finished the job. However, sometimes this slows down the background task. A typical example would be sending notifications about the progress to the main thread. Each time Synchronize is called, the worker thread pauses for some time, which makes the CPUs underutilized.

In such cases, it is better to use `TThread.Queue` instead of `Synchronize`. This method accepts the same parameters as `Synchronize` and works almost completely the same, with one exception. It does not wait for the main thread to execute the anonymous method. Instead of that, it returns immediately, which allows the background task to continue processing data.

Result processing in the `PartialResult` method is completely the same as in `MsgTaskDone`. I'm just using different methods in different approaches so that each implementation is separated from the others. It also allows me to log appropriate method names in the log:

```
procedure TfrmIncDecComm.PartialResult(value: integer);
begin
  Inc(FValue, value);
  Inc(FNumDone);
  if FNumDone = 2 then
    Done('Synchronize');
end;
```

# Polling

Instead of reacting to notifications from the thread, we can also periodically check the status of background calculation from the main thread. In other words, we *poll* their status.

If we want to send some data from a background worker, we can simply insert it into a `TLockedList<T>` or, for a faster operation, into `TThreadedQueue<T>`. In the main thread, we must then periodically check if something has appeared in this queue and process the data.

As the `TThreadedQueue<T>` has quite an unwieldy user interface which doesn't allow us to check whether the queue is empty, we have to take care while creating it. The following code initializes the queue with two parameters (queue size—we know that we'll only put two values in the queue), *0* (push timeout), and *0* (pop timeout). The last parameter is the most important because it allows our polling code to work correctly. I'll return to that shortly.

The polling is done from a `TimerCheckQueue` timer, which is set to trigger every *10* milliseconds but is disabled when the program starts. The following code also starts this timer:

```
procedure TfrmIncDecComm.btnThQueueAndTImerClick(Sender: TObject);
begin
  FValue := 0;
  FNumDone := 0;
  FResultQueue := TThreadedQueue<integer>.Create(2, 0, 0);
  RunInParallel(IncThQueue, DecThQueue);
  TimerCheckQueue.Enabled := true;
end;
```

The worker task starts with a now standard `for` loop. After that, it stores the partial result in the queue by calling `PushItem`:

```
procedure TfrmIncDecComm.IncThQueue(startValue: integer);
var
  i: integer;
  value: integer;
begin
  value := startValue;
  for i := 1 to CNumRepeat do
    value := value + 1;
  Assert(FResultQueue.PushItem(value) = wrSignaled);
end;
```

If the queue is full, `PushItem` waits for some user-configurable timeout before it returns. If a free space appears in the queue in that time, the item is pushed to the queue and the call returns `wrSignaled`. If, after the timeout, the queue is still full, the call returns `wrTimeout`. It would be great if we could specify the timeout as a parameter to `PushItem` but, sadly, this is not implemented. We have to pass it to the constructor and it defaults to infinite waiting (constant `INFINITE`).

The timer method triggers every *10* milliseconds and tries to fetch a value from the queue. If the queue is empty, `PopItem` waits up to a configurable timeout before it returns `wrTimeout`. If there's data in the queue, the method returns `wrSignaled`. As with the `PushItem`, we can only configure the timeout in the constructor. The default value for timeout is again `INFINITE`.

When the timer manages to retrieve partial data from the queue, it aggregates it to the result, increments the number of tasks, and terminates the operation when both tasks are completed. After that it breaks out of the `while` loop because the `Done` method destroys the queue, so we can't read from it anymore:

```
procedure TfrmIncDecComm.TimerCheckQueueTimer(Sender: TObject);
var
  qsize: integer;
  value: integer;
begin
  while FResultQueue.PopItem(qsize, value) = wrSignaled do begin
    FValue := FValue + value;
    Inc(FNumDone);
    if FNumDone = 2 then begin
      Done('TThreadedQueue + TTimer');
      break; //while
    end;
  end;
end;
```

In the `Done` method, we have to stop the timer and destroy the thread in addition to stopping the worker tasks:

```
TimerCheckQueue.Enabled := false;
FreeAndNil(FResultQueue);
```

The `TThreadedQueue<T>` is also useful in combination with the *push* notifications. We can, for example, store some complex data type in a queue and then send a simple Windows message to notify the main thread that it should read from the queue.

# Performance

Let's complete this section by examining the execution times of different communication approaches. Even more importantly, let's compare them with the original single-threaded implementation and with locking methods.

The original single-threaded code needed *75* ms to increment and decrement values. Critical section based synchronization needed *1017* ms, `TMonitor` implementation took *700* ms, spinlock needed *493* ms, and the fastest parallel implementation so far, `TInterlocked`, used *407* ms.

In comparison, communication-based approaches are blindingly fast. Both message-based mechanisms needed only *23-24* milliseconds, Synchronize and Queue are even faster with *17* milliseconds, and even the slowest timer- based code needed *36* milliseconds at worst:

It is obvious why the timer-based code is the slowest in the pack. After the last value is calculated, we may have to wait up to *10* ms for the timer to trigger.

What is interesting is that other approaches are more than twice as fast as the single-threaded code. The main reason for that is the incrementation and decrementation of a value, which is in the new code done in one line (value := value + 1), while in the old code it needed two assignments:

```
value := FValue;
  FValue := value + 1;
```

If we correct the original code, then it needs around *34* ms to do the job. In other words, the Synchronize and Queue-based approaches are exactly twice as fast as the original code, which is the best possible result we can get from running parallel code on two cores.

# Third-party libraries

While this book focuses almost exclusively on the out-of-the-box Delphi experience, sometimes I do point to external libraries that can simplify your programming experience. In the context of this chapter, such libraries are Spring4D (www.spring4d.org) and OmniThreadLibrary (www.omnithreadlibrary.com).

**Spring4D** is a multipurpose library with very limited support for parallel programming. It is, however, widely used in the Delphi community. If you are already using it, you may find the following notes helpful.

I've said before that creating and destroying TCriticalSection objects is a pain. To fix that, Spring4D introduces a Lock record which doesn't require initialization. You just declare a variable of that type and then use its Enter and Leave methods.

Another useful Spring4D addition is the optimistic initializer, TLazyInitializer. In the section *Object life cycle*, I've shown how to safely initialize the FSharedObject: TSharedObject variable and it was not very simple. With TLazyInitializer we can do it in one line:

```
TLazyInitializer.EnsureInitialized<TSharedObject>(FSharedObject);
```

As opposed to Spring4D, **OmniThreadLibrary** has everything to do with parallel programming. Similar to Spring4D, it contains an easy-to-use critical section, TOmniCS, with the Acquire and Release methods. It also implements an optimistic initializer, Atomic<T>, which can be used as in the next example:

```
Atomic<TSharedObject>.Initialize(FSharedObject);
```

OmniThreadLibrary also implements very fast multiple readers, and an exclusive writer synchronization mechanism called TOmniMREW. It should only be used to lock very short parts of code because access methods never sleep when access is locked. They always use the spinning mechanism, which can use lots of CPU time when waiting for a longer time. This mechanism is also not re-entrant and should be used with care.

At the end, I would like to mention OmniThreadLibrary lock-free data structures. There's a fixed-size stack, TOmniBoundedStack, fixed-size queue, TOmniBoundedQueue, and a very fast dynamically-allocated queue, TOmniBaseQueue. All of them can easily be used with standard Delphi multithreading code.

# Summary

In this chapter, we finally started learning to write parallel code. I started with a short introduction about processes and threads, single and multithreading, single-tasking, and multitasking. I also explained the most important differences between processes and threads.

After that, we started learning what **not** to do when writing multithreaded code. Firstly, I brought up the most important dogma—"Never access the user interface from a background thread". Such strong words deserve proof and I gave you one.

In the next, largest part of the chapter, I slowly explained why you should be extremely careful if you want to access shared data from multiple threads. While simultaneous reading is OK, you should always use protection when reading and writing at the same time.

In the context of parallel programming and data sharing, this protection is implemented by the introduction of one of the synchronization mechanisms. I spent quite some time introducing critical sections, mutexes, semaphors, TMonitor, spinlocks, and the terribly named TMultiReadExclusiveWriteSynchronizer. Using synchronization inevitably brings in new problems, and so I also spent some time discussing deadlocks. I also mentioned three data structures that implement locking internally—TThreadList, TThreadList<T>, and TThreadedQueue<T>.

After that I introduced a less powerful but faster way of locking—interlocked operations. We examined the TInterlocked class and all the interlocked operations it implements. As interlocked operations are frequently used in optimistic initialization, we also dealt with the object life cycle in the parallel world.

Towards the end, I introduced a much faster replacement for synchronization—communication. We saw how a parallel program can use data duplication and aggregation to achieve the highest possible speed. I went over four communication techniques, namely Windows messages, Synchronize, Queue, and polling. We also saw how TThreadedQueue<T> can be used in practice.

To wrap things up, I introduced two libraries that contain helpful parallel programming helpers—Spring4D and OmniThreadLibrary.

In the next chapter, we'll finally start writing parallel code. I'll talk about threads, tasks, and writing parallel code with TThread and with the Parallel Programming Library, which has been part of Delphi since release XE7.

---

# 6
# Working with Parallel Tools

After using one whole chapter to warn you about the traps of parallel programming, it is now finally time to write some code! Although I always prefer using modern multithreading approaches—and we'll spend all of the next chapter learning them—it is also good to know the basics. Because of that, I have dedicated this chapter to the good old `TThread` class.

In this chapter, we will cover the following topics:

- How can you use `TThread` to write multithreading code?
- What different approaches to thread management does `TThread` support?
- How can exceptions in threads be handled?
- Which additional functions does `TThread` implement?
- How can we implement a communication channel sending messages to a thread?
- How can we centralize thread-message handling in the owner form?
- How can we simplify thread writing to the max by implementing a specific framework for one usage pattern?

## TThread

Multithreading support has been built into Delphi since its inception.

The very first 32-bit version, Delphi 2, introduced a `TThread` class. At that time, `TThread` was a very simple wrapper around the Windows `CreateThread` function. In later Delphi releases, `TThread` was extended with multiple functions and with support for other operating systems, but it still remained a pretty basic tool.

The biggest problem with TThread is that it doesn't enforce the use of any programming patterns. Because of that, you can use it to create parallel programs that are hard to understand, hard to debug, and which work purely by luck. I should know—I shudder every time I have to maintain my old TThread-based code.

Still, the TThread approach can be very effective and completely readable, provided that you use it correctly. On the next pages, I'll firstly show the basic TThread usage patterns and then improve the basic approach by introducing the *communication* techniques into the old framework.

A TThread class is declared in the System.Classes unit. You cannot use it directly, as it contains an abstract method, Execute, which you have to override in a derived class:

```
TMyThread = class(TThread)
protected
  procedure Execute; override;
end;
```

When you create an instance of this class, Delphi uses operating system functions to create a new thread and then runs the Execute method in that thread. When that method exits, the thread is terminated.

The **TThread** and **Stop** button in the Threads demo one way of using TThread to create a thread. The former creates the thread descendant and starts the thread. It also sets up an event handler, which gets triggered when the thread is terminated:

```
procedure TfrmThreads.btnThreadClick(Sender: TObject);
begin
  FThread := TMyThread.Create;
  FThread.OnTerminate := ReportThreadTerminated;
end;
```

By default, TThread.Create creates and **starts** the thread. It is also possible to create a thread in a **suspended** (paused) state by providing True as an argument to the constructor. In that case, you have to call TThread.Start at some time, to actually start the thread.

The following code fragment is functionally equivalent to the previous code, except that it initially creates a thread in a suspended state. This approach is safer if we are doing additional initialization on the thread object, (FThread), as it makes sure that the thread did not start up before it was fully initialized:

```
procedure TfrmThreads.btnThreadClick(Sender: TObject);
begin
  FThread := TMyThread.Create(True);
```

```
    FThread.OnTerminate := ReportThreadTerminated;
    FThread.Start;
  end;
```

In our case, the thread will only stop when we tell it to. It is therefore safe to assign the `OnTerminate` handler to a running (not suspended) thread, as we did in the initial version.

 Although the `TThread` object implements the methods `Suspend` and `Resume`, which pause and start the thread, you should never use them in your code! Unless they are used with great care, you cannot know exactly in what state the thread is when you suspend it. Using these two functions will only bring you great pain and weird, hard-to-repeat problems.

The traditional way to stop a thread is to firstly call a `Terminate` method, which sets a `Terminated` flag. The `Execute` method should check this flag periodically and exit when it is set. (I'll show you an example of that in a moment). Next, we should call the `WaitFor` method, which waits on a thread to finish execution. After that, we can destroy the thread object. The following code is executed when you click the **Stop** button:

```
procedure TfrmThreads.btnStopThreadClick(Sender: TObject);
begin
  FThread.Terminate;
  FThread.WaitFor;
  FreeAndNil(FThread);
end;
```

A simpler way is to just destroy the thread object, as it will internally call `Terminate` and `WaitFor` itself. Sometimes, though, it is good to know that we can do this in three separate steps:

```
procedure TfrmThreads.btnStopThreadClick(Sender: TObject);
begin
  FreeAndNil(FThread);
end;
```

Let's now move away from the thread management to actual code running in the thread. It is implemented in the `TMyThread.Execute` method. In the `Threads` demo, this code just checks the `Terminated` flag to see whether it should terminate, posts a message to the main window, and sleeps for a second. As we learned in the previous chapter, we could also use the `Synchronize` or `Queue` methods to do the same:

```
procedure TMyThread.Execute;
begin
  while not Terminated do
```

```
  begin
    PostMessage(frmThreads.Handle, WM_PING, ThreadID, 0);
    Sleep(1000);
  end;
end;
```

 Every thread in a system has a unique integer ID, which we can access through the `ThreadID` property.

Terminating a thread is always a cooperative process. The main program sets a flag that tells the thread to terminate, and the thread must cooperate by checking this flag as frequently as possible. Later in this chapter, we'll also see how to do thread termination without constant checking (without *polling*).

The form implements a simple `MsgPing` method, which handles the `WM_PING` message handler. Inside the method, the code logs the thread ID passed in the `wParam` message parameter:

```
procedure TfrmThreads.MsgPing(var msg: TMessage);
begin
  ListBox1.Items.Add('Ping from thread ' + msg.WParam.ToString);
end;
```

When we terminate the thread, the `OnTerminated` event handler is called. The thread object being destroyed is passed in the `Sender` parameter. The code just logs the thread ID of the thread being destroyed:

```
procedure TfrmThreads.ReportThreadTerminated(Sender: TObject);
begin
  Assert(Sender is TThread);
  ListBox1.Items.Add('Terminating thread ' +
    TThread(Sender).ThreadID.ToString);
end;
```

This concludes the first example. As you can see, managing a thread is not that hard. The problems appear when we want to do some useful work in the `Execute` method and especially when we want to communicate with the thread. Before I deal with that, however, I'd like to show you some simplifications that `TThread` supports.

The thread management that I've shown is most appropriate when we have a long-running thread providing some service. The main program starts the thread when it needs that service and stops it when the service is no longer needed. Lots of times, though, the background thread runs some operations and then stops. At times, it is simpler to allow the thread to terminate itself.

We can do that by making one simple change—by setting the `FreeOnTerminate` property to `True`. The demo program does that when you click on the **Free on terminate** button. Although not strictly required in this case, the code creates the thread in a suspended state so it can be safely initialized:

```
procedure TfrmThreads.btnFreeOnTermClick(Sender: TObject);
begin
  FThreadFoT := TFreeThread.Create(True);
  FThreadFoT.FreeOnTerminate := true;
  FThreadFoT.OnTerminate := ReportThreadTerminated;
  FThreadFoT.Start;
end;
```

The `TFreeThread` class—just as the `TMyThread`—overrides only the `Execute` method:

```
procedure TFreeThread.Execute;
var
  i: Integer;
begin
  for i := 1 to 5 do
  begin
    PostMessage(frmThreads.Handle, WM_PING, GetCurrentThreadID, 0);
    Sleep(1000);
    if Terminated then
      Exit;
  end;
end;
```

There's no need to destroy the `FThreadFoT` object, as Delphi will do that for us. We should, however, still clear the field when the thread is destroyed so that we don't keep a reference to the destroyed object in the code. The simplest way to do that is with the `OnTerminated` event handler:

```
procedure TfrmThreads.ReportThreadTerminated(Sender: TObject);
begin
  Assert(Sender is TThread);
  ListBox1.Items.Add('Terminating thread ' +
    TThread(Sender).ThreadID.ToString);
  FThreadFoT := nil;
end;
```

If you need to run a shorter operation, but you still want to be able to abort it, both approaches can be combined. The thread can check the `Terminated` flag even when it is run in `FreeOnTerminate` mode. The main program can then just call `Terminate` to terminate the thread, and the thread will terminate itself.

The demo program uses this approach to destroy both threads when the form is closed:

```
procedure TfrmThreads.FormDestroy(Sender: TObject);
begin
  FreeAndNil(FThread);
  if assigned(FThreadFoT) then
    FThreadFoT.Terminate;
end;
```

Sometimes, we don't care much about thread management because we know that the thread will only run for a short time. In such a cases, we can forego the creation of a derived class and simply call the `CreateAnonymousThread` method, which creates a slightly misnamed *anonymous thread*.

This method takes an anonymous method (`TProc`) as a parameter. Internally, it creates an instance of a `TAnonymousThread` class (found in `System.Classes`) and returns it as a function result. When the `Execute` method of that class runs, it executes your anonymous method.

An anonymous thread is always created in the suspended state and has the `FreeOnTerminate` flag set. In the simplest form, you can create and start such a thread and ignore any returned value:

```
TThread.CreateAnonymousThread(PingMe).Start;
```

The code in the demo assigns the result to a temporary `thread` variable, so that it can set the termination handler:

```
procedure TfrmThreads.btnAnonymousClick(Sender: TObject);
var
  thread: TThread;
begin
  thread := TThread.CreateAnonymousThread(PingMe);
  thread.OnTerminate := ReportThreadTerminated;
  thread.Start;
end;
```

The background code is now implemented as a normal method of the `TfrmThreads` form object. This makes such an approach inherently dangerous, as it blurs the boundaries between the user interface (accessible through the form methods) and the background thread, which has full access to the form object. When you work with anonymous threads, you should always be careful and respect the separation between objects used in the main and background threads. (And never, *never!* access user interface from the background thread!)

As the `PingMe` method isn't implemented in a class derived from `TThread`, it cannot access the `ThreadID` property directly. It can, however, access the `TThread.Current` property, which returns the `TThread` instance of the current thread:

```
procedure TfrmThreads.PingMe;
var
  i: Integer;
begin
  for i := 1 to 5 do
  begin
    PostMessage(Handle, WM_PING, TThread.Current.ThreadID, 0);
    Sleep(1000);
  end;
end;
```

# Advanced TThread

The `TThread` class offers the programmer a collection of various properties and methods. In this section, I'll take you through the most useful ones.

The `FatalException` property deals with exceptions. If an exception arises inside your `Execute` method and is not caught, it will be handled inside the system code:

```
if not Thread.Terminated then
try
  Thread.Execute;
except
  Thread.FFatalException := AcquireExceptionObject;
end;
```

The best place to check whether this property is assigned is the `OnTerminate` handler. If the `FatalException` is not `nil`, we can log the exception and call `ReleaseExceptionObject` to destroy the exception object or we can reraise the exception. The following code from the `Threads` demo shows how to implement such logging:

```
procedure TfrmThreads.ReportThreadTerminated(Sender: TObject);
var
  thread: TThread;
begin
  thread := Sender as TThread;
  if assigned(thread.FatalException) then
  begin
    ListBox1.Items.Add(Format('Thread raised exception: [%s] %s',
      [thread.FatalException.ClassName,
        Exception(thread.FatalException).Message]));
    ReleaseExceptionObject;
  end;
end;
```

The demo contains a `TExceptThread` class, which just raises an exception so we can test the exception-handling mechanism. To run a thread of this class, click on the **Exception in a thread** button:

```
procedure TExceptThread.Execute;
begin
  Sleep(1000);
  raise Exception.Create('Thread exception');
end;
```

A thread can return an integer value by setting its `ReturnValue` property. This property is, however, protected and hard to access from the main thread. Delphi offers better implementation of such functionality with a `Future<T>` pattern, which we'll explore in the next chapter.

Next come the communication methods `Synchronize`, `Queue` and `ForceQueue`. The first two I've mentioned already in the previous chapter, while the `ForceQueue` is a special version of `Queue`. If you call `Queue` from the main thread, the code detects that and executes your anonymous method immediately (without queuing). In contrast to that, `ForceQueue` always queues the anonymous method, even when called from the main thread.

All communication methods accept a TThread parameter, which in all the previous examples we passed simply as nil. This parameter, when set, connects the anonymous method with a thread. We can use that to remove all queued but unhandled events by calling the TThread.RemoveQueueEvents function. For example, we can call this method from a thread's OnTerminate handler to prevent any queued events for that thread from being executed, after the thread was destroyed.

At the end, I'd like to mention methods that are useful when you are tuning the multithreading performance. A class property, the ProcessorCount, will give you the total number of processing cores in the system. This includes all hyper-threading cores, so in a system with 4 cores where each of them is hyper-threaded, the ProcessorCount would be *8*.

 Running a system with multiple processing cores doesn't necessarily mean that all of them are available for your program. In Windows, it is possible to limit the number of cores that a program can see. To get a real number of available cores on Windows, call the GetProcessAffinityMask function declared in the Winapi.Windows unit.

The property, Priority can be used to read and set the thread's *priority*. A priority represents how important that thread is in the system. In Windows, this property can have the following values:

```
TThreadPriority = (tpIdle, tpLowest, tpLower, tpNormal, tpHigher,
tpHighest, tpTimeCritical);
```

tpIdle represents a very low-priority thread, which only runs when the system is idle. tpTimeCritical, on the other hand, represents a thread which must always be running, if at all possible. In reality, a high-priority thread cannot completely stop a low-priority thread from running, as Windows dynamically adjusts the thread priorities to allow all of them at least a small chance of executing.

I would strongly recommend that you never set the priority to tpTimeCritical. If you run multiple CPU intensive threads with this priority, this can really cripple your system.

Thread priority should always be left at the default value of tpNormal. Windows is extremely good at scheduling threads and tuning thread priorities. Only in very special situations should it be necessary to raise or lower a thread priority, but even then you should not go above tpHighest.

On non-Windows systems the `Priority` property has the type `integer`. A range of allowed values may differ from platform to platform but at least on POSIX compliant systems (OS X, Linux) you can assume that the allowed range is from *0* to *31* with *0* representing the lowest priority.

A thread that is running in a loop may want to give some slice of its CPU time to other threads, from time to time. One way to do it is to call `Sleep(0)`, which signals to the operating system that a thread has finished its job at the moment but that it would like to continue executing soon, please. The code can also call `TThread.Yield`, instead. This also pauses the thread and allows the execution of another thread that is ready to run on the *current processor*. Calling `Yield` instead of `Sleep` generally means that your thread will be woken again a bit sooner.

# Setting up a communication channel

The biggest problem of `TThread` is that it only allows communication to flow from the background thread to the owner. As you've seen in the previous chapter, we can use different mechanisms for that—Windows messages, `Synchronize`, `Queue`, and polling. There is, however, no built-in way to send messages in a different direction, so you have to build such a mechanism yourself. This is not entirely trivial.

Another problem with built-in mechanisms is that they make for unreadable code. `Synchronize` and `Queue` are both inherently messy because they wrap a code that executes in one thread inside a code executing in a different thread. Messages and polling have a different problem. They decouple code through many different methods, which sometimes makes it hard to understand the system.

To fix all these problems (and undoubtedly introduce some new ones as, sadly, no code is perfect), I have built a better base class `TCommThread`. You can find it in unit `DHPThreads`, which is part of this book's code archive. The demonstration program for the new class is called `ThreadsComm`. You can use this unit without any limitations in your projects.

This thread contains two parts. Firstly, there is communication channel running from the owner to the thread. Secondly, there's a channel running in a different direction, from the thread to the owner. I'll explain them one by one.

The code needs some container mechanism that will store messages sent from the owner, but not yet processed by the thread. Although it is hard to use, I've decided to go with the TThreadedQueue, which doesn't need a separate synchronization mechanism. As I have no idea what kind of data you'll be storing in the queue, I've implemented the queue as TThreadedQueue<T>. This type from the System.Rtti unit can store any Delphi data structure inside, so it's very appropriate for such task.

It is true that the flexibility of TValue means that it is a bit slower then using a specific data type directly. On the other hand—as I always say—if your code depends on millions of messages to be processed each second, then the problem lies not in the implementation but in your architecture. For all normal usage patterns, TValue is more than fast enough.

The code also needs a way to tell the thread that something has happened when a message is sent. I've chosen to use a TEvent, as it allows the thread to completely sleep while nothing is going on. This removes the need for constant *polling*, which would use a bit of CPU time.

The following code fragment shows how the two are declared in the TCommThread object. The Event field is declared protected, as it was designed to be used directly from the derived class:

```
strict private
  FQueueToThread : TThreadedQueue<TValue>;
protected
  Event: TEvent;
```

Both fields are initialized in the constructor, which, in addition to the standard CreateSuspended parameter, accepts a queue size. It is set to 1,024 elements by default, but you can make this value larger or smaller, if that's required. In the actual unit the constructor is a bit more complicated, as it also initializes the second communication channel. I've removed that part in the code shown here, to make it clearer:

```
constructor TCommThread.Create(CreateSuspended: boolean = False;
  ToThreadQueueSize: integer = 1024);
begin
  inherited Create(CreateSuspended);
  FQueueToThread := TThreadedQueue<TValue>.Create(ToThreadQueueSize, 0, 0);
  Event := TEvent.Create;
end;
```

The constructor creates both fields *after* the inherited constructor was called, even when CreateSuspended is False. This doesn't cause problems because the thread is actually not started in the TThread constructor. It is only started in the TThread.AfterConstruction method, which is executed *after* TCommThread.Create finishes its job.

To send a message to the thread, the code has to call the SendToThread public function. This very simple method pushes an item into the queue and sets the event, if the push was successful. If the queue is full, the function returns False:

```
function TCommThread.SendToThread(const value: TValue): boolean;
begin
  Result := (FQueueToThread.PushItem(value) = wrSignaled);
  if Result then
    Event.SetEvent;
end;
```

To process these messages, the code in the Execute method must be written in a specific manner. It must periodically check the Event, or it can even spend all of the time waiting on the Event to get set. The TMyThread from the ThreadCommMain unit of the example program can serve as a good starting point for your code.

This method calls Event.WaitFor(5000) to wait for a new message. WaitFor will either return wrSignaled, if a message has been received; wrTimeout, if nothing happened in five seconds; and something else, if something unexpected happened. In the latter case, the code exits the thread, as there's nothing better that can be done at the moment.

If wrSignaled or wrTimeout is received, the code enters the loop. Firstly, it resets the event by calling Event.ResetEvent. This is mandatory and allows for proper functioning of the code. Without that call, the event would stay *signalled* (set), and the next time around, WaitFor would immediately return wrSignaled, even though no new messages would be received.

After that, the code calls GetMessage to fetch messages from the queue. You should always empty the entire queue, otherwise there's a possibility that messages could get stuck inside for an unknown time (until next message is sent). The code also exits when the Terminated flag is set.

At the end, the code sends a message back to the owner. This part is omitted in the code shown here, as I haven't discussed that part of the mechanism yet:

```
procedure TMyThread.Execute;
var
  pingMsg: integer;
  value: TValue;
begin
  while Event.WaitFor(5000) in [wrSignaled, wrTimeout] do
  begin
    Event.ResetEvent;
    // message processing
    while (not Terminated) and GetMessage(value) do
      pingMsg := value.AsInteger;
    // termination
    if Terminated then
      break;
    // send message to the owner ...
  end;
end;
```

A careful reader may have started thinking about the thread termination now. Doesn't this implementation mean that when we request the thread to terminate, we will have to wait for up to five seconds for the thread to do so? After all, `WaitFor` may just have been called, and we have to wait until it reports a timeout. Even worse—what if the thread is completely message-driven and does no other processing? In that case, we can wait with `Event.WaitFor(INFINITE)`, but wouldn't that prevent the thread from exiting?

Indeed, careful reader, these are all valid worries. Do not fear, though, as there's a simple solution already built into the `TCommThread`! Besides the message-handling code, it also overrides the `TerminatedSet` virtual method, which `TThread` calls when the `Terminated` flag is set. Inside this overridden method, the code signals the `Event` event, and this causes the `WaitFor` to immediately exit:

```
procedure TCommThread.TerminatedSet;
  begin
  Event.SetEvent;
  inherited;
  end;
```

The only missing part of this half of the puzzle is the `GetMessage` method. That one is again trivial and just reads from the queue:

```
function TCommThread.GetMessage(var value: TValue): boolean;
begin
  Result := (FQueueToThread.PopItem(value) = wrSignaled);
end;
```

# Sending messages from a thread

The second part of the solution deals with sending messages back to the parent. As I've mentioned before, you already have several possibilities to do the same with built-in Delphi functions. They all work well in combination with the previously described method for sending messages to a thread. This second part is therefore purely optional, but I believe it is a good solution, because it centralizes the message-handling for each thread.

Again, the code starts by creating a `TThreadedQueue<TValue>` to store sent values. We cannot use an event to signal new messages, though. Delphi forms interact with the operating system and with the user by constantly processing messages, and we cannot block this message processing by waiting on an event, or the whole user interface will freeze. Instead of that, `TCommThread` uses `Queue` to call a method of your own choosing to process messages. You pass this method to the constructor as a parameter.

The following code fragment shows relevant types and fields, together with (now complete) constructor. Besides the user-provided `MessageReceiver` method that will process messages, you can also set the queue size:

```
public type
  TMessageReceiver = TProc<TValue>;
strict private
  FQueueToMain : TThreadedQueue<TValue>;
  FMessageReceiver: TMessageReceiver;

constructor TCommThread.Create(MessageReceiver: TMessageReceiver;
  CreateSuspended: boolean = False;
  ToThreadQueueSize: integer = 1024; ToMainQueueSize: integer = 1024);
begin
  inherited Create(CreateSuspended);
  FQueueToThread := TThreadedQueue<TValue>.Create(ToThreadQueueSize, 0, 0);
  Event := TEvent.Create;
  FMessageReceiver := MessageReceiver;
  if assigned(MessageReceiver) then
    FQueueToMain := TThreadedQueue<TValue>.Create(ToMainQueueSize, 0, 0);
end;
```

The message-receiver parameter is optional. If you set it to `nil`, the channel for sending messages back to the owner won't be created, and this part of the functionality will be disabled.

The code also overrides the standard `TThread` constructor to create a `TCommThread` with only one communication channel—the one towards the thread:

```
constructor TCommThread.Create(CreateSuspended: Boolean);
begin
  Create(nil, CreateSuspended);
end;
```

The code can use the protected method, `SendToMain`, to send messages back to the owner. It checks whether the necessary queue was created, posts a message to the queue, and, if that was successful, queues a `PushMessagesToReceiver` method. If the queue is full, this method returns `False`:

```
function TCommThread.SendToMain(const value: TValue): boolean;
begin
  if not assigned(FQueueToMain) then
    raise Exception.Create('MessageReceiver method was not set in
constructor!');
  Result := (FQueueToMain.PushItem(value) = wrSignaled);
  if Result then
    TThread.Queue(nil, PushMessagesToReceiver);
end;
```

The `PushMessagesToReceiver` method is implemented in the `TCommThread` object. It reads messages from the queue, and, for each message, calls the user-provided `FMessageReceiver` method:

```
procedure TCommThread.PushMessagesToReceiver;
var
  value: TValue;
begin
  // This method executes from the main thread!
  while FQueueToMain.PopItem(value) = wrSignaled do
    FMessageReceiver(value);
end;
```

The value of this approach is twofold. Firstly, all message processing for a thread is concentrated in one method. Secondly, you can pass different types of data through this channel—from basic types to objects, interfaces, and even records.

A word of caution is necessary. Never destroy the thread object from inside the message receiver. Instead, use the `ForceQueue` method to queue a code to destroy the thread object. That will cause that code to execute *after* the message receiver does its job.

In the `ThreadCommMain` unit, all this comes together. The **Start thread** button creates a new thread and immediately sends a number 42 to it. It only sets the message receiver method (`ProcessThreadMessages`) and leaves other parameters at default:

```
procedure TfrmThreadComm.btnStartClick(Sender: TObject);
begin
  FThread := TMyThread.Create(ProcessThreadMessages);
  FThread.SendToThread(42);
end;
```

The **Change** button sends the current value of a spin edit to the thread via the communication mechanism:

```
procedure TfrmThreadComm.btnChangePingClick(Sender: TObject);
begin
  FThread.SendToThread(inpPing.Value);
end;
```

The **Stop thread** button just destroys the thread object:

```
procedure TfrmThreadComm.btnStopClick(Sender: TObject);
begin
  FreeAndNil(FThread);
end;
```

The `TMyThread` object overrides the `Execute` method. We've seen a part of that method before. The full implementation is shown here.

The code immediately sends a message of a `TPingMsg` type back to the owner. This message carries the current value of the local variable, `pingMsg`, and the current thread ID. The message is sent over the built-in communication mechanism.

Next, the code starts the `while` loop, which I have already described. The only new part here appears under the `// workload` comment, when the code again sends the current `pingMsg` and thread ID to the owner:

```
type
  TPingMsg = TPair<integer, cardinal>;

procedure TMyThread.Execute;
var
```

```
    pingMsg: integer;
    value: TValue;
  begin
    pingMsg := 0;
    if not SendToMain(TValue.From<TPingMsg>(
            TPingMsg.Create(pingMsg, ThreadID)))
    then
      raise Exception.Create('Queue full!');
    while Event.WaitFor(5000) in [wrSignaled, wrTimeout] do
    begin
      Event.ResetEvent;
      // message processing
      while (not Terminated) and GetMessage(value) do
        pingMsg := value.AsInteger;
      // termination
      if Terminated then
        break;
      // workload
      if not SendToMain(TValue.From<TPingMsg>(
              TPingMsg.Create(pingMsg, ThreadID)))
      then
        raise Exception.Create('Queue full!');
    end;
  end;
```

The behavior of this method can be described in a few words. It sends pingMsg back to the owner every five seconds. When it receives a message, it assumes that it contains an integer and stores that integer in the pingMsg variable. The code terminates when the Terminated flag is set.

The only part I haven't shown yet is the ProcessThreadMessages method, which simply shows the data stored inside the TPingMsg:

```
procedure TfrmThreadComm.ProcessThreadMessages(value: TValue);
var
  pingMsg: TPingMsg;
begin
  pingMsg := value.AsType<TPingMsg>;
  ListBox1.Items.Add(Format('%s: %d from thread %d',
    [FormatDateTime('hh:nn:ss.zzz', Now), pingMsg.Key, pingMsg.Value]));
end;
```

And there you have it—a thread with two communication channels!

# Implementing a timer

If you play with the demo application, you'll soon find that it works fine, just not exactly as I described before. I stated that "(the code) sends `pingMsg` back to the owner every five seconds." As the following image shows, that isn't exactly so.

This image shows one short testing session. During the testing, I started the thread. That caused two messages to be logged. The initial value of *0* is sent from the thread immediately when the thread is started. After that, the main thread sent a new value *42* to the worker thread, and that resulted in an immediate *ping* response.

After that, I didn't click anything for 11 seconds, which generated two *ping* messages, each sent 5 seconds after the previous message. Next, I clicked **Change** twice, which resulted in two *ping* messages. After that, I changed the value to *8, 9,* and *0,* and each time a *ping* was immediately received:

A proper description of the worker thread would therefore be this: It sends a message every 5 seconds, unless a new message is received, in which case it sends it back immediately.

If that's OK with you, fine! Feel free to use this framework. But sometimes you need a better timer. I could fix that in the `TMyThread` with a better calculation of the timeout parameter passed to the `WaitFor`. I would also have to fix the code, which now works the same, regardless of the `WaitFor` result (`wrSignaled` or `wrTimeout`). I could do that, but then you would have to repeat my steps each time you needed a thread with a built-in timer. Instead of that, I did something better and implemented a generic parent for all such tasks, a `TCommTimerThread`.

This time my implementation is closer to the approach used in all modern parallel libraries. It is not a multipurpose tool, such as TThread or TCommThread, but a specific solution that satisfies one *usage pattern*. Because of that, you don't have to implement any of the nasty multithreading plumbing to use it—such as when we had to implement a very specific Execute method in the previous example. Using a TCommTimerThread is more akin to using the VCL. You just plug in a few methods, and the framework does the rest. We'll see this approach a lot in the next chapter.

This approach has numerous advantages over the classical TThread. Firstly, it is easier to write the code, as all the hard stuff has already been taken care of. Secondly, the code will have less bugs, as you don't have to write error-prone multithreading plumbing. As many people are using the same framework, any potential bugs in the framework can be found quickly.

The usage pattern my implementation covers is "a background task that can send and receive messages and process timer-based events". While this looks simple, and even primitive, it can be used to solve many different kinds of problems, especially as you can ignore the message-processing part or the timer event part, if you don't need them.

Let us look at the implementation now. TCommTimerThread is derived from the TCommThread class so that it can reuse its communication mechanism. It exposes a public property Interval, which you can use to set the timer interval, in milliseconds. Setting Interval to a value equal to or smaller than zero disables the timer. In addition to that, the code uses a FTimer: TStopwatch record to determine the time to the next timer event.

Instead of overriding the Execute function, you override four methods (or just some of them). Initialize is called immediately after the thread is created, and Cleanup is called just before it is destroyed. You can do your own initialization and cleanup inside them. ProcessTimer is called each time a timer event occurs, and ProcessMessage is called for each received message. The code fragment here shows all the important parts of the TCommTimerThread:

```
TCommTimerThread = class(TCommThread)
strict private
  FInterval: integer;
  FTimer: TStopwatch;
protected
  procedure Cleanup; virtual;
  procedure Execute; override;
  procedure Initialize; virtual;
  procedure ProcessMessage(const msg: TValue); virtual;
  procedure ProcessTimer; virtual;
```

```
public
  property Interval: integer read GetInterval write SetInterval;
end;
```

All important parts of the functionality are implemented in the overridden `Execute` method. It is very similar to `TMyThread.Execute`, except that the `WaitFor` timeout is calculated dynamically and that processing depends on the value returned from the `WaitFor`. If it returns `wrSignaled`, the code checks the `Terminated` flag and fetches waiting messages. If it returns `wrTimeout`, the timer is restarted, and the timer-handling function is called:

```
procedure TCommTimerThread.Execute;
var
  awaited: TWaitResult;
  timeout: Cardinal;
  value: TValue;
begin
  Initialize;
  try
    repeat
      awaited := Event.WaitFor(CalculateTimeout);
      event.ResetEvent;
      case awaited of
        wrSignaled:
          begin
            while (not Terminated) and GetMessage(value) do
              ProcessMessage(value);
            if Terminated then
              break;
          end;
        wrTimeout:
          begin
            FTimer.Reset;
            FTimer.Start;
            ProcessTimer;
          end
        else
          break; //Terminate thread
      end;
    until false;
  finally
    Cleanup;
  end;
end;
```

The demonstration program implements TMyTimerThread, which uses this approach to implement the same functionality as the TMyThread. Instead of using a monolithic Execute, the code implements three very small overridden methods. Another change is that the local variable pingMsg is now a field, as it must be shared between different methods:

```
TMyTimerThread = class(TCommTimerThread)
strict private
  FPingMsg: integer;
protected
  procedure Initialize; override;
  procedure ProcessMessage(const msg: TValue); override;
  procedure ProcessTimer; override;
end;
```

The code to create this thread looks almost the same as the code that creates TMyThread, except that it also sets the interval between messages:

```
procedure TfrmThreadComm.btnStartTimerClick(Sender: TObject);
begin
  FTimerThread := TMyTimerThread.Create(ProcessThreadMessages);
  FTimerThread.Interval := 5000;
  FTimerThread.SendToThread(42);
end;
```

Sending a message to the thread and stopping the thread looks completely the same as before. This thread also uses the same *message receiver* function in the main form, ProcessThreadMessage.

When a thread is initialized, the code sends a *ping* message to the owner. There's no need to initialize FPingMsg, as all of the object fields are initialized to zero when an object is created. The timer event handler, ProcessTimer, just calls the same helper function, SendPing, to send a message to the owner. And the message processing is trivial—it just sets the shared field:

```
procedure TMyTimerThread.Initialize;
begin
  SendPing;
end;

procedure TMyTimerThread.ProcessMessage(const msg: TValue);
begin
  FPingMsg := msg.AsInteger;
end;
```

```
procedure TMyTimerThread.ProcessTimer;
begin
  SendPing;
end;

procedure TMyTimerThread.SendPing;
begin
  if not SendToMain(TValue.From<TPingMsg>(
          TPingMsg.Create(FPingMsg, ThreadID)))
  then
    raise Exception.Create('Queue full!');
end;
```

When the code is written in such way, it becomes clear why I prefer using patterns and communication over standard `TThread` code. There is no data sharing, no weird communication calls and, best of all, no mess.

# Summary

While this chapter focused on a single topic, it was still quite diverse. You've learned everything about the `TThread` class, which is a basis for all multithreading code in Delphi. Even the task-based approach that we'll explore in the next chapter uses `TThread` as a basic building block.

I have shown three different ways of creating a `TThread`-based, multithreading solution. A program can take complete ownership of a thread so that it is created and destroyed by the owner. This approach is best used when a thread implements a *service,* as in such cases the main program knows best when the service is needed.

Another way, more appropriate for *background calculations*, is `FreeOnTerminate` mode. With this approach, a thread object is immediately destroyed when a thread's `Execute` function exits. The thread owner can set up an `OnTerminate` event to catch this condition and process the result of the calculation.

Instead of writing a separate class for each background operation, we can also create a thread that executes an *anonymous method*. This approach is most appropriate for short-lived tasks that don't require any interaction with the thread's owner.

After that, we looked into exception handling inside a thread. I've also discussed a few other important `TThread` methods and properties.

The second half of the chapter focused on writing better threading tools. Firstly, I have extended a `TThread` with two communication channels. The result, `TCommThread,` can be used as a base class for your own threads, which can use these channels to communicate with the thread owner.

For the finishing touch, I have implemented a specific solution for one usage pattern—a background task that can send and receive messages and react to timer events. I have then shown how you can produce very clean and understandable code, by using such threading implementation.

In the next chapter, we'll focus even more on a usage-pattern approach. We'll dig deeply into Delphi's **Parallel Programming Library** (**PPL**), which is all about usage patterns. For good measure, I'll also implement a few patterns that PPL doesn't cover.

# 7

# Exploring Parallel Practices

You made it! I admit that the previous two chapters were not much fun and that they mostly tried to scare you away from multithreaded code. Now it's time for something completely different.

In this chapter, I'll cover the fun parts of multithreaded programming by moving to high-level concepts—tasks and patterns. We will not create any threads in the code, no we won't. Instead, we'll just tell the code what we need, and it will handle all the nitty-gritty details.

When you have read this chapter to its conclusion, you'll know all about the following topics:

- What are tasks, and how are they different from threads?
- How do we create and destroy tasks?
- What are our options for managing tasks?
- How should we handle exceptions in tasks?
- What is thread pooling, and why is it useful?
- What are patterns, and why are they better than tasks?
- How can we use the Async/Await pattern to execute operations in a thread?
- How can we use Join pattern to execute multiple parts of code in parallel?
- What is a Future, and how can it help when calculating functions?
- How can we convert a normal loop into a parallel loop with Parallel For?
- How can a pipeline help us parallelize many different problems?

# Tasks and patterns

Traditionally, parallel programming was always implemented with a focus on threads and data sharing. The only support we programmers got from the operating system and the language runtime libraries were thread—and synchronization—related functions. We were able to create a thread, maybe set some thread parameters (like thread priority), and kill a thread. We were also able to create some synchronization mechanisms—a critical section, mutex, or a semaphore. But that was all.

As you are not skipping ahead and you read the previous two chapters, you already know that being able to start a new thread and do the locking is not nearly enough. Writing parallel code that way is a slow, error-prone process. That's why in the last decade the focus in parallel code has shifted from threads to *tasks* and *patterns*. Everyone is doing it—Microsoft with the .NET Task Parallel Library, Intel with Thread Building Blocks, Embarcadero with the Parallel Programming Library and third-party extensions such as OmniThreadLibrary, and so on.

The difference between threads and tasks is simple. A **thread** is an operating system concept that allows executing multiple parts of a process simultaneously. A **task** is merely a part of the code that we want to execute in that way. Or, to put it in different words—when you focus on threads, you tell the system *how* to do the work. When you work with tasks you tell the library *what* you want to be done. You don't lose time with *plumbing*, with setting up threads, communication mechanisms, and so on. Everything is already ready and waiting for you.

As it turns out, working with tasks is usually still too low level. For example, if you want the program to iterate over some loop with multiple tasks in parallel, you would not want to do that by using basic tasks. I'll create such an example in this chapter and you'll see that it still takes some work. A much simpler approach is to use a specific usage *pattern* —a *parallel for* in this example.

Many such patterns exist in modern parallel libraries. Delphi's Parallel Programming Library offers *join*, *future*, and *parallel for*. .NET has *async* and *await*. Thread Building Blocks offers an incredibly powerful *flow graph*. OmniThreadLibrary gives you *background worker*, *pipeline*, *timed task*, and more.

In this chapter, I'll cover all the patterns implemented by the Parallel Programming Library, and then some. I'll extend the set with patterns that you can freely use in your code. Before that, however, we have to cover the basics and deal with *tasks*.

# Variable capturing

Before I start writing parallel code, I have to cover something completely different. As you'll see in this chapter, the big part of the incredible usefulness of tasks and patterns is the ability to use them in combination with anonymous methods and variable capturing. As powerful as that combination is, however, it also brings in some problems.

The code in this chapter will frequently run into the problem of capturing a *loop variable*. Instead of trying to explain this problem at the same time as dealing with the already hard concepts of parallel code, I decided to write a simple program that demonstrates the problem and does nothing more.

The code in the AnonMethod project tries to write out the numbers from *1* to *20* in a convoluted way. For each value of i, the code calls TThread.ForceQueue and passes in an anonymous method that calls Log(i) to write the value into a ListBox.

The problem with the following code lies in the programmer's assumptions. When you write code like this, you should not forget that by writing an anonymous method you are creating a completely separate part of the code that will be executed at some other time. In this example, Log will be called *after* btnAnonProblemClick finishes the execution:

```
procedure TfrmAnonMthod.btnAnonProblemClick(Sender: TObject);
var
  i: Integer;
begin
  ListBox1.Items.Add('');
  for i := 1 to 20 do
    TThread.ForceQueue(nil,
      procedure
      begin
        Log(i);
      end);
end;

procedure TfrmAnonMthod.Log(i: integer);
begin
  ListBox1.Items[ListBox1.Items.Count - 1] :=
  ListBox1.Items[ListBox1.Items.Count - 1] + i.ToString + ' ';
end;
```

To support this, the compiler must somehow make the value of i available to our anonymous method when it is executed. This is done through the magic of *variable capturing*. I'm not going to go into specifics here, as this is a book about high performance computing and not about Delphi implementation details. The only important part you have to know is that the compiler doesn't capture the current *value* of i (as the author of the preceding code fragment assumed) but a *reference* to the value (a pointer to i).

Because of that, all Log calls will receive the same parameter—a value that some pointer points to. It will contain whatever was left inside i after the for loop completed, namely 21. That is just how Delphi works. After a for loop, a loop variable will contain upper bound plus *1*. (Or *minus 1*, if the loop is counting downwards.)

A trick that solves the problem of capturing a loop variable is to write an intermediate function that creates an anonymous method. If we pass our loop variable (i) to such a function, the compiler captures the parameter to the function and not the loop variable, and everything works as expected.

Don't worry if you did not understand any of the mumbo-jumbo from the previous paragraph. Writing about anonymous methods is hard, but luckily they are easily explained through the code. The following example shows how we can fix the code in AnonMethod. The MakeLog function creates an anonymous method that logs the value of parameter i. In the loop, we then call MakeLog for each value of i and pass the output of this function to the ForceQueue call:

```
function TfrmAnonMthod.MakeLog(i: integer): TThreadProcedure;
begin
  Result :=
    procedure
    begin
      Log(i);
    end;
end;

procedure TfrmAnonMthod.btnAnonFixClick(Sender: TObject);
var
  i: Integer;
begin
  ListBox1.Items.Add('');
  for i := 1 to 20 do
    TThread.ForceQueue(nil, MakeLog(i));
end;
```

The following screenshot shows both the unexpected output from the original code and good output from the fixed code:

# Tasks

Let's get back to business, and in this chapter business means tasks. I don't want to spend all the time talking about the theory and classes and interfaces, so I will start by introducing some code. Actually, it is not my code—I got it from our good friend, Mr. Smith.

For the past few chapters, he was quite busy, working on things botanical, so I let him be. (He gave me a comprehensive overview of his activities, but I'm just a programmer, and I didn't really understand him.) Now he has more spare time, and he returned to his great love—prime numbers. He is no longer trying to improve `SlowCode`. Now he studies how the probability of finding a prime number changes when numbers become larger. To do so, he wrote two simple functions (shown as follows) that check a range of numbers and count how many prime numbers are in this range:

```
function IsPrime(value: integer): boolean;
var
  i: Integer;
begin
  Result := (value > 1);
  if Result then
    for i := 2 to Round(Sqrt(value)) do
      if (value mod i) = 0 then
        Exit(False);
end;

function FindPrimes(lowBound, highBound: integer): integer;
var
  i: Integer;
begin
```

```
  Result := 0;
  for i := lowBound to highBound do
    if IsPrime(i) then
      Inc(Result);
end;
```

He soon found out that his code is using only one CPU on his 64-core machine. As he found out that I'm writing about parallel programming, he asked me to change his code so that all the CPUs will be used. I didn't have the heart to tell him that his approach is flawed from the beginning and that he should use mathematical theory to solve his problem. Rather, I took his code and used it as a starting point for this chapter. There are different ways to parallelize such code. It probably won't surprise you that I'll start with the most basic one, *tasks*.

In Delphi's Parallel Programming Library, tasks are objects that implement the ITask interface. They are created through methods of the TTask class. Both the class and the interface are implemented in the System.Threading unit.

The code in the ParallelTasks demo shows basic operations on the tasks. The following method is executed if you click on the **Run tasks** button.

The first task is created by calling the TTask.Run method. This method creates a new task and immediately starts it. The task will be started in a thread, run the SleepProc code, and terminate. Run returns an ITask interface, which we can use to query and manipulate the task.

The second task is created by calling the TTask.Create method. This method creates a new task but does not start it. It returns an ITask interface, just as Run does. In this second example, the task payload is a simple anonymous method. As we want it to start running immediately, the code then calls the ITask.Start method, which starts the task. Start returns the task's ITask interface, which the code saves in the tasks array.

The code then waits for both tasks to complete by calling the TTask.WaitForAll method. It will wait until both the anonymous method and SleepProc exit. The program will be blocked for about 2.5 seconds in WaitForAll, which is not optimal. Later we'll look into different techniques to work around the problem:

```
procedure SleepProc;
begin
  Sleep(2500);
end;

procedure TfrmParallelTasks.btnRunTasksClick(Sender: TObject);
var
```

```
    tasks: array [1..2] of ITask;
  begin
    tasks[1] := TTask.Run(SleepProc);
    tasks[2] := TTask.Create(procedure begin Sleep(2000) end).Start;
    TTask.WaitForAll(tasks);
  end;
```

If we don't want to block the main program, we have to use a different technique to find out when the task has finished its work. We can apply any of the notification methods from the previous chapter—Windows messages, Synchronize, Queue, or polling. In this example, I used the Queue.

When you click the **Async TTask** button in the ParallelTasks demo, the btnAsyncTaskClick method (shown as follows) is executed. This method creates a task by calling TTask.Run and stores the task interface into the form field FTask: ITask. The code also disables the button to give a visual indication that the task is running.

The task then executes the LongTask method in its own thread. After the hard work (Sleep) is done, it queues the notification method, LongTaskCompleted, to the main thread. This method cleans up after the finished task by setting the FTask field to nil and reactivates the btnAsyncTask button:

```
procedure TfrmParallelTasks.LongTask;
begin
  Sleep(2000);
  TThread.Queue(nil, LongTaskCompleted);
end;

procedure TfrmParallelTasks.LongTaskCompleted;
begin
  FTask := nil;
  btnAsyncTask.Enabled := True;
end;

procedure TfrmParallelTasks.btnAsyncTaskClick(Sender: TObject);
begin
  FTask := TTask.Run(LongTask);
  btnAsyncTask.Enabled := False;
end;
```

When you have to wait for multiple tasks to complete, the code becomes a bit more complicated. You have to keep count of running tasks and only trigger the notification when the last task completes. You'll have to wait a bit for the practical example. Later in this chapter, I'll implement a custom join pattern, and I'll return to the notification problem then.

# Exceptions in tasks

Handling exceptions in tasks is a tricky business. The best approach is to handle exceptions explicitly by wrapping the task code in a `try..except` block.

The following code shows how exceptions are handled in the `ExplicitExceptionTask` task. This task is executed when the user clicks on the **Exception 1** button in the `ParallelTasks` demo.

The code always raises an exception, so `LongTaskCompleted` is never called. Instead of that, the code always executes the `except` block, which queues `LongTaskError` to be executed in the main thread.

As the queued code is not executed immediately, we have to *grab* the exception object by calling the `AcquireExceptionObject` method. Variable capturing will take care of the rest. If we did not call the `AcquireExceptionObject` method, the exception object would be already destroyed by the time the queued anonymous method was called:

```
procedure TfrmParallelTasks.ExplicitExceptionTask;
var
  exc: TObject;
begin
  try
    raise Exception.Create('Task exception');
    TThread.Queue(nil, LongTaskCompleted);
  except
    on E: Exception do
    begin
      exc := AcquireExceptionObject;
      TThread.Queue(nil,
        procedure
        begin
          LongTaskError(exc);
        end);
    end;
  end;
end;
```

The `LongTaskError` just logs the details about the exception and calls
`ReleaseExceptionObject` to release exception acquired with
the `AcquireExceptionObject`.

```
procedure TfrmParallelTasks.LongTaskError(exc: Exception);
begin
  ListBox1.Items.Add(Format('Task raised exception %s %s', [exc.ClassName,
exc.Message]));
  ReleaseExceptionObject;
end;
```

Another option is to not use the `try..except` block in the task but to periodically check
the `ITask.Status` property. If a task raises an unhandled exception, `TTask`
implementation will catch it, store the exception object away, and set the status to
`TTaskStatus.Exception`.

A click on the **Exception 2** button in the demo program calls the `btnException2Click`
method, which starts such a task. At the same time, the code enables a timer, which
periodically checks the status of the `FTask` task:

```
procedure TfrmParallelTasks.btnException2Click(Sender: TObject);
begin
  FTask := TTask.Run(ExceptionTask);
  TimerCheckTask.Enabled := true;
end;

procedure TfrmParallelTasks.ExceptionTask;
begin
  Sleep(1000);
  raise Exception.Create('Task exception');
end;
```

The code in the timer event handler jumps through lots of hoops to get the exception
information from the task. It looks like the designer of the `ITask` decided that you ought to
always explicitly handle task exceptions, and he made this second approach needlessly
complicated.

The full code for the timer method is shown as follows. Firstly, it checks the task's status. If
it is one of `Completed`, `Canceled`, or `Exception` then the task has finished its work.
`Completed` is used to indicate a normal task completion. `Canceled` means that somebody
called the `ITask.Cancel` method of that task. `Expection` tells us that an unhandled
exception was raised by the task.

In all three cases, the code clears the `FTask` field and disables the timer. If the status was `Exception`, it goes through more steps to log that exception.

Unfortunately, there's no clean way to access the exception object raised by the task. We can only see its contents by calling the `ITask.Wait` method. This method waits for a specified time on a task to complete (in our code, the time is set to *0* milliseconds). It returns `True` if the task has completed, `False` if timeout was reached and the task is still running, or it raises an exception if the task was cancelled or an exception was caught.

 The `Deadlock` demo from Chapter 5, *Getting Started with the Parallel World*, shows how to cancel a task.

We must wrap the `Wait` call in a `try..except` block to catch that exception. It will not be a simple exception object but an instance of the `EAggregateException` class, which can contain multiple *inner* exceptions. The code then uses a loop to log all caught exceptions:

```
procedure TfrmParallelTasks.TimerCheckTaskTimer(Sender: TObject);
var
  i: integer;
begin
  if assigned(FTask) then
  begin
    if FTask.Status in [TTaskStatus.Completed, TTaskStatus.Canceled,
TTaskStatus.Exception] then
    begin
      if FTask.Status = TTaskStatus.Exception then
      try
        FTask.Wait(0);
      except
        on E: EAggregateException do
          for i := 0 to E.Count - 1 do
            ListBox1.Items.Add(Format('Task raised exception %s %s',
              [E[i].ClassName, E[i].Message]));
      end;
      FTask := nil;
      TimerCheckTask.Enabled := true;
    end;
  end;
end;
```

All in all, this is terribly complicated, which is why I strongly support explicit exception handling in task code.

# Parallelizing a loop

Let us now return to Mr. Smith's problem. He is calling the `FindPrimes` method, which checks the primality of natural numbers in a `for` loop. I've shown that code at the beginning of the chapter, but for convenience I'll reprint it here:

```
function FindPrimes(lowBound, highBound: integer): integer;
var
  i: Integer;
begin
  Result := 0;
  for i := lowBound to highBound do
    if IsPrime(i) then
      Inc(Result);
end;
```

When he calls, for example, `FindPrimes(1, 10000000)`, the computer spends a long time doing the calculation during which time only one CPU is busy. That is not surprising given that in any Delphi program only one thread is running by default. If we want to make other CPUs busy too, we have to run multiple threads.

In his case, it is quite simple to split the job between multiple tasks. Let's say we want to check numbers from 1 to 100,000 with four tasks. We'll let the first task scan the numbers from 1 to 25,000, the second from 25,001 to 50,000, and so on. The tricky part is collecting partial results back together. Each thread will count the number of primes in its subrange, and we have to collect and aggregate (add together) all the partial results. I'll show two different ways to do that.

The first approach is implemented in the `btnCheckPrimes1Click` method, which is activated by clicking the **Check primes 1** button. The number of tasks created is dictated by the `inpNumTasks` spin edit so the code allocates a `tasks: TArray<ITask>` array of that length. It also allocates a `results: TArray<Integer>` array, which will be used to collect partial results.

After that, the code creates and starts all the tasks. Some simple mathematics makes sure that each task gets the subrange of approximately the same size. The actual anonymous method that is run in the task is returned by the `PrepareTask` function to circumvent the problem of capturing a `for` variable. Each task receives three parameters—lower and upper bound for the search range (`lowBound` and `highBound`) and a pointer to the slot, which will receive the partial result (`@results[i-1]`).

When all tasks are created and started, the code waits for all of them to complete. After that a simple `for` loop aggregates the partial results:

```
function TfrmParallelTasks.PrepareTask(lowBound, highBound: integer;
taskResult: PInteger): TProc;
begin
  Result :=
    procedure
    begin
      taskResult^ := FindPrimes(lowBound, highBound);
    end;
end;

procedure TfrmParallelTasks.btnCheckPrimes1Click(Sender: TObject);
var
  aggregate: Integer;
  i: Integer;
  highBound: Integer;
  lowBound: Integer;
  numTasks: Integer;
  results: TArray<Integer>;
  sw: TStopwatch;
  tasks: TArray<ITask>;
begin
  sw := TStopwatch.StartNew;
  numTasks := inpNumTasks.Value;
  SetLength(tasks, numTasks);
  SetLength(results, numTasks);

  lowBound := 0;
  for i := 1 to numTasks do
  begin
    highBound := Round(CHighestNumber / numTasks * i);
    tasks[i-1] := TTask.Run(PrepareTask(lowBound, highBound,
      @results[i-1]));
    lowBound := highBound + 1;
  end;
  TTask.WaitForAll(tasks);
```

```
aggregate := 0;
for i in results do
  Inc(aggregate, i);

sw.Stop;
ListBox1.Items.Add(Format(
  '%d prime numbers from 1 to %d found in %d ms with %d tasks',
  [aggregate, CHighestNumber, sw.ElapsedMilliseconds, numTasks]));
end;
```

The second approach uses a variable, shared between tasks (`aggregate`), to store the number of found prime numbers. To ensure a proper operation, it is updated with a call to `TInterlocked.Add`. The code in `btnCheckPrimes2Click` implements that. As it looks mostly the same as the preceding code, I'll show here just the worker function that creates the task method:

```
function TfrmParallelTasks.PrepareTask2(lowBound, highBound: integer;
taskResult: PInteger): TProc;
begin
  Result :=
    procedure
    begin
      TInterlocked.Add(taskResult^, FindPrimes(lowBound, highBound));
    end;
end;
```

If you start the program and test the code with different numbers of tasks, you may be in for a surprise. I said "may be" because the behavior depends on the way you test the code and on the Delphi version you are using.

There's a nasty bug in the `System.Threading` code that was introduced in Delphi 10.2 Tokyo. I certainly hope that it will be fixed in the next release, as it makes the Parallel Programming Library hard to use. It sometimes causes new threads *not* to be created when you start a task. That forces your tasks to execute one by one, not in parallel.

To demonstrate this, I have enhanced the code executed when you click the **Check primes 2** button. It counts the number of tasks that are executing in parallel and reports that at the end.

If you compile the demo with Tokyo and then start it with four tasks, then two tasks, and finally one task, you'll get the expected result. In my case, calculations run for 2.5, 4.2, and 6.6 seconds, respectively, which is exactly what we would expect. The log window also shows that four, two, and one tasks were running in parallel during the tests, which is again what we wanted.

On the other hand, if you first run the code with one task, then with two, and finally with four, you'll see that each operation takes about the same time and that they all run only one operation in parallel. This is caused by the aforementioned bug. The following screenshot shows both test runs on my test computer:

As far as I know, there are two ways around the problem. One is to insert a little delay after each `TTask.Run`. The `btnCheckPrimes2Click` method contains a commented-out `Sleep(1)` call. If you uncomment it, everything will work as expected. (By the way, `Sleep(0)` is not enough to fix the problem.)

Another workaround is to create a new *thread pool* and limit the minimum number of running threads in that pool. (I know I haven't yet mentioned thread pools, but I'll fix that in a moment.) We can then tell the task to run in that thread pool.

The demo program has a method called `btnCustomThreadPoolClick`, which does exactly that. It is almost completely equal to `btnCheckPrimes2Click`, except in four places.

Firstly, it declares an internal thread pool variable, `tp: TThreadPool`. Secondly, it creates this thread pool and limits the minimum number of threads it will run. This will prevent the thread pool from starting too few worker threads. Thirdly, the `tp` variable is passed as an additional parameter to `TTask.Run`. That tells `TTask` to start the task in our thread pool and not in the default one. Lastly, the `tp` threadpool is destroyed after all tasks are done with their job.

The following code fragment shows only the central part of that method, enough to see how the thread pool is put to use:

```
tp := TThreadPool.Create;
if not tp.SetMinWorkerThreads(numTasks) then
  ListBox1.Items.Add('Failed to set minimum number of worker threads');

lowBound := 0;
for i := 1 to numTasks do
begin
  highBound := Round(CHighestNumber / numTasks * i);
  tasks[i-1] := TTask.Run(PrepareTask2(lowBound, highBound, @aggregate),
tp);
  lowBound := highBound + 1;
end;
TTask.WaitForAll(tasks);

FreeAndNil(tp);
```

# Thread pooling

While starting a thread is much faster than creating a new process, it is still a relatively slow operation. It may easily take few milliseconds to create a new thread. Because in high-performance applications every millisecond counts, most task- and pattern-based libraries use a concept of a *thread pool*.

A thread pool is just a storage that manages unused threads. For example, let's say that your application—which was working in a single thread until now—has just created (and started) its first task. The Parallel Programming Library will then ask a thread pool to run that task. Unless you pass a custom thread pool parameter to `TTask.Create` or `TTask.Run`, a default thread pool will be used.

The thread pool will then create a new thread to run your task in. After the task completes its job, the thread will not die, but will be stored in the list of inactive threads.

If the program now starts another task, the thread pool will not create a new thread, but will reuse the previous one. If a new task is started while the previous one is still active, a new thread will be created.

This creation and storage of inactive threads can be controlled by changing the properties of the `TThreadPool` object, which implements a thread pool. The following code fragment shows the public interface exposed by a thread pool:

```
function SetMaxWorkerThreads(Value: Integer): Boolean;
function SetMinWorkerThreads(Value: Integer): Boolean;

property MaxWorkerThreads: Integer read GetMaxWorkerThreads;
property MinWorkerThreads: Integer read GetMinWorkerThreads;
```

Calling `SetMinWorkerThreads` limits the minimum number of worker threads—except that it does not. The comment inside the code states that *"The actual number of pool threads could be less than this value depending on actual demand"*. So this call is actually just a hint to the library. The `MinWorkerThreads` property gives you a read access to that value. By default, this value is initialized to the number of CPU cores in the system.

Calling `SetMaxWorkerThreads` limits the maximum number of worker threads. If that number of threads is active and you start a new task, it will have to wait for another task to complete its work. The `MaxWorkerThreads` property gives you a read access to that value. By default, this value is initialized to the number of CPU cores in the system **times 25,** which is a pretty high value—much too high if your tasks are CPU-intensive.

# Async/Await

Tasks are powerful but clumsy. The real power of modern multithreading libraries comes not from them, but from specialized code designed to solve specific usage patterns (*pattern* or a *parallel pattern* for short). Although I intend to cover all of the patterns implemented in the Parallel Programming Library, I'll start with a pattern you won't find there.

The *Async/Await* pattern comes from .NET. It allows you to start a background task (*async*) and execute some code in the main thread after the task completes its work (*await*). In Delphi, we cannot repeat the incredible usefulness of the .NET syntax, as it requires support from the compiler, but we can approximate it with something that is useful enough. Such an implementation can be found in my OmniThreadLibrary. For the purpose of this book, I have re-implemented it in the unit `DHPThreading`, which you can freely use in your code.

The `AsyncAwait` demo shows when this pattern can be useful and how to use it. The **Long task** button calls a method that simulates a typical old-school Delphi code.

Firstly, the user interface (the button) is disabled. Then, some time-consuming operation is executed. For example, a program could fetch data from a database, generate a report, export a long XML file, and so on. In this demo program, the `LongTask` method simply executes `Sleep(5000)`. At the end, the user interface is enabled again:

```
procedure TfrmAsyncAwait.btnLongTaskClick(Sender: TObject);
begin
  btnLongTask.Enabled := false;
  btnLongTask.Update;
  LongTask;
  btnLongTask.Enabled := true;
end;
```

This typical pattern has one big problem. It blocks the user interface. While the code is running, the user cannot click into the program, move the window around, and so on. Sometimes the long operation can easily be adapted to run in a background thread, and in such cases a pattern, such as *Async/Await* (or, as we'll later see, a *Future*), can be really helpful.

Async/Await allows you to rewrite the code, shown as follows. The code still disables the user interface but does not call `btnLongTask.Update`. This method will exit almost immediately, and the normal Delphi message loop will take over, redrawing the controls as required.

The code then calls `Async(LongTask)` to start the long task in a background thread. The second part of the command, `.Await`, specifies a *termination event*, a code that is called after the `LongTask` method exits. This event will execute in a main thread, and so it is a good place to update the user interface:

```
TfrmAsyncAwait.btnLongTaskAsyncClick(Sender: TObject);
begin
  btnLongTaskAsync.Enabled := false;
  Async(LongTask)
  .Await(
    procedure
    begin
      btnLongTaskAsync.Enabled := true;
    end
  );
end;
```

If you click the **Long task async** button in the demo program, it will call this method. The time-consuming task will start, but the program will still be responsive. After 5 seconds, the button will be re-enabled, and you'll be able to start the task again.

Actually, the program has three buttons, which all start the same code. If you click all three, three background threads will be created, and `LongTask` will be started in each of them. The following screenshot shows what happens inside the program if you do that. The screenshot proves that the long tasks are started in three threads (*Long task started ...*) and that *await* handlers are executed in the main thread (*Await in thread ...*):

The `DHPThreads` unit implements `Async` as a method returning an `IAsync` interface, which implements the `Await` method:

```
type
  IAsync = interface ['{190C1975-FFCF-47AD-B075-79BC8F4157DA}']
    procedure Await(const awaitProc: TProc);
  end;

function Async(const asyncProc: TProc): IAsync;
```

The implementation of `Async` creates an instance of the `TAsync` class and returns it. The `TAsync` constructor is also trivial; it just stores the `asyncProc` parameter in an internal field:

```
function Async(const asyncProc: TProc): IAsync;
begin
  Result := TAsync.Create(asyncProc);
end;

constructor TAsync.Create(const asyncProc: TProc);
begin
  inherited Create;
  FAsyncProc := asyncProc;
end;
```

Everything else happens inside the `Await` call. It stores the `awaitProc` parameter in an internal field and starts the `Run` method in a task.

The tricky part is hidden in assignment `FSelf := Self`. In the main program, `Async` creates a new `IAsync` interface but doesn't store it away in a form field. Because of that, this interface would be destroyed on exit from the `btnLongTaskAsyncClick` method. To prevent that, `Await` stores a reference to itself in a `FSelf` field. This increases the reference count and prevents the interface from being destroyed:

```
procedure TAsync.Await(const awaitProc: TProc);
begin
  FSelf := Self;
  FAwaitProc := awaitProc;
  TTask.Run(Run);
end;
```

The `Run` method simply runs `FAsyncProc` and then queues an anonymous method to the main thread. This method firstly calls `FAwaitProc` in the main thread and then clears the `FSelf` field. This decrements the reference count and destroys the `ITask` interface:

```
procedure TAsync.Run;
begin
  FAsyncProc();

  TThread.Queue(nil,
    procedure
    begin
      FAwaitProc();
      FSelf := nil;
    end
  );
end;
```

The *Async/Await* pattern is intentionally simple. It offers no capability for processing exceptions, no communication channel to return a value, no interface to stop the running task, and so on. Later we'll see more complicated patterns that offer better control, but sometimes simplicity is exactly what you need.

# Join

The next pattern I want to present is *Join*. This is a very simple pattern that starts multiple tasks in parallel. In the Parallel Programming Library, *Join* is implemented as a class method of the `TParallel` class. To execute three methods, `Task1`, `Task2`, and `Task3`, in parallel, you simply call `TParallel.Join` with parameters collected in an array:

```
TParallel.Join([Task1, Task2, Task3]);
```

This is equivalent to the following implementation, which uses tasks:

```
var
  tasks: array [1..3] of ITask;

tasks[1] := TTask.Run(Task1);
tasks[2] := TTask.Run(Task2);
tasks[3] := TTask.Run(Task3);
```

 Although the approaches work the same, that doesn't mean that `Join` is implemented in this way. Rather than that, it uses a pattern that I haven't yet covered, a *parallel for* to run tasks in parallel.

The `Join` starts tasks but doesn't wait for them to complete. It returns an `ITask` interface representing a new, composite task, which only exits when all of its subtasks finish execution. You can do with this task anything you can with a *normal* instance of `TTask`. For example, if you want to wait for the tasks to finish, you can simply call `Wait` on the resulting interface.

The following line of code starts two tasks in parallel and waits on both of them to finish. An overload of the `Join` function allows you to pass in two `TProc` parameters without the array notation:

```
TParallel.Join(Task1, Task2).Wait;
```

There's not much to say about `Join`, except that in current Delphi it doesn't work correctly. A bug in the 10.1 Berlin and 10.2 Tokyo implementations causes `Join` to not start enough threads. For example, if you pass in two tasks, it will only create one thread and execute tasks one after another. If you pass in three tasks, it will create two threads and execute two tasks in one and one in another.

The `ParallelJoin` program demonstrates this problem. You can use it to check whether the version of Delphi you are using is affected.

A **Join 2 tasks** button executes the following code:

```
procedure TfrmParallelJoin.btnJoin2Click(Sender: TObject);
begin
  ListBox1.Items.Add('Starting tasks');
  TParallel.Join(Task1, Task2);
end;
```

Both tasks look the same. They log a message, wait a little, log another message, and exit:

```
procedure TfrmParallelJoin.QueueLog(const msg: string);
begin
  TThread.Queue(nil,
    procedure
    begin
      ListBox1.Items.Add(msg);
    end);
end;

procedure TfrmParallelJoin.Task1;
begin
  QueueLog('Task1 started in thread ' + TThread.Current.ThreadID.ToString);
  Sleep(1000);
  QueueLog('Task1 stopped in thread ' + TThread.Current.ThreadID.ToString);
end;

procedure TfrmParallelJoin.Task2;
begin
  QueueLog('Task2 started in thread ' + TThread.Current.ThreadID.ToString);
  Sleep(1000);
  QueueLog('Task2 stopped in thread ' + TThread.Current.ThreadID.ToString);
end;
```

The **Join 3 tasks** button starts a similar code that executes three tasks all working in the same fashion as the preceding two tasks.

If you start the program and click **Join 2 tasks,** you'll see that both tasks are executed in the same thread. Because of that—as a thread can only do one thing at a time—the second task is only started when the first task finishes execution. Of course, this only happens if the Join implementation is buggy. With good implementation, the tasks will be started at the same time in two different threads.

If you click the **Join 3 tasks** button, two tasks will be started immediately, each in their own thread. After the first of them exits, its thread will be reused to run the third task. Again, a good implementation will start three tasks in three threads at (almost) the same time.

The following screenshot shows the behavior with the buggy implementation of `Join`:

A simple workaround for this problem is to start one task too many. The extra task should not do anything and should be executed first. When it exits (which will be almost immediately), a new, real task will be started in the same thread.

The `ParallelJoin` program has the **Join 1+2 tasks** button, which demonstrates this behavior. Clicking on a button starts tasks `NullTask`, `Task1`, and `Task2`. A bad implementation will start `NullTask` and `Task1` in two threads. As `NullTask` immediately exits, its thread is reused to start `Task2`:

```
procedure NullTask;
begin
end;

procedure TfrmParallelJoin.btnJoin1p2Click(Sender: TObject);
begin
  ListBox1.Items.Add('Starting tasks');
  TParallel.Join([NullTask, Task1, Task2]);
end;
```

The following screenshot shows this workaround in action:

# Join/Await

Another way to work around the `TParallel.Join` problem is to create a different implementation of the same pattern. As with the *Async/Await* pattern, I've created a version that supports the *Join/Await* pattern.

As with the `TParallel` version, `Join` accepts multiple `TProc` parameters. It, however, doesn't return an `ITask` interface but `IJoin`. This interface is similar to the `IAsync` interface used for the *Async/Await* pattern. It implements two versions of the `Await` method. One is the same as in the `IAsync` version, while the other can be used to catch exceptions raised in tasks:

```
type
  IJoin = interface ['{ED4B4531-B233-4A02-A09A-13EE488FCCA3}']
    procedure Await(const awaitProc: TProc); overload;
    procedure Await(const awaitProc: TProc<Exception>); overload;
  end;

function Join(const async: array of TProc): IJoin;
```

Full implementation of the *Join/Await* pattern can be found in the `DHPThreading` unit. In this book, I'll only show the interesting parts.

A trivial function `Join` creates and returns an instance of a `TJoin` class. The `TJoin` constructor makes a copy of Join's `async` parameter and nothing more.

The interesting things start happening in `Await`. It stores `FAwaitProc` away, initializes a counter of running tasks, `FNumRunning`, makes sure that it cannot be destroyed by using the `FSelf := nil` trick, and starts all tasks. The helper function, `GetAsyncProc`, is used to work around the problem of capturing a `for` loop variable.

If compiled with Delphi 10.2 Tokyo, the code also inserts a short `Sleep` after `TTask.Run` to work around the problem I mentioned previously in this chapter. I certainly hope this bug will be fixed in the next release.

```
function TJoin.GetAsyncProc(i: integer): TProc;
begin
  Result :=
    procedure
    begin
      Run(FAsyncProc[i]);
    end;
end;
```

```
procedure TJoin.Await(const awaitProc: TProc<Exception>);
var
  i: integer;
begin
  FAwaitProc := awaitProc;
  FNumRunning := Length(FAsyncProc);
  FSelf := Self;
  for i := Low(FAsyncProc) to High(FAsyncProc) do begin
    TTask.Run(GetAsyncProc(i));
    {$IF CompilerVersion = 32}Sleep(1);{$IFEND}
  end;
end;
```

The main part of the *Join/Await* implementation is the `Run` method, which is started once for each task passed to the `Join` call. First it calls the `asyncProc` parameter (executing your task in the process) and catches all exceptions. Any exception will be passed to the `AppendException` function, which I'll cover in a moment.

After that, the code decrements the number of running tasks in a thread-safe manner. If the counter has dropped to *0* (as `TInterlocked` is used, this can only happen in one task), the code queues an anonymous method that calls the *Await* handler and drops the reference to itself so that the `TJoin` object can be destroyed. The `CreateAggregateException` function will be shown in a moment.

```
procedure TJoin.Run(const asyncProc: TProc);
begin
  try
    asyncProc();
  except
    on E: Exception do
      AppendException(AcquireExceptionObject as Exception);
  end;

  if TInterlocked.Decrement(FNumRunning) = 0 then
    TThread.Queue(nil,
      procedure
      begin
        FAwaitProc(CreateAggregateException);
        FSelf := nil;
      end);
end;
```

The `AppendException` function adds the caught exception object to an `FExceptions` array. As it may be called from multiple threads at once (if more than one task fails simultaneously), locking is used to synchronize access to `FExceptions`:

```
procedure TJoin.AppendException(E: Exception);
begin
  TMonitor.Enter(Self);
  try
    SetLength(FExceptions, Length(FExceptions) + 1);
    FExceptions[High(FExceptions)] := e;
  finally
    TMonitor.Exit(Self);
  end;
end;
```

The `CreateAggregateException` exception is only called when all tasks have finished execution and so doesn't need any locking. If the `FExceptions` array is empty, the function returns nil. Otherwise, it creates an `EAggregateException` object containing all caught exceptions:

```
function TJoin.CreateAggregateException: Exception;
begin
  if Length(FExceptions) = 0 then
    Result := nil
  else
    Result := EAggregateException.Create(FExceptions);
end;
```

What about the second `Await` overload? It simply calls the `Await` that we've already seen. If any of the tasks raises an exception, it will be reraised inside the `Await` code. Otherwise, your `awaitProc` will be called:

```
procedure TJoin.Await(const awaitProc: TProc);
begin
  Await(
    procedure (E: Exception)
    begin
      if assigned(E) then
        raise E;
      awaitProc();
    end);
end;
```

The **DHP Join Exception** button on the `ParallelJoin` demo shows how to use the exception-handling mechanism. The code starts three tasks. One works as in the previous `Join` examples, while the other two tasks raise exceptions (only one of those tasks is shown as follows):

```
procedure TfrmParallelJoin.Task2E;
begin
  QueueLog('Task2E started in thread ' +
    TThread.Current.ThreadID.ToString);
  Sleep(1000);
  QueueLog('Task2E raising exception in thread ' +
    TThread.Current.ThreadID.ToString);
  raise Exception.Create('Task2 exception');
end;

procedure TfrmParallelJoin.btnDHPJoinExcClick(Sender: TObject);
begin
  ListBox1.Items.Add('Starting tasks');
  Join([Task1, Task2E, Task3E]).Await(TasksStopped);
end;
```

The termination handler, `TasksStopped`, is called in the main thread after all tasks have finished their job. If the `E` parameter is nil, there was no exception—but we already know that in the demo program this is not so.

When at least one exception is raised (and not handled) in a task, the `E` parameter will contain an `EAggregateException` object. The code in `TaskStopped` iterates over all inner exceptions stored in that object and logs them on the screen:

```
procedure TfrmParallelJoin.TasksStopped(E: Exception);
var
  i: Integer;
begin
  ListBox1.Items.Add('Tasks stopped');
  if assigned(E) then
    for i := 0 to EAggregateException(E).Count - 1 do
      ListBox1.Items.Add('Task raised exception: ' +
        EAggregateException(E)[i].Message);
end;
```

The demo program also contains a **DHP Join** button, which starts the same three tasks that we used to test the `TParallel.Join` implementation. In addition to the `TParallel` demo, the code logs the moment when all tasks are completed:

```
procedure TfrmParallelJoin.btnDHPJoinClick(Sender: TObject);
begin
```

```
ListBox1.Items.Add('Starting tasks');
Join([Task1, Task2, Task3]).Await(
  procedure
  begin
    ListBox1.Items.Add('Tasks stopped');
  end);
end;
```

In the following screenshot, we can see how with this implementation all three tasks start in each in their own thread. The screenshot also shows an output of the exception-handling code:

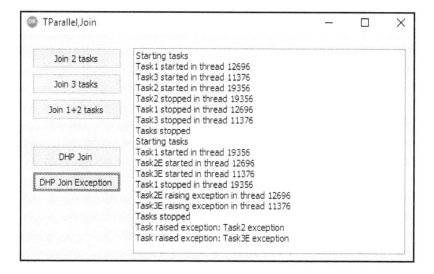

# Future

A big category of operations that we would like to execute in a background thread can be summarized with the words "do something and return a result". Such operations are represented by a pattern called *Future*.

A *Future* always wraps some function. In Delphi's Parallel Programming Library, a Future is represented by an IFuture<T> interface, where T is the data type returned from the function. This interface is created by calling the TTask.Future<T> function. IFuture<T> is derived from ITask, so it supports all ITask methods and properties, such as Status, Cancel, Wait, and so on.

The `ParallelFuture` demo shows two ways of using an `IFuture<T>`. In the first scenario, the code creates a Future, does some other work, and then asks the Future about the result of the calculation. If the background calculation is not yet finished, the code waits until the result is ready. That could block the user interface, so this approach should only be used if you know that the Future will be calculated relatively quickly.

In the demo, the **Create Future** button starts the calculation, while the **Get value** button reads the result of the calculation. The calculation is performed by the `CountPrimes` function, which counts prime numbers from 2 to *5,000,000*:

```
function CountPrimes: integer;
var
  i: Integer;
begin
  Result := 0;
  for i := 2 to 5000000 do
    if IsPrime(i) then
      Inc(Result);
end;
```

A Future is created simply by calling `TTask.Future<integer>`, passing in `CountPrimes` as a parameter:

```
procedure TfrmFuture.btnFutureClick(Sender: TObject);
begin
  FFuture := TTask.Future<integer>(CountPrimes);
end;
```

Getting a result of a Future—if you don't mind waiting until the result is calculated—is as simple as accessing its `Value` property. After that, the code destroys the Future interface by assigning it a `nil` value:

```
procedure TfrmFuture.btnGetValueClick(Sender: TObject);
begin
  ListBox1.Items.Add('Result = ' + FFuture.Value.ToString);
  FFuture := nil;
end;
```

The second approach is more appropriate for general use. First, it calculates the resulting value and then notifies the main thread that the value was calculated. We can use any notification mechanism to do that—Windows messages, `TThread.Queue`, polling, and so on.

A click on the **Create Future 2** button in the demo program starts the
btnFuture2Click method, which uses this approach. As before, the code begins by calling
the TTask.Future<integer> function, but this time its argument is an anonymous
function returning an Integer. When a background thread executes this anonymous
function, it first calls our real calculation—CountPrimes—and then queues a
method, ReportFuture, to be executed in the main thread:

```
procedure TfrmFuture.btnFuture2Click(Sender: TObject);
begin
  FFuture := TTask.Future<integer>(
    function: Integer
    begin
      Result := CountPrimes;
      TThread.Queue(nil, ReportFuture);
    end);
end;
```

The ReportFuture reads the Value property to access the result of the calculation:

```
procedure TfrmFuture.ReportFuture;
begin
  ListBox1.Items.Add('Result = ' + FFuture.Value.ToString);
  FFuture := nil;
end;
```

The big difference between the two approaches is that, in the first case, reading from
FFuture.Value may block until the result is calculated. In the second case, the result is
guaranteed to be ready at that point, and the value is returned immediately.

If a Future calculation raises an exception, this exception is caught by the TTask and will be
reraised when main thread accesses the Value property. You can use the technique
described in the section *Exceptions in tasks* or—what I would wholeheartedly
recommend—catch and handle all exceptions in the background task itself.

# Parallel for

The Parallel Programming Library implements only one pattern that I haven't talked about
yet—*Parallel for*, a multithreaded version of a for loop. This pattern allows for very simple
parallelization of loops, but this simplicity can also get you into trouble. When you use
*Parallel for*, you should always be very careful that you don't run into some data sharing
trap.

For comparison reasons, the `ParallelFor` demo implements a normal `for` loop (shown as follows), which goes from 2 to 10 million, counts all prime numbers in that range, and logs the result:

```
const
  CHighestNumber = 10000000;

procedure TbtnParallelFor.btnForClick(Sender: TObject);
var
  count: Integer;
  i: Integer;
  sw: TStopwatch;
begin
  sw := TStopwatch.StartNew;
  count := 0;

  for i := 2 to CHighestNumber do
    if IsPrime(i) then
      Inc(count);

  sw.Stop;
  ListBox1.Items.Add('For: ' + count.ToString + ' primes. ' +
    'Total time: ' + sw.ElapsedMilliseconds.ToString);
end;
```

To change this `for` loop into a Parallel for, we just have to call `TParallel.For`, instead of using `for`, and pass in both range boundaries and workloads as parameters. A **Parallel for - bad** button in the demo program activates the `btnParallelForBadClick` method, which implements this approach—with a small (intentional) mistake.

The three parameters passed to `TParallel.For` in the following code are lower bound for the iteration (2), higher bound (`CHighestNumber`), and a worker method (an anonymous method). A worker method must accept one parameter of type `integer`. This parameter represents the loop variable (`i`) of a standard `for` statement:

```
procedure TbtnParallelFor.btnParalleForBadClick(Sender: TObject);
var
  count: Integer;
  i: Integer;
  sw: TStopwatch;
begin
  sw := TStopwatch.StartNew;
  count := 0;

  TParallel.For(2, CHighestNumber,
    procedure (i: integer)
```

```
  begin
    if IsPrime(i) then
      Inc(count);
  end);

sw.Stop;
ListBox1.Items.Add('Parallel for - bad: ' + count.ToString +
  ' primes. ' + 'Total time: ' + sw.ElapsedMilliseconds.ToString);
end;
```

This code demonstrates the classical data-sharing problem. It is so easy to replace `for` with `TParallel.For` that sometimes you forget that the body of this iteration executes in multiple parallel copies and that all access to shared variables (`count` in this example) must be protected.

We could use locking to solve that problem, but we've already seen that interlocked operations are faster. The code activated by the **Parallel for - good** button therefore uses `TInterlocked.Increment` instead of `Inc` to fix the problem.

The following code fragment shows the Parallel for loop from the `btnParallelForClick` method. All other parts of the method are the same as in the preceding code fragment.

```
TParallel.For(2, CHighestNumber,
  procedure (i: integer)
  begin
    if IsPrime(i) then
      TInterlocked.Increment(count);
  end);
```

The following screenshot compares all three versions. We can clearly see that the parallel version is about four times faster than the single-threaded code. The test machine had four physical cores, so this is not surprising. We can also see that the "bad" code produces a different value each time. The code runs without any other problems, and that's why such errors are usually hard to detect:

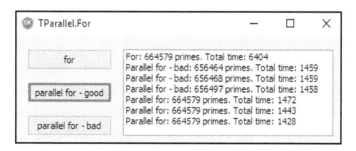

What the screenshot doesn't show is that `TParallel.For` stops the main thread until all the work is done. This is completely understandable. A Parallel for is meant as an in-place replacement for a `for` loop, and with this approach you can sometimes speed up a program with very little work.

If this behavior blocks the user interface for too long, you can still wrap a *Parallel for* pattern inside a *Future* pattern. A Future will take care of a non-blocking execution, while the Parallel for will speed up the program.

 Alternatively, you can wrap a *Parallel for* in an *Async/Await* pattern.

The **Async Parallel for** button in the demo program does exactly that. When you click it, a code starts a computation function, `ParallelCountPrime` in a Future. This function will return a number of primes in the tested range:

```
procedure TbtnParallelFor.btnAsyncParallelForClick(Sender: TObject);
begin
  FStopWatch := TStopwatch.StartNew;
  FParallelFuture := TTask.Future<Integer>(ParallelCountPrimes);
end;
```

The `ParallelCountPrimes` function is executed in a background thread by the Future pattern. It uses `TParallel.For` and `TInterlocked.Increment` to quickly and correctly count prime numbers. After that it assigns the `count` variable to the `Result` function so that the main thread will be able to read it via the `Value` property. At the end, the code queues an anonymous function that will log the result in the main thread and destroy the Future interface:

```
function TbtnParallelFor.ParallelCountPrimes: integer;
var
  count: Integer;
begin
  count := 0;
  TParallel.For(2, CHighestNumber,
    procedure (i: integer)
    begin
      if IsPrime(i) then
        TInterlocked.Increment(count);
    end);
  Result := count;
```

```
TThread.Queue(nil,
  procedure
  begin
    FStopwatch.Stop;
    ListBox1.Items.Add('Async parallel for: ' +
      FParallelFuture.Value.ToString +
      ' primes. Total time: ' + FStopwatch.ElapsedMilliseconds.ToString);
    FParallelFuture := nil;
  end);
end;
```

If your parallel iteration code raises an exception, it will be caught and reraised in the main thread. In theory, you should be able to wrap `TParallel.For` with a `try .. except` block and process the exception there. In practice, however, the implementation of exception catching is buggy (as are many parts of the Parallel Programming Library), and you are likely to run into trouble that way.

A click on the **Parallel for exception** button runs a code, shown as follows, which demonstrates the exception-catching technique. It starts multiple background tasks to process a small range of integers (from 1 to 10) and raises an exception in each task. When Parallel for catches an exception, it tries to shut down the background operation, but during that time a different thread may have already raised the exception too. As the multithreading is unpredictable by nature, a different number of exceptions will be raised each time.

The Parallel for pattern collects all exceptions and joins them in an `EAggregateException`. The following code iterates over all exceptions in this object and logs them on screen:

```
procedure TbtnParallelFor.btnParallelForExceptionClick(Sender: TObject);
var
  i: Integer;
begin
  ListBox1.Items.Add('---');
  try
    TParallel.For(1, 10,
      procedure (i: integer)
      begin
        Sleep(100);
        raise Exception.Create('Exception in thread ' +
          TThread.Current.ThreadID.ToString);
      end);
  except
    on E: EAggregateException do
      for i := 0 to E.Count - 1 do
        if not assigned(E) then
          ListBox1.Items.Add(i.ToString + ': nil')
```

```
        else
          ListBox1.Items.Add(i.ToString + ': ' + E[i].ClassName + ': ' +
            E[i].Message);
      on E: Exception do
        ListBox1.Items.Add(E.ClassName + ': ' + E.Message);
    end;
  end;
```

If you try to run this code, you should do it without the debugger. I was not able to successfully run the program inside the debugger, as, after a few exceptions, the debugger stopped responding.

Even if you run the program without the debugger, it may report weird results from time to time. The preceding code has a special `if` clause that checks whether an inner exception, `E[i]`, is assigned at all. As you can see from the following screenshot, this is necessary, because sometimes an inner exception is not correctly captured. In such cases, `E[i]` contains `nil`:

I did some debugging and found out that this is caused by an improperly designed code in the Parallel Programming Library, which sometimes tries to access fields from a destroyed object. As we can have no idea what additional problems that may cause, it is best that the parallel iteration code doesn't raise any exceptions.

# Pipelines

So far, I have discussed two different categories of problems that can be solved using patterns. In the first category, there are long operations that we just want to push into the background. We are happy with the execution time, but we would like to keep the user interface responsive, and so we need to execute them in a background thread. *Async/Await* and *Future* are tools for this occasion.

In the second category, there are problems that can be split into parts that are independent or mostly independent of each other. We can use *Join*, *Join/Await*, or *Parallel for* to parallelize them and implement the "mostly" part with locking or interlocked operations.

This, however, doesn't even nearly cover all the use cases. There's at least one big category left that is hard to parallelize with the Parallel Programming Library tools. I'm talking about problems that are hard to split into parts but where operations executed on a given data item (an atomic part of the input data) can be split into stages.

To work on such problems, we need a pattern that can transfer data from one stage to another. In Thread Building Blocks, such a pattern is called the *Flow graph*, while OmniThreadLibrary implements the less powerful *Pipeline*. As OmniThreadLibrary is much easier to use with Delphi, I'll focus on the latter.

 OmniThreadLibrary is simple to set up. You can use Delphi's GetIt Package Manager, or you can surf to `www.omnithreadlibrary.com` and follow the instructions on the *Download* page.

Explaining the *pipeline* concept is easiest with a concrete example. And describing an example is much less confusing if it is backed with code. I'll therefore focus on the `ParallelPipeline` demo, which is included with the book. The code archive also contains a copy of OmniThreadLibrary, so you can just open the demo, press *F9*, and the code will compile.

The `ParallelPipeline` demo implements a very simple source code analyzer. It runs on all files with the extension `.pas` in some folder (including subfolders), for each file counts the number of lines, words, and characters in a file, and displays cumulative statistics for all found files.

From the implementation view, the program must enumerate over the folders and for each file do the following:

- Read the file from the disk into the buffer
- Count the number of lines, words, and characters in that buffer
- Update cumulative statistics with information about that file

We can parallelize this operation by first finding all files in the folder, storing their names in a string list, and using *Parallel for* to process that list. If we do so, however, we have to wait until the initial file list is built, and that can take some time, especially if there's lots of files and they are stored on a network server. We would rather start working immediately after the first filename is known, and a pipeline is designed exactly for that.

To create a pipeline, we must think about the problem in a different way: as a series of work stages, connected with communication channels. In a way, we are implementing my favorite technique of speeding up programs—*changing the algorithm.*

In our problem, the first stage is just enumerating files. Its input is the name of the folder that is to be scanned, and its output is a list of files with extension .pas files found in that folder and its subfolders. Instead of storing the names of found files in some list, the stage is writing them into a communication channel.

The second stage is a simple file reader. It is connected to the first stage by using a shared communication channel—the first stage is writing into the channel, and the second stage is reading from it. This stage reads the next filename from the channel, opens the file, reads its content into some buffer, and writes that buffer into its own output channel.

This pattern of stage - channel - stage - channel ... then continues. The third stage reads data buffers from its input (which is at the same time the output of the second stage), performs analysis on the data, and writes the result of the analysis into its own output.

The last, fourth stage collects all of the partial analysis results and generates the summary report, which the main program accesses after the job is done.

In that way, we can create a sequence of small workers, connected with communication channels. The nice part about this approach is that the workers are completely independent and because of that simple to parallelize. None of them are accessing any shared data at all. The only shared parts are communication channels, but they are implemented and managed by the pattern, and so your code doesn't have to care about them.

This independence of stages also means that we can execute more than one instance of some stage if we think that the stage will be executing slower than other stages in the chain. To support this, the communication channel used to connect stages must support multiple simultaneous readers and writers. This can be achieved either by locking (as in Delphi's `TThreadedQueue<T>`) or by using interlocked operations (in OmniThreadLibrary's `TOmniQueue` and `IOmniBlockingCollection`).

The pipeline built by the demo program uses that extensively. It implements only one instance of the first and last stage, two instances of the statistics analysis stage, and multiple instances (depending on the number of cores in the system) of the file-reading stage. Accessing files is a relatively slow operation that doesn't use much CPU, and it makes sense to run it in parallel.

The following diagram shows the pipeline created by the `ParallelPipeline` demo. You will notice that there are two additional communication channels that I only hinted at. The first stage also has a communication channel on the input, and the last stage on the output. They will be typically used by the main program to provide initial data (the starting folder in our example) and to read the result (cumulative statistics). In OmniThreadLibrary, they are accessed through the pipeline's `Input` and `Output` properties:

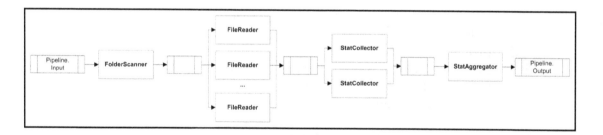

# Creating the pipeline

Let's look at the code now. The user interface has one button that can both start and stop the parallel operation. It's `OnClick` event is shown as follows. When starting the process, it calls the `CreatePipeline` method. To stop the process, it just calls the pipeline's `Cancel` method. The pipeline object will be destroyed later, through a termination event. I'll return to that part later.

```
procedure TfrmPipeline.btnStartClick(Sender: TObject);
begin
  if btnStart.Tag = 0 then begin
    ListBox1.Items.Add(inpStartFolder.Text);
```

```
      CreatePipeline;
      btnStart.Caption := 'Stop';
      btnStart.Tag := 1;
      TimerUpdateProcessing.Enabled := true;
   end
   else
      if assigned(FPipeline) then
         FPipeline.Cancel;
   end;
```

The `CreatePipeline` method (shown as follows) creates, configures, and starts the pipeline. First, `FPipeline: IOmniPipeline` (a form field) is created by calling the `Parallel.Pipeline` method. In OmniThreadLibrary, the `Parallel` class functions as a factory for all patterns, similar to Delphi's own `TParallel` class.

Next, the code creates all four stages by calling the `Stage` function for each of them. Some stages require additional configuration to set the number of instances, to specify message handlers, and to limit the size of the output queue. For example, the first stage (`FolderScanner`) and the last stage (`StatAggregator`) are created without any additional configuration, while the code specifies that there should be two instances of the third stage (`StatCollector`) by calling `NumTasks(2)` after specifying the stage method.

In OmniThreadLibrary, functions usually follow the *fluent* programming style. Almost every `IOmniPipeline` method is implemented as a function that returns `Self`. That allows you to chain method calls. In the following code, this behavior is used when configuring the second stage (`Stage().NumTasks().Throttle()`) and the third stage (`Stage().NumTasks()`).

The configuration of the second stage (`FileReader`) is the most complex. Besides setting the number of parallel tasks for this stage to the number of CPUs that are available to the process, we also limit the size of the output queue to 1,000 items (`Throttle(1000)`) and specify the function that will process messages sent from the stage to the main thread (`Parallel.TaskConfig.OnMessage`).

The code also sets up an event handler, which will be called (in the main thread) after all the pipeline tasks complete their execution (`OnStopInvoke`). This event handler is also called when the process is cancelled by the user.

After all the configuration is done, the code calls `Run` to start the pipeline. Tasks for all stages will be created, and each will try to read from its own communication channel. As there is no data present in the channels yet, they will all simply go to sleep until some data appears. At this point, the pipeline doesn't use any CPU.

To kickstart the process, the code writes the starting folder into the pipeline's input (`FPipeline.Input.Add`). This will wake the `FolderScanner` stage, which will scan the folder, send all found files to the output channel, and so on. After that, it will try to read the next starting folder from the input, and, as there will be no data present, the stage will again go to sleep.

As the code knows that there's only one input element to be processed, we want to prevent that. After the first stage is done with its input, it should exit and not try to read the next element. We can enforce that by calling the `CompleteAdding` method on the input channel. This puts the channel into *completed* mode, which indicates that no more data can be written into the channel, thus allowing the first stage to stop:

```
procedure TfrmPipeline.CreatePipeline;
begin
  FPipeline := Parallel.Pipeline;
  FPipeline.Stage(FolderScanner);
  FPipeline.Stage(FileReader,
                  Parallel.TaskConfig.OnMessage(HandleFileReaderMessage))
    .NumTasks(Environment.Process.Affinity.Count)
    .Throttle(1000);
  FPipeline.Stage(StatCollector)
    .NumTasks(2);
  FPipeline.Stage(StatAggregator);

  FPipeline.OnStopInvoke(ShowResult);

  FPipeline.Run;

  FPipeline.Input.Add(inpStartFolder.Text);
  FPipeline.Input.CompleteAdding;
end;
```

When the first stage is done processing the data, it will put its output channel into *completed* mode, which will allow the second stage to stop. In that way, the indication that the pipeline is finished with its work trickles down the communication channels. A similar mechanism is used by the `Cancel` method, which is used to cancel currently running operations.

A note on communication channel size and throttling is in order at this point. By default, each communication channel can store up to 10,240 elements. After that number is reached, the *producer* (the task writing into the channel) will go to sleep when it tries to write a new data item to the channel. Only when the channel becomes partially empty (by default that happens when it is under 75% full), will the producer awaken.

This mechanism was implemented so that one very fast task cannot produce so much data that it fills up the computer's memory. The default value sometimes needs manual adjustment, though. That's why the second stage limits its output to 1,000 data buffers. A content of a file can be relatively big, especially compared with other outputs (a filename outputted from stage one and statistics data outputted from stage three).

I must admit that the number of tasks I specified for stages two and three was not determined scientifically, but by guesswork. In a real-life application, it would be prudent to test such a program with different configuration parameters (different number of tasks and different communication channel sizes) on local and network folders. A true *flow graph* implementation should do such tuning automatically, but `IOmniPipeline` was never designed to do that but to be a simple and powerful pattern that can be easily controlled.

# Stages

Let us now see how the stages are implemented. The first stage, `FolderScanner`, scans a folder and writes all found Pascal files to the output. Its implementation is shown as follows.

The stage method receives two parameters of type `IOmniBlockingCollection`, which represent its input and output communication channel, and an optional parameter that allows access to the task that runs the stage code (`task: IOmniTask`).

An `IOmniBlockingCollection` channel contains items of type `TOmniValue`, which is a fast variation of Delphi's `Variant` or `TValue`. This type can store any other Delphi data type inside.

A typical stage would run a `for value in input` loop to read all the data from the input. This `for` doesn't exit if there is no data on the input but simply enters a *wait* state, which uses no CPU power. Only when the `input` is put into *completed* mode *and* there is no data inside will the `for` exit.

 We know that the input will only contain one item, so we could also just call the `input.TryTake` function to read that value. The approach implemented in the `FolderScanner` method is more flexible, though.

The code then uses the helper function, `DSiEnumFilesEx`, from the `DSiWin32` library, which is included with the OmniThreadLibrary. This function scans folders and their subfolders and calls an anonymous method for each found file.

This anonymous method first checks whether the operation should be aborted by calling `task.CancellationToken.IsSignalled`. If so, it will set the `stopEnum` flag, which tells `DSIEnumFilesEx` to stop enumerating files and to exit. If everything is OK, however, it concatenates the folder and filename parts and writes them to the output. A `TryAdd` method is used instead of `Add`, as this call may fail when the pipeline is cancelled (when the code calls `IOmniPipeline.Cancel`):

```
procedure TfrmPipeline.FolderScanner(
  const input, output: IOmniBlockingCollection;
  const task: IOmniTask);
var
  value: TOmniValue;
begin
  for value in input do begin
    DSiEnumFilesEx(
      IncludeTrailingPathDelimiter(value) + '*.pas', 0, true,
      procedure (const folder: string; S: TSearchRec;
                 isAFolder: boolean; var stopEnum: boolean)
      begin
        stopEnum := task.CancellationToken.IsSignalled;
        if (not stopEnum) and (not isAFolder) then
          output.TryAdd(IncludeTrailingPathDelimiter(folder) + S.Name);
      end);
  end;
end;
```

The second stage, `FileReader`, is implemented with a similar loop. It also checks the cancellation token and exits if it is signaled. Without that check, the stage would always process all data waiting in its input queue before exiting, even if the pipeline was cancelled.

Inside the loop, the code loads the contents of a file to a string list. An implicit operator converts `value` into a string parameter, needed in the `LoadFromFile` method. After that, the `TStringList` is sent to the output queue. To assure that somebody will always destroy this object, even if the list is canceled, it is best to store it as an *owned object*. It will then be reference-counted and destroyed when appropriate:

```
procedure TfrmPipeline.FileReader(
  const input, output: IOmniBlockingCollection;
  const task: IOmniTask);
var
  sl: TStringList;
  value: TOmniValue;
  outValue: TOmniValue;
begin
  for value in input do begin
```

```
      if task.CancellationToken.IsSignalled then
        break;

      sl := TStringList.Create;
      try
        sl.LoadFromFile(value);
        outValue.AsOwnedObject := sl;
        sl := nil;
        output.TryAdd(outValue);
        task.Comm.Send(MSG_OK, value);
      except
        task.Comm.Send(MSG_ERROR, value);
        FreeAndNil(sl);
      end;
    end;
  end;
```

The preceding code sends a message to the main thread when a file is read or when an exception is raised when accessing a file. This message is sent via OmniThreadLibrary's built-in message channel (task.Comm) and is dispatched to the HandleFileReaderMessage method, which was specified as a message handler while building the pipeline.

This following method displays all errors on the screen but only stores the currently processed file in a global field. It would be useless to overflow the user interface with information on all processed files, and so the code is using a timer (not shown in the book), which every quarter of a second displays the current FLastProcessed on screen:

```
procedure TfrmPipeline.HandleFileReaderMessage(
  const task: IOmniTaskControl;
  const msg: TOmniMessage);
begin
  if msg.MsgID = MSG_ERROR then
    ListBox1.ItemIndex := ListBox1.Items.Add('*** ' + msg.MsgData)
  else
    FLastProcessed := msg.MsgData;
end;
```

Let's move to the third stage, StatCollector, which analyzes one file. It is implemented as a *simple stage,* meaning that the for .. in loop is implemented in the pipeline pattern itself. The pattern also handles the cancellation.

This approach is ideal when each input value produces zero or one output value. The stage method is called once for each item read from the input channel. If the stage writes anything into its `output` parameter, that value is written to the stage's output channel. If the stage leaves `output` untouched, nothing is written out.

The third stage calls the `GenerateStatistics` function to generate the statistics. I decided not to show it in the book, as the implementation is not relevant for the pipeline pattern. The resulting record is assigned to the `output` parameter via a special `FromRecord<T>` function, which can store a record inside `TOmniValue`.

There's no need to destroy the `TStringList` that is contained in each input `TOmniValue`. Because it was assigned to the `AsOwnedObject` property, it will be destroyed automatically:

```
type
  TStatistics = record
    Files: Int64;
    Lines: int64;
    Words: int64;
    Chars: int64;
  end;

procedure TfrmPipeline.StatCollector(const input: TOmniValue;
  var output: TOmniValue);
var
  stat: TStatistics;
begin
  stat := GenerateStatistics(input.ToObject<TStringList>);
  output := TOmniValue.FromRecord<TStatistics>(stat);
end;
```

The last stage, `StatAggregator`, reads all `TStatistics` records from the input queue. The `ToRecord<T>` function is used to extract record from a `TOmniValue` item. The `Merge` function, which is not shown in the book, merges current aggregate and new partial statistics data together.

Only after all the data is processed (when the `for` loop exits), will the resulting aggregate value be written to the pipeline's output:

```
procedure TfrmPipeline.StatAggregator(const input,
  output: IOmniBlockingCollection; const task: IOmniTask);
var
  aggregate: TStatistics;
  stat: TStatistics;
  value: TOmniValue;
begin
```

```
    aggregate := Default(TStatistics);

    for value in input do begin
      if task.CancellationToken.IsSignalled then
        break;

      stat := value.ToRecord<TStatistics>;
      Merge(aggregate, stat);
    end;

    output.TryAdd(TOmniValue.FromRecord<TStatistics>(aggregate));
  end;
```

If we wanted to implement the parallalelization in some other way (for example, with a *Parallel for* pattern), then this part would need to implement locking to access the shared aggregate state. As the pipeline pattern gently guides you to use the data duplication and communication instead, there is no need for sharing, locking, and other complications.

# Displaying the result and shutting down

When all tasks have finished execution, the `ShowResult` method is called. It tries to read the result of the computation from the pipeline's output channel by calling `FPipeline.Output.TryTake`. This function will return `false` if the pipeline was cancelled, so no result will be displayed in that case:

```
procedure TfrmPipeline.ShowResult;
var
  value: TOmniValue;
  stat: TStatistics;
begin
  if FPipeline.Output.TryTake(value) then begin
    stat := value.ToRecord<TStatistics>;
    ListBox1.Items.Add(Format(
      'Files: %d, Lines: %d, Words: %d, Characters: %d',
      [stat.Files, stat.Lines, stat.Words, stat.Chars]));
  end;
  Cleanup;
end;
```

At the end, ShowResult calls the Cleanup method, which destroys the pipeline interface by setting it to nil. It also clears and resets the user interface and prepares it for a new operation:

```
procedure TfrmPipeline.Cleanup;
begin
  FPipeline := nil;
  TimerUpdateProcessing.Enabled := false;
  lblProcessing.Visible := false;
  btnStart.Caption := 'Start';
  btnStart.Tag := 0;
end;
```

Pipelines are a very interesting concept that implements the *data duplication* and *communication* paradigms to the max. It allows for the parallelization of many different problems that don't fit into other patterns.

# Summary

This was the final chapter, dedicated to multithreading, which put a finishing touch on a story line that started in Chapter 5, *Getting Started with the Parallel World*. I started by describing all the bad things that can happen when writing parallel code, then spent one chapter showing the cumbersome TThread, which makes multithreaded code such an unnecessary pain, and then in this chapter I finally moved on to the nice parts of the puzzle—tasks and patterns.

The chapter opened with a discussion of tasks and patterns—what they are and how they can be used to simplify multithreaded programming. For a bonus, I threw in a short treatise about variable capturing, which focused only on one problematic part—the capturing of a loop variable.

Then we looked at how we can use tasks to split a loop into multiple parallel loops. We saw that there's quite some work involved, particularly around task creation and setup. On the way, we also learned about the thread-pooling concept.

The last part of the very long section on tasks discussed the exception handling. We learned that it is quite hard to correctly capture in the main thread exceptions that were raised inside a task and that it is better to catch all task exceptions explicitly in the code.

After that, we finally moved from the (merely acceptable) tasks to (fun and simple) patterns. For starters, I've shown how to implement a very simple *Async/Await* pattern, something that is missing from the Parallel Programming Library.

Next on the list was the *Join* pattern. This very simple tool sometimes allows for very efficient parallelization of completely independent pieces of code. Sadly, I also had to demonstrate a failing in the current Delphi implementation, and I provided two workarounds. I also implemented a more powerful and simpler *Join/Await,* which allows you to capture exceptions raised in tasks.

After that, we looked into the *Future* (with a capital F). This interesting and powerful pattern allows you to execute a function in a task, while it simplifies accessing the function result in the main thread. The Delphi implementation of this pattern is quite flexible and can be used in different ways.

As the last Parallel Programming Library pattern, I covered *Parallel For*. This pattern allows for a very simple parallelization of a standard `for` loop. I cautioned you about the problems that can sprout from its use, and I added a short trick that demonstrated how to create a non-blocking Parallel for.

At the end of the chapter, I moved to my own OmniThreadLibrary. From all the patterns it implements, I picked the one that is, in my opinion, the most powerful—the *Pipeline*. I used it to implement a small utility: a filesystem scanner that generates simple file statistics. If you are interested in knowing more about OmniThreadLibrary, you should read the book that focuses on this topic, *Parallel Programming with OmniThreadLibrary* (`www.omnithreadlibrary.com/tutorials.htm`).

I could spend a lot longer discussing parallel programming and parallel patterns. I could fill up a whole book, without doubt. As this is not a book on parallel programming, but a book about high-performance practices, I have to move on to the last topic. In the next chapter, we'll see what we can do if Delphi can't handle something and we have to bring in another compiler.

# 8
# Using External Libraries

We've seen many different ways of improving program speed in this book. We've changed algorithms, reduced the number of memory allocations, fine-tuned the code, made parts of programs parallel, and more. Sometimes, however, all of this is not enough. Maybe the problem is too hard and we give up, or maybe the fault lies in Delphi; more specifically, in the compiler.

In such cases, we will look outside the boundary of a local computer or company, and search the internet for a solution. Maybe, somebody has already solved the problem and created a nicely wrapped solution for it. Sometimes, we'll be able to find it. Most of the time, it will **not** be written with Delphi in mind.

Face it, Delphi programmers (even though there are millions of us) are still a minority in a world of C, Java, and Python. It is much simpler to find a C or C++ solution for hard problems than a Delphi one. This is, however, not a reason to give up. It is always possible—with a bit of hard work—to use such a solution in a Delphi program, even if it is pre-packaged for C or C++ users.

In this chapter, we'll answer the following questions:

- What are the types of C and C++ files that you can use in your projects?
- What are the most frequently used object file formats?
- Which object formats can be used in Delphi projects?
- What traps await you when you try to link object files to Delphi?
- How can you use C++ libraries in Delphi projects?

# Using object files

Before I jump into the complicated world of interfacing with C and C++, I'll introduce a simpler example—a library written in Delphi. The motivation for its use comes not from a bad algorithm that Mr. Smith wrote, but from a badly performing 64-bit compiler. This is not something that I am claiming without proof. Multiple Delphi programmers have pointed out that the 64-bit Windows compiler (dcc64) generates pretty bad floating point code that is 2-3 times slower than the floating point generated from an equivalent source by a C compiler.

When you have already explored all the standard approaches of speeding up the program, and the compiler is the only source of the problem, you cannot do much. You can only rewrite parts of the program in the assembler, or use an external library that works faster than the native code. Such a library will either use lots of assembler code or—most of the time—contain a bunch of object files compiled with an optimizing C compiler.

Sometimes, such an external library will only cover your basic needs. For example, the FastMath library, which is written in Delphi (https://github.com/neslib/FastMath) contains floating-point functions that operate on vectors and matrices. Others, such as *Intel's Math Kernel Library* (https://software.intel.com/en-us/mkl/) also add more complicated mathematical algorithms, such as Fast Fourier Transform.

For a short example, let's look into FastMath and how it implements a Radians function that converts a vector of four floating-point numbers (TVector4) from degrees to radians. For your convenience, the copy of the FastMath repository is included in the code archive for this chapter, in the FastMath-master folder.

As a fallback, the library implements a pure Pascal Radians function in the Neslib.FastMath.Pascal.inc file. The trivial implementation shown in the following, only calls the Radians function for a single-precision argument four times:

```
function Radians(const ADegrees: Single): Single;
begin
  Result := ADegrees * (Pi / 180);
end;

function Radians(const ADegrees: TVector4): TVector4;
begin
  Result.Init(Radians(ADegrees.X), Radians(ADegrees.Y),
    Radians(ADegrees.Z), Radians(ADegrees.W));
end;
```

A different implementation in unit `Neslib.FastMath.Sse2_32.inc` (shown in the following) implements the same method with much faster Intel SSE2 assembler instructions. A similar code in `Neslib.FastMath.Sse2_64.inc` (which is not shown in the book but can be found in the `FastMath` folder in the code archive) does the same for a 64-bit Intel target:

```
function Radians(const ADegrees: TVector4): TVector4; assembler;
asm
  movups xmm0, [ADegrees]
  movups xmm1, [SSE_PI_OVER_180]
  mulps xmm0, xmm1
  movups [Result], xmm0
end;
```

For ARM platforms (Android and iOS) the same code is implemented in `trig_32.S` (and `trig_64.S` for 64-bit platforms). A fragment of that file showing 32-bit implementation is reproduced in the following:

```
_radians_vector4: // (const ADegrees: TVector4; out Result: TVector4);
  adr r2, PI_OVER_180
  vld1.32 {q0}, [r0]
  vld1.32 {q1}, [r2]
  vmul.f32 q0, q0, q1
  vst1.32 {q0}, [r1]
  bx lr
```

The batch files in `fastmath-android` and `fastmath-ios` folders use native development tools, made by Google and Apple, to compile assembler sources into the object libraries, `libfastmath-android.a` and `libfastmath-ios.a`. Functions are then linked to this library in the `Neslib.FastMath.Internal.inc` unit with a mechanism that we'll explore in the continuation of this chapter.

A simple series of `$IF`/`$INCLUDE` statements then links those include files in one unit, `Neslib.FastMath.pas`:

```
{$IF Defined(FM_PASCAL)}
// Pascal implementations
{$INCLUDE 'Neslib.FastMath.Pascal.inc'}
{$ELSEIF Defined(FM_X86)}
// 32-bit SSE2 implementations
{$INCLUDE 'Neslib.FastMath.Sse2_32.inc'}
{$ELSEIF Defined(FM_X64)}
// 64-bit SSE2 implementations
{$INCLUDE 'Neslib.FastMath.Sse2_64.inc'}
{$ELSEIF Defined(FM_ARM)}
```

```
// Arm NEON/Arm64 implementations
{$INCLUDE 'Neslib.FastMath.Arm.inc'}
{$ENDIF}
```

This design allows the library to present a unified application interface that uses the best implementation for each platform to your Delphi application.

In this case, the implementation is linked against a static library (.a). This will not be the case when trying to include a C-specific solution in a Delphi project. You'll have a bunch of object files (.obj, .o) instead.

Object files are a complicated topic, as there is not a single standard governing them, but a bunch of competing specifications. Before we start using them in Delphi, we should therefore have at least some understanding of what is encountered in the wild.

# Object file formats

Object files come in different formats and not all are useful for linking with Delphi. The three most common file formats that you'll encounter are *OMF*, *COFF*, and *ELF*.

The **Relocatable Object Module Format** (**OMF**) is a format developed by Intel. It was extensively used in DOS times. Support for linking OMF object files was already included in Turbo Pascal DOS compilers and is still present in modern Delphi.

 This format can be linked with Delphi's Win32 and compilers. It is generated by the C++Builder's Win32 compiler (bcc32).

To analyze an OMF file you can use the tdump utility (part of the Delphi and C++Builder standard installation) with the -d switch. A command such as tdump -d object_file.obj will output a bunch of information about the OMF file. It is best if you *redirect* this output into a file by using the command-line redirect functionality. For example, you can type tdump -d object_file.obj > object_file.txt to redirect the output to object_file.txt.

Once you have the file, search for entries with labels PUBDEF or PUBD32 to find names of exported functions. You can also use the command-line parameter -oiPUBDEF (or -oiPUBD32) to limit output to PUBDEF (PUBD32) records.

The following output shows the results of the command `tdump -d -oiPUBDeF` `LzmaDec.obj`. The file, `LzmaDec.obj` is part of the code archive for this chapter and will be used as an example in the next section. We can see that this object file contains the functions, `LzmaDec_InitDicAndState`, `LzmaDec_Init`, and so on. These functions can, with some work, be used from a Delphi program:

```
Turbo Dump Version 6.5.4.0 Copyright (c) 1988-2016 Embarcadero
Technologies, Inc.
Display of File lzmadec.obj
002394 PUBDEF 'LzmaDec_InitDicAndState' Segment: _TEXT:172E
0023B5 PUBDEF 'LzmaDec_Init' Segment: _TEXT:176B
0023CB PUBDEF 'LzmaDec_DecodeToDic' Segment: _TEXT:17D2
0023E8 PUBDEF 'LzmaDec_DecodeToBuf' Segment: _TEXT:1A6E
002405 PUBDEF 'LzmaDec_FreeProbs' Segment: _TEXT:1B40
002420 PUBDEF 'LzmaDec_Free' Segment: _TEXT:1B78
002436 PUBDEF 'LzmaProps_Decode' Segment: _TEXT:1B9B
002450 PUBDEF 'LzmaDec_AllocateProbs' Segment: _TEXT:1C9A
00246F PUBDEF 'LzmaDec_Allocate' Segment: _TEXT:1CE5
002489 PUBDEF 'LzmaDecode' Segment: _TEXT:1D6D
```

The second file format that you'll frequently encounter is **Common Object File Format (COFF)**. It was introduced in *Unix System V* and is generated by Microsoft's Visual C++ compilers. Delphi Win32 and Win64 compilers can link to it.

To dump this file, use Embarcadero's `tdump` with the `-E` switch, or Microsoft's `dumpbin` utility, which is part of Visual Studio.

The third most popular object format is **Executable and Linkable Format (ELF)**. It is mostly used on Unix platforms. This format is used in the *LLVM* compiler infrastructure and as such, is supported by some Delphi and C++Builder compilers—namely the ones that use the LLVM toolchain. This file format is not supported by the `tdump` utility.

ELF format is not supported by current Win32 and Win64 Delphi compilers. Usually, that would not present a big problem, except that the Win64 C++Builder compiler (bcc64) uses the LLVM infrastructure and therefore generates object files in ELF format. As far as I can tell, there's currently no way to use the C++Builder to generate 64-bit object files that can be linked to Delphi.

# Object file linking in practice

To demonstrate some typical problems that you may run into when trying to link object files to Delphi, I picked two simple examples from the *Abbrevia* open source library. Abbrevia was originally a commercial compression library developed by TurboPower. They were selling multiple libraries—AsyncPro, Orpheus, and SysTools, which were later donated to the open source community. Their current home is at `https://github.com/TurboPack`.

For simplicity, I have included the complete Abbrevia repository in the code archive. All demos are already configured so you can just press *F9* in Delphi and enjoy.

The first demo is called `LzmaDecTest` and it links in a single object file—`LzmaDec.obj`. That file is stored in the `Abbrevia\source\Win32` folder (or `Win64` if you are compiling for 64-bit Windows). This demo is a standard Windows console application with one additional line linking the object file:

```
{$L LzmaDec.obj}
```

If you try to compile the test project, you'll notice that compilation fails with the following error message:

```
[dcc32 Error] LzmaDecTest.dpr(22): E2065 Unsatisfied forward or external
declaration: 'memcpy'
```

This happens a lot when linking object files created with C compilers. An object file can contain references to functions that are not implemented inside the object file. The same situation happens with Delphi—a `.dcu` file can (and most probably will) contain references to methods implemented in different units.

An experienced programmer will try to minimize these dependencies when writing a library, simply because that helps with portability, but there are always some basic functions that are necessary in almost all C programs. Think of the Delphi's *System unit*—all units in your program implicitly depend on it and most of the time you are not aware of that (and you don't have to be). Most of the object files that you'll have to link to will be compiled with Microsoft's C compiler, and typically they will depend on a `msvcrt` library.

There are two ways out of this problem. Firstly, you can write the missing functions yourself. They are implemented by the `MSVCRT.DLL` dynamic library and you only have to link to them.

For example, in our case we would need the missing `memcpy` function. We can simply import it from the appropriate DLL by adding the following line to the program. We would also have to add the `Windows` unit to the `uses` list as the `size_t` type is defined in it:

```
function memcpy(dest, src: Pointer; count: size_t): Pointer; cdecl;
  external 'msvcrt.dll';
```

Alternatively, we can just add the `System.Win.Crtl` unit to the `uses` list. It links to all functions from the `MSVCRT.DLL` dynamic library.

Be aware though, `MSVCRT.DLL` is not part of the operating system. If you want to distribute an application that links to this DLL, you should also include the *Microsoft Visual C++ Redistributable* package, which you can download from the Microsoft web server.

For the second demo, I wanted to link to the `decompress.obj` file, which is also part of Abbrevia and is stored in the same folder as `LzmaDec.obj`. This demo is named `DecompressTest`.

Again, I started with an empty console application to which I added `{$LINK decompress.obj}`. (`{$L}` and `${LINK}` are synonyms.) The compiler reported four errors:

```
[dcc32 Error] DecompressTest.dpr(45): E2065 Unsatisfied forward or external
declaration: 'BZ2_rNums'
[dcc32 Error] DecompressTest.dpr(45): E2065 Unsatisfied forward or external
declaration: 'BZ2_hbCreateDecodeTables'
[dcc32 Error] DecompressTest.dpr(45): E2065 Unsatisfied forward or external
declaration: 'BZ2_indexIntoF'
[dcc32 Error] DecompressTest.dpr(45): E2065 Unsatisfied forward or external
declaration: 'bz_internal_error'
```

To fix such problems, you'll always have to use the documentation that comes with the object files. There's no way to know what those symbols represent simply by looking at the object file. In this case, I found out that the first is an initialization table (so the symbol is actually a name of a global variable). The second and third functions are implemented in other object files, and the last one is an error handling function that we have to implement in the code. Adding the following code fragment to the file left me with two errors:

```
var
  BZ2_rNums: array[0..511] of Longint;

procedure bz_internal_error(errcode: Integer); cdecl;
begin
  raise Exception.CreateFmt('Compression Error %d', [errcode]);
end;
```

Take note of the calling convention used here. C object files will almost invariably use the `cdecl` convention.

To find the object files with missing functions, you can use a full-text search tool that handles binary files, and search for missing names. This will give you false positives as it will also return object files that are *using* those functions. You can then use the `tdump` utility to examine potential candidates and find the true source of those units.

Or, you can look into the documentation. But who does that?

I found `BZ2_hbCreateDecodeTables` in `huffman.obj` and `BZ2_indexIntoF` in `bzlib.obj`. Only two lines are needed to add them to the project:

```
{$LINK huffman.obj}
{$LINK bzlib.obj}
```

That fixes the two errors about missing symbols but introduces three new errors:

```
[dcc32 Error] DecompressTest.dpr(40): E2065 Unsatisfied forward or external
declaration: 'BZ2_crc32Table'
 [dcc32 Error] DecompressTest.dpr(40): E2065 Unsatisfied forward or
external declaration: 'BZ2_compressBlock'
 [dcc32 Error] DecompressTest.dpr(40): E2065 Unsatisfied forward or
external declaration: 'BZ2_decompress'
```

`BZ2_crc32Table` is an initialization table (says the documentation) so we need another variable:

```
var
  BZ2_crc32Table: array[0..255] of Longint;
```

Further detective work found `BZ2_compressBlock` in the file `compress.obj`, so let's add this to the project. We only have to add one line:

```
{$LINK compress.obj}
```

The second error is trickier. Research showed that this function is actually implemented in the `decompress.obj` unit, which is already linked to the project! Why is the error reported then? Simply because that's how the single-pass Delphi compiler works.

As it turns out, the compiler will happily resolve symbols used by object file *A* if they are defined in object file *B*, which is loaded **after** file *A*. It will, however, **not** resolve symbols used by object file *B* if they are defined in object file *A*.

In our case, the `compress.obj` file needs the `BZ2_decompress` symbol, which is defined in `decompress.obj`, but as the latter is linked **before** the former, we get the error. You could try rearranging the units but then some other symbol will not be found.

Luckily, this problem is very simple to fix. We just have to tell the compiler that `BZ2_decompress` exists. The compiler is happy with that and produces workable code. When all units are compiled, *linker* kicks in to collect them in the EXE file. Linker is smarter than the compiler and finds the correct implementation, regardless of the include order.

If we add the following line to the code, the error about *unsatisfied* `BZ2_decompress` *declaration* goes away. I also like putting in a comment that marks the source of the function:

```
procedure BZ2_decompress; external; //decompress.obj
```

Linking `compress.obj` causes three new errors to appear:

```
[dcc32 Error] DecompressTest.dpr(45): E2065 Unsatisfied forward or external
declaration: 'BZ2_hbMakeCodeLengths'
[dcc32 Error] DecompressTest.dpr(45): E2065 Unsatisfied forward or external
declaration: 'BZ2_hbAssignCodes'
[dcc32 Error] DecompressTest.dpr(45): E2065 Unsatisfied forward or external
declaration: 'BZ2_blockSort'
```

The first two are defined in `huffman.obj`, which is already linked, so we have to add the following two lines to the code:

```
procedure BZ2_hbMakeCodeLengths; external; //huffman.obj
procedure BZ2_hbAssignCodes; external;     //huffman.obj
```

The last one comes from `blocksort.obj`, which we have yet to link in. After that, the code finally compiles:

```
{$LINK blocksort.obj}
```

This is, of course, just the first step toward a working program. Now we have to check how functions exported from these object files are actually defined. Then, we have to add appropriate `external` declarations to the Delphi source.

If we look at the previous example, `LzmaDecTest`, we can implement functions to initialize and free the decoder by adding the following two lines:

```
procedure LzmaDec_Init(var state); cdecl; external;
procedure LzmaDec_Free(var state; alloc: pointer); cdecl; external;
```

This declaration is actually incomplete, as the first parameter to both functions should be a complicated record, which I didn't want to try to decipher just for this simple demo. Rather than do that (and a whole lotta additional work), I would use the already-prepared Abbrevia library.

By now, you've probably noticed that linking in object files is hard work. If at all possible, you should try to find a Delphi (or at least a Free Pascal) wrapper. Even if it covers only a part of the functionality you need, it will spare you hours and hours of work.

# Using C++ libraries

Using C object files in Delphi is hard but possible. Linking to C++ object files is, however, nearly impossible. The problem does not lie within the object files themselves, but in C++.

While C is hardly more than an assembler with improved syntax, C++ represents a sophisticated high-level language with runtime support for strings, objects, exceptions, and more. All these features are part of almost any C++ program and are as such compiled into (almost) any object file produced by C++.

The problem here is that Delphi has no idea how to deal with any of that. A C++ object is not equal to a Delphi object. Delphi has no idea how to call functions of a C++ object, how to deal with its inheritance chain, how to create and destroy such objects, and so on. The same holds for strings, exceptions, streams, and other C++ concepts.

If you can compile the C++ source with C++Builder then you can create a package (`.bpl`) that can be used from a Delphi program. Most of the time, however, you will not be dealing with a source project. Instead, you'll want to use a commercial library that only gives you a bunch of C++ header files (`.h`) and one or more static libraries (`.lib`). Most of the time, the only Windows version of that library will be compiled with Microsoft's Visual Studio.

A more general approach to this problem is to introduce a *proxy* DLL created in C++. You will have to create it in the same development environment as was used to create the library you are trying to link into the project. On Windows, that will in most cases be Visual Studio. That will enable us to include the library without any problems.

To allow Delphi to use this DLL (and as such use the library), the DLL should expose a simple interface in the Windows API style. Instead of exposing C++ objects, the API must expose methods implemented by the objects as normal (non-object) functions and procedures. As the objects cannot cross the API boundary we must find some other way to represent them on the Delphi side.

Instead of showing how to write a DLL wrapper for an existing (and probably quite complicated) C++ library, I have decided to write a very simple C++ library that exposes a single class, implementing only two methods. As compiling this library requires Microsoft's Visual Studio, which not all of you have installed, I have also included the compiled version (DllLib1.dll) in the code archive.

The Visual Studio solution is stored in the StaticLib1 folder and contains two projects. StaticLib1 is the project used to create the library while the Dll1 project implements the proxy DLL.

The static library implements the CppClass class, which is defined in the header file, CppClass.h. Whenever you are dealing with a C++ library, the distribution will also contain one or more header files. They are needed if you want to use a library in a C++ project—such as in the proxy DLL Dll1.

The header file for the demo library StaticLib1 is shown in the following. We can see that the code implements a single CppClass class, which implements a constructor (CppClass()), destructor (~CppClass()), a method accepting an integer parameter (void setData(int)), and a function returning an integer (int getSquare()). The class also contains one integer private field, data:

```
#pragma once
class CppClass
{
    int data;
public:
    CppClass();
    ~CppClass();
    void setData(int);
    int getSquare();
};
```

The implementation of the CppClass class is stored in the CppClass.cpp file. You don't need this file when implementing the proxy DLL. When we are using a C++ library, we are strictly coding to the interface—and the interface is stored in the header file.

In our case, we have the full source so we can look inside the implementation too. The constructor and destructor don't do anything and so I'm not showing them here. The other two methods are as follows. The setData method stores its parameter in the internal field and the getSquare function returns the squared value of the internal field:

```
void CppClass::setData(int value)
{
    data = value;
```

```
}

int CppClass::getSquare()
{
  return data * data;
}
```

This code doesn't contain anything that we couldn't write in 60 seconds in Delphi. It does, however, serve as a perfect simple example for writing a proxy DLL.

Creating such a DLL in Visual Studio is easy. You just have to select **File** | **New** | **Project**, and select the **Dynamic-Link Library (DLL)** project type from the **Visual C++** | **Windows Desktop** branch.

The Dll1 project from the code archive has only two source files. The file, dllmain.cpp was created automatically by Visual Studio and contains the standard DllMain method. You can change this file if you have to run project-specific code when a program and/or a thread attaches to, or detaches from, the DLL. In my example, this file was left just as the Visual Studio created it.

The second file, StaticLibWrapper.cpp fully implements the proxy DLL. It starts with two include lines (shown in the following) which bring in the required RTL header stdafx.h and the header definition for our C++ class, CppClass.h:

```
#include "stdafx.h"
#include "CppClass.h"
```

The proxy has to be able to find our header file. There are two ways to do that. We could simply copy it to the folder containing the source files for the DLL project, or we can add it to the project's search path. The second approach can be configured in **Project** | **Properties** | **Configuration Properties** | **C/C++** | **General** | **Additional Include Directories**. This is also the approach used by the demonstration program.

The DLL project must be able to find the static library that implements the CppClass object. The path to the library file should be set in project options, in the **Configuration Properties** | **Linker** | **General** | **Additional Library Directories** settings. You should put the name of the library (StaticLib1.lib) in the **Linker** | **Input** | **Additional Dependencies** settings.

The next line in the source file defines a macro called EXPORT, which will be used later in the program to mark a function as *exported*. We have to do that for every DLL function that we want to use from the Delphi code. Later, we'll see how this macro is used:

```
#define EXPORT comment(linker, "/EXPORT:" __FUNCTION__ "=" __FUNCDNAME__)
```

The next part of the StaticLibWrapper.cpp file implements an IndexAllocator class, which is used internally to cache C++ objects. It associates C++ objects with simple integer identifiers, which are then used outside the DLL to represent the object. I will not show this class in the book as the implementation is not that important. You only have to know how to use it.

This class is implemented as a simple static array of pointers and contains at most MAXOBJECTS objects. The constant MAXOBJECTS is set to 100 in the current code, which limits the number of C++ objects created by the Delphi code to *100*. Feel free to modify the code if you need to create more objects.

The following code fragment shows three public functions implemented by the IndexAllocator class. The Allocate function takes a pointer obj, stores it in the cache, and returns its index in the deviceIndex parameter. The result of the function is FALSE if the cache is full and TRUE otherwise.

The Release function accepts an index (which was previously returned from Allocate) and marks the cache slot at that index as empty. This function returns FALSE if the index is invalid (does not represent a value returned from Allocate) or if the cache slot for that index is already empty.

The last function, Get, also accepts an index and returns the pointer associated with that index. It returns NULL if the index is invalid or if the cache slot for that index is empty:

```
bool Allocate(int& deviceIndex, void* obj)
bool Release(int deviceIndex)
void* Get(int deviceIndex)
```

Let's move now to functions that are exported from the DLL. The first two—Initialize and Finalize—are used to initialize internal structures, namely the GAllocator of type IndexAllocator and to clean up before the DLL is unloaded. Instead of looking into them, I'd rather show you the more interesting stuff, namely functions that deal with CppClass.

The CreateCppClass function creates an instance of CppClass, stores it in the cache, and returns its index. The important three parts of the declaration are: extern "C", WINAPI, and #pragma EXPORT.

`extern "C"` is there to guarantee that `CreateCppClass` name will not be changed when it is stored in the library. The C++ compiler tends to *mangle* (change) function names to support method overloading (the same thing happens in Delphi) and this declaration prevents that.

`WINAPI` changes the *calling convention* from `cdecl`, which is standard for C programs, to `stdcall`, which is commonly used in DLLs. Later, we'll see that we also have to specify the correct calling convention on the Delphi side.

The last important part, `#pragma EXPORT`, uses the previously defined `EXPORT` macro to mark this function as *exported*.

The `CreateCppClass` returns *0* if the operation was successful and −1 if it failed. The same approach is used in all functions exported from the demo DLL:

```
extern "C" int WINAPI CreateCppClass (int& index)
{
#pragma EXPORT
  CppClass* instance = new CppClass;
  if (!GAllocator->Allocate(index, (void*)instance)) {
    delete instance;
    return -1;
  }
  else
    return 0;
}
```

Similarly, the `DestroyCppClass` function (not shown here) accepts an index parameter, fetches the object from the cache, and destroys it.

The DLL also exports two functions that allow the DLL user to operate on an object. The first one, `CppClass_setValue`, accepts an index of the object and a value. It fetches the `CppClass` instance from the cache (given the index) and calls its `setData` method, passing it the value:

```
extern "C" int WINAPI CppClass_setValue(int index, int value)
{
#pragma EXPORT
  CppClass* instance = (CppClass*)GAllocator->Get(index);
  if (instance == NULL)
    return -1;
  else {
    instance->setData(value);
    return 0;
  }
```

```
}
```

The second function, CppClass_getSquare also accepts an object index and uses it to access the CppClass object. After that, it calls the object's getSquare function and stores the result in the output parameter, value:

```
extern "C" int WINAPI CppClass_getSquare(int index, int& value)
{
#pragma EXPORT
  CppClass* instance = (CppClass*)GAllocator->Get(index);
  if (instance == NULL)
    return -1;
  else {
    value = instance->getSquare();
    return 0;
  }
}
```

A proxy DLL that uses a mapping table is a bit complicated and requires some work. We could also approach the problem in a much simpler manner—by treating an address of an object as its external identifier. In other words, the CreateCppClass function would create an object and then return its address as an untyped pointer type. A CppClass_getSquare, for example, would accept this pointer, cast it to a CppClass instance, and execute an operation on it. An alternative version of these two methods is shown in the following:

```
extern "C" int WINAPI CreateCppClass2(void*& ptr)
{
#pragma EXPORT
  ptr = new CppClass;
  return 0;
}

extern "C" int WINAPI CppClass_getSquare2(void* index, int& value)
{
#pragma EXPORT
  value = ((CppClass*)index)->getSquare();
  return 0;
}
```

This approach is simpler but offers far less security in the form of error checking. The table-based approach can check whether the index represents a valid value, while the latter version cannot know if the pointer parameter is valid or not. If we make a mistake on the Delphi side and pass in an invalid pointer, the code would treat it as an instance of a class, do some operations on it, possibly corrupt some memory, and maybe crash.

Finding the source of such errors is very hard. That's why I prefer to write more verbose code that implements some safety checks on the code that returns pointers.

# Using a proxy DLL in Delphi

To use any DLL from a Delphi program, we must firstly import functions from the DLL. There are different ways to do this—we could use *static* linking, *dynamic* linking, and static linking with *delayed loading*. There's plenty of information on the internet about the art of DLL writing in Delphi so I won't dig into this topic. I'll just stick with the most modern approach—delay loading.

The code archive for this book includes two demo programs, which demonstrate how to use the `DllLib1.dll` library. The simpler one, `CppClassImportDemo` uses the DLL functions directly, while `CppClassWrapperDemo` wraps them in an easy-to-use class.

Both projects use the `CppClassImport` unit to import the DLL functions into the Delphi program. The following code fragment shows the `interface` part of that unit which tells the Delphi compiler which functions from the DLL should be imported, and what parameters they have.

As with the C++ part, there are three important parts to each declaration. Firstly, the `stdcall` specifies that the function call should use the `stdcall` (or what is known in C as `WINAPI`) calling convention. Secondly, the name after the `name` specifier should match the exported function name from the C++ source. And thirdly, the `delayed` keyword specifies that the program should not try to find this function in the DLL when it is started but only when the code calls the function. This allows us to check whether the DLL is present at all before we call any of the functions:

```
const
  CPP_CLASS_LIB = 'DllLib1.dll';

function Initialize: integer;
  stdcall; external CPP_CLASS_LIB name 'Initialize' delayed;
function Finalize: integer;
  stdcall; external CPP_CLASS_LIB name 'Finalize' delayed;
function CreateCppClass(var index: integer): integer;
  stdcall; external CPP_CLASS_LIB name 'CreateCppClass' delayed;
function DestroyCppClass(index: integer): integer;
  stdcall; external CPP_CLASS_LIB name 'DestroyCppClass' delayed;
function CppClass_setValue(index: integer; value: integer): integer;
  stdcall; external CPP_CLASS_LIB name 'CppClass_setValue' delayed;
function CppClass_getSquare(index: integer; var value: integer): integer;
  stdcall; external CPP_CLASS_LIB name 'CppClass_getSquare' delayed;
```

The `implementation` part of this unit (not shown here) shows how to catch errors that occur during *delayed loading*—that is, when the code that calls any of the imported functions tries to find that function in the DLL.

> If you get an `External exception C06D007F` exception when you try to call a delay-loaded function, you have probably mistyped a name—either in C++ or in Delphi. You can use the `tdump` utility that comes with Delphi to check which names are exported from the DLL. The syntax is `tdump -d <dll_name.dll>`.
>
> If the code crashes when you call a DLL function, check whether both sides correctly define the calling convention. Also check if all the parameters have correct types on both sides and if the `var` parameters are marked as such on both sides.

To use the DLL, the code in the `CppClassMain` unit firstly calls the exported `Initialize` function from the form's `OnCreate` handler to initialize the DLL. The cleanup function, `Finalize` is called from the `OnDestroy` handler to clean up the DLL. All parts of the code check whether the DLL functions return the `OK` status (value 0):

```
procedure TfrmCppClassDemo.FormCreate(Sender: TObject);
begin
  if Initialize <> 0 then
    ListBox1.Items.Add('Initialize failed')
end;

procedure TfrmCppClassDemo.FormDestroy(Sender: TObject);
begin
  if Finalize <> 0 then
    ListBox1.Items.Add('Finalize failed');
end;
```

When you click on the **Use import library** button, the following code executes. It uses the DLL to create a `CppClass` object by calling the `CreateCppClass` function. This function puts an integer value into the `idxClass` value. This value is used as an identifier that identifies a `CppClass` object when calling other functions.

The code then calls `CppClass_setValue` to set the internal field of the `CppClass` object and `CppClass_getSquare` to call the `getSquare` method and to return the calculated value. At the end, `DestroyCppClass` destroys the `CppClass` object:

```
procedure TfrmCppClassDemo.btnImportLibClick(Sender: TObject);
var
```

```
    idxClass: Integer;
    value: Integer;
  begin
    if CreateCppClass(idxClass) <> 0 then
      ListBox1.Items.Add('CreateCppClass failed')
    else if CppClass_setValue(idxClass, SpinEdit1.Value) <> 0 then
      ListBox1.Items.Add('CppClass_setValue failed')
    else if CppClass_getSquare(idxClass, value) <> 0 then
      ListBox1.Items.Add('CppClass_getSquare failed')
    else begin
      ListBox1.Items.Add(Format('square(%d) = %d',
        [SpinEdit1.Value, value]));
      if DestroyCppClass(idxClass) <> 0 then
        ListBox1.Items.Add('DestroyCppClass failed')
    end;
  end;
```

This approach is relatively simple but long-winded and error-prone. A better way is to write a wrapper Delphi class that implements the same public interface as the corresponding C++ class. The second demo, `CppClassWrapperDemo` contains a unit `CppClassWrapper` which does just that.

This unit implements a `TCppClass` class, which maps to its C++ counterpart. It only has one internal field, which stores the index of the C++ object as returned from the `CreateCppClass` function:

```
type
  TCppClass = class
  strict private
    FIndex: integer;
  public
    class procedure InitializeWrapper;
    class procedure FinalizeWrapper;
    constructor Create;
    destructor Destroy; override;
    procedure SetValue(value: integer);
    function GetSquare: integer;
  end;
```

I won't show all of the functions here as they are all equally simple. One—or maybe two—will suffice.

The constructor just calls the `CreateCppClass` function, checks the result, and stores the resulting index in the internal field:

```
constructor TCppClass.Create;
begin
  inherited Create;
  if CreateCppClass(FIndex) <> 0 then
    raise Exception.Create('CreateCppClass failed');
end;
```

Similarly, `GetSquare` just forwards its job to the `CppClass_getSquare` function:

```
function TCppClass.GetSquare: integer;
begin
  if CppClass_getSquare(FIndex, Result) <> 0 then
    raise Exception.Create('CppClass_getSquare failed');
end;
```

When we have this wrapper, the code in the main unit becomes very simple—and very Delphi-like. Once the initialization in the `OnCreate` event handler is done, we can just create an instance of the `TCppClass` and work with it:

```
procedure TfrmCppClassDemo.FormCreate(Sender: TObject);
begin
  TCppClass.InitializeWrapper;
end;

procedure TfrmCppClassDemo.FormDestroy(Sender: TObject);
begin
  TCppClass.FinalizeWrapper;
end;

procedure TfrmCppClassDemo.btnWrapClick(Sender: TObject);
var
  cpp: TCppClass;
begin
  cpp := TCppClass.Create;
  try
    cpp.SetValue(SpinEdit1.Value);
    ListBox1.Items.Add(Format('square(%d) = %d',
      [SpinEdit1.Value, cpp.GetSquare]));
  finally
    FreeAndNil(cpp);
  end;
end;
```

# Summary

I would be the first to admit that this chapter presents only sketches of ideas rather than fully reusable solutions. That is a direct consequence of the topic, which is too open to give definite answers. Rather than that, I have tried to give you enough information to do your own research on the topic.

The chapter started with a discussion of the possible reasons for including external libraries in your application. They may cover a topic you are unfamiliar with, or they may implement some specific algorithm faster than you are able to—or faster than the Delphi compiler can do it.

That brought us to the `FastMath` Delphi library, which implements fast functions for working with vectors (series of numbers) and matrices (two-dimensional arrays of numbers). This library uses an assembler intermixed with Pascal to give you the best performance in each case. We saw how assembler code is sometimes included internally and sometimes as an external file, and how a unified front is built on top of that.

After that, I took a short detour and inspected most of the popular types of object files that you'll encounter in your work. Object files are frequently used when linking C code with Delphi and it is good to know what you can run into.

I followed up with a longer example on how to link C object files with Delphi, and what problems you can encounter. We saw how to replace the standard Microsoft C library, `msvcrt` with a Delphi equivalent, how to write Delphi functions that plug a hole expected by the object file, and how to include multiple files that use each other in a circular fashion.

Then I moved from C to C++. This is currently the most popular Windows development tool and you'll find it used in most open source and commercial libraries. I explained why we cannot use C++ directly in Delphi applications and how to work around that.

The chapter ended with a practical demonstration that linked a very simple C++ library through a proxy DLL written in C++ to a Delphi application. I looked into two different ways of implementing a proxy DLL and into two ways of using this DLL in a Delphi application.

Linking to C and C++ code is hard and certainly not for everyone, but in critical situations it can save your skin.

The long and winding path that has led you through the many different topics in this book is coming to an end. There's only two things left: to take a deep breath and get some R&R. The next chapter will take care of that. Instead of introducing new topics, it will return to the beginning. In it, I'll revisit the most important topics of the book to help you *relax* and *remember*.

# 9
# Best Practices

This book has covered lots of different topics. I believe that, right now, it has all become a big mess from which you can only remember bits and pieces. I know *I* can't handle it all in my head at this moment. There's just too much information packed inside.

To help you remember as much as possible, this last chapter will revisit all the topics of the book, chapter by chapter. I'll repeat the most important ideas from each chapter, while you can just relax and remember all the details. For good measure, I'll throw in some additional tips, tricks, and techniques that didn't find a place in the "regular" chapters.

## About performance

As I stated in the opening statement of this book—performance matters. But what exactly is performance? What do we mean when we use this word? Sometimes we just want to say that the program runs so fast that the users don't detect any delays. We can say that the program is not *lagging* and that the user interface does not *block*. In other situations, *performance* means that a program finishes its execution quickly, or that a server can handle a large number of clients.

Knowing what we mean when we use the word will help us determine the best way to fix the problem. Whatever the approach will be, we still have to find out why the application is not performing as we expect. The original suspect should always be the *algorithm*, and to examine it we need to know more about how algorithms behave.

Algorithms are different in their nature. What we want to know about them when we are designing a program is how they behave when their input set gets larger and larger. Some run in *constant time*, meaning that the size of the data doesn't matter. Accessing array elements behaves in this way. Some are *linear* and have processing time proportional to the size of the input. A typical example is searching in an unordered list. And some are worse. *Exponential* algorithms get slower so quickly that they are completely useless for large input.

The complexity of an algorithm is encompassed by a *big O* notation, which—very simply put—tells you how much slower an algorithm will run when it gets more input to process. We say that (for example) naive sort algorithms, such as Bubble sort, have time complexity of $O(n^2)$. In other words, if we enlarge the input size by a factor of 1000, the execution time will get slower by a factor of a million ($1000^2$).

It is good to know big O complexities for popular algorithms. I have already mentioned array access, searching in unordered lists, and naive sorting algorithms. You should also know that searching in a sorted list (bisection) has a complexity of only $O(log\ n)$, while a good sorting algorithm runs in $O(n\ log\ n)$. These two approaches are **much** faster than $O(n)$ and $O(n^2)$, and `Chapter 1`, *About Performance*, contains a table to prove that.

Good performance starts with using data structures that are appropriate for the job. You should know how standard Delphi structures behave when you are adding or removing elements and when you are trying to locate a specific element. We saw that all *lists* behave more or less the same, and that performance depends on whether you want to keep them sorted (fast lookup) or not (fast element insertion). A special case is a *dictionary*, which executes all operations in $O(1)$ time. It gets that speed increase by forgetting the insertion order and by using lots of memory space—more than is required for just storing the data.

In the chapter itself, I didn't have enough space to discuss another great data structure that is not supported out-of-the-box in Delphi. There's actually a family of related algorithms called *trees*, which don't have the fastest insertion or removal speed, nor are they the fastest at locating data. They are, however, very balanced and do every operation in a reasonable time of $O(log\ n)$. They also keep data in sorted order.

If you want to play with trees, I'd recommend using either GPL'd LibRBTree (`http://www.demonak.com/delphi/rbtree.shtml`) or Spring4D (`https://bitbucket.org/sglienke/spring4d`) which comes with the commercial-friendly Apache License 2.0.

Even if you know how fast or slow the algorithms that your program is using are, you should never just assume that you know which parts of the program are slowing you down. You should always measure the execution speed.

Don't guess, measure!

The simplest way to time parts of a program is to use Delphi's `TStopwatch`. It is useful when you think you know where the problem lies, and want only to confirm your suspicions and (later) verify that the improved solution is indeed faster than the original.

If you don't know exactly which parts of the program are slow, you need to measure with a special tool, a *profiler*. They come in two varieties—*sampling* and *instrumentation*. As always, it is a question of balance. Sampling profilers are fast, but will give you approximate results, while instrumenting profilers are very precise, can generate a *call graph* to show you exactly what goes on inside the program, but make the program run slower.

`Chapter 1`, *About Performance*, describes AsmProfiler, Sampling Profiler, AQTime, and Nexus Quality Suite in more detail. Sadly, I didn't have space to include ProDelphi, which should definitely be on your list of profilers to test.

# Fixing the algorithm

My preferred approach to improving performance is—always—fixing the algorithm. Look at it this way—if we need *1* time unit to process one data item, and the algorithm is $O(n^2)$, we need *10,000* time units to process an input of size *100*. If you fine-tune the code and speed up the operation by 50% (which is an excellent result), the code will need *5000* time units to do the job. If you, however, change the algorithm to $O(n \log n)$, it will need in the order of *1000* time units or less. Even if processing one item takes 100% longer than in the original code, the whole process will run in, say, *2000* time units.

An algorithm with lower complexity will beat an algorithm with higher complexity, even if the latter executes its steps faster.

As it's impossible to give one piece of advice that will fix all your problems, `Chapter 2`, *Fixing the Algorithm*, looked into different user stories. The first topic was about responsive user interfaces. A program's UI can lag or block for different reasons, but the two most common are that some non-visual operations inside the program take too much time, or updating the UI itself causes a problem.

In the latter case, the solution is simple although, sometimes, not obvious at first glance. If updating the UI takes too long, then do less updates. In the chapter, we saw how constant updates to a progress bar can slow down the program, and how we should **always** use `BeginUpdate` / `EndUpdate` when updating more than one line of a listbox or memo.

Another option for speeding up the user interface is to not do anything until the data is visible on the screen. Instead of a standard listbox, we can use its *owner draw* mechanism. Alternatively, we can throw the listbox away and use a *virtual tree* control, `TVirtualStringTree`.

When part of the code takes too long to run, sometimes it is best not to execute it at all. This brings us to the concept of *caching*. If we find out that some values are frequently calculated, we can just store them away in some list, array, or dictionary and not calculate them the next time they are needed. The chapter introduced a size-limited cache component, `TDHPCache<K,V>`, which does everything in *O(1)* time.

The whole concept of caching is also helpful when you are doing lots of repainting of a user interface. Sometimes, you can precalculate some of the display and store it in a bitmap (or multiple bitmaps). Later, you can just paint them on screen, potentially one over another to create layers.

# Fine-tuning the code

When the algorithm is as perfect as it can get, and the program is still not running fast enough, it is time to fine-tune the code. In a process we call *optimization*, we can change the Delphi code so that it will execute in less time, or we can convert it to assembler code. The latter option should be used sparingly, as assembler code is hard to maintain; it also prevents us from compiling to multiple platforms. The last option, which I discussed in `Chapter 8`, *Using External Libraries*, is to replace the code with an external library.

As a first step in fine-tuning the code, you should always check the compiler settings. The most important setting is probably *Optimization*, which can sometimes make a big difference. My recommendation, however, is to disable optimization in the DEBUG version and enable it for RELEASE. Disabling optimization can make a big improvement in the debugging experience.

Another setting that makes a big difference is *Range checking*. Disabling range checking can make accessing array elements significantly faster. As arrays are used in all kinds of places, for example, inside list classes (`TList` and its brethren), this can seriously affect the code. On the other hand, range checking catches the worst kinds of programming errors that could lead to corrupt data and hard-to-find errors. I **always** enable range checking for my code, and then only disable it for small and well-tested parts of code.

 Range checking is disabled by default in a fresh Delphi installation, which is—in my opinion—a big mistake. Always enable range checking, at least in the DEBUG version.

Changing the *Overflow checking* doesn't affect code speed much, but sometimes you'll still want to disable it. This option is enabled by default, which is a good thing.

The chapter also covered the effects of using *Record field alignment*. Surprisingly, it has relatively little effect on the program. Modern CPUs are great when accessing unaligned data, but the biggest difference—on the slow side—is observed when record field alignment is set to 8. That points to the fact that the most important way to speed up operations with a modern CPU is to put as much data in the processor cache as possible.

If you want to write fast code, you should know about Delphi data types and how they behave. Delphi has a plethora of built-in types—in the chapter I enumerated some 40 of them, and I only covered basic types. I covered *simple* types—integers, reals, Booleans, and so on—just briefly, and focused on string, and structured types.

Strings in Delphi are particularly interesting as they can be implemented as statically allocated data (`string[42]`), dynamically allocated data (`WideString`), or dynamically allocated data with reference counting and *copy on write* mechanisms (`string` and `AnsiString`). The latter minimize the amount of operations when assigning a string to a new variable.

Another interesting data type is arrays, especially dynamic ones. The main topic of interest was dynamic arrays, which are reference-counted (just as strings and interfaces) but don't implement the *copy on write* mechanism.

Structured types are also interesting, each in their own way. Records are not initialized by default, except if they contain *managed* data (strings, interfaces, and dynamic arrays). There can be a big speed difference between a record that uses such fields and one that does not. Classes are less interesting as their content is always initialized to zero. Interfaces (and classes on ARC platforms—Android, iOS, and Linux) bring in additional slowdown because of the reference counting mechanism, which makes sure that an interface is destroyed when no one is using it.

Another coding mechanism which affects the execution speed is parameter passing. It can make a difference whether the parameter is marked as var or const or not marked at all. This will greatly affect static arrays and records and—to a lesser extent—strings and interfaces. Interesting things happen when you are passing dynamic arrays to a method, but they are far too weird to explain in a few words. You will have to reread that part of the chapter to experience all the weirdness.

# Memory management

Understanding how built-in data types work also means knowing how Delphi manages the memory for them. It helps if you know at least something about Delphi and memory in general. Admittedly, this is a deep topic; something that most programmers—even excellent programmers—only understand in general terms. In other words, don't worry, you can safely forget 90% of the stuff I told you in Chapter 4, *Memory Management*, and you'll still know enough.

When a Delphi program is running, memory is constantly being allocated, reallocated, and freed. This happens when classes are created and destroyed, when the length of a dynamic array is changed, when strings are modified, lists appended, and so on. If you want your code to perform well, you should be aware of this.

Instead of appending to a string, character by character, you would call SetLength to *preallocate* the target length (or some approximation of it) and then store characters in a string. Dynamic arrays can be handled in a similar manner. Various list classes, such as TList<T>, offer a different way—the SetCapacity method, which preallocates the storage.

Memory can also be managed by calling specialized functions, such as GetMem to get a memory block, ReallocMem to change its size, and FreeMem to release (free) it. Or you can use New to allocate memory and Dispose to release it. These two functions will also correctly initialize/clean up records containing managed fields. Alternatively, you can do it manually by calling Initialize and Finalize.

Memory management functions allow you to dynamically allocate and release records. By using these functions, you can use records instead of classes when you create a myriad of small objects. Records are created and initialized faster because they don't have to use inheritance mechanisms as objects do. It is also possible to dynamically allocate generic records (`TRecord<T>`).

The internal details of the FastMM memory manager—the default Delphi memory manager—are interesting, but most of the time serve no practical purpose. It does, however, help us understand why multithreaded Delphi programs sometimes exhibit bad performance. The reason, surprisingly, lies not in allocating memory but in releasing it. FastMM implements some performance enhancements that help multiple threads allocate memory (for example, create objects) at the same time, but they will have to wait for their turn to have their memory released (objects are destroyed).

Two recent additions to FastMM, contributed by yours truly, help with that. To use any of them, you'll need the latest version from the official repository (`https://github.com/pleriche/FastMM4`) and not the version that comes with Delphi.

Compiling with the `LogLockContention` symbol defined enables a special detection mode that helps you find parts of program that are fighting to access the memory manager. You can think of it as a specialized *profiler*, one that is not interested in execution times, but in memory management.

Alternatively, you can compile your program with the `UseReleaseStack` symbol defined. This will enable a special mode that minimizes the problem of releasing memory. Everything comes with a price; this solution does its magic by using more memory than standard FastMM.

You could also replace the built-in memory manager, which is a simple matter of calling two functions—`GetMemoryManager` and `SetMemoryManager`. One good and tested alternative, written in Delphi and assembler, is ScaleMM (`https://github.com/andremussche/scalemm`). Another good alternative is Intel's TBBMalloc. It is written in C but can be linked to Delphi by using techniques from `Chapter 8`, *Using External Libraries*. The simplest way to use it is to download a compiled version and Delphi wrappers from `https://sites.google.com/site/aminer68/intel-tbbmalloc-interfaces-for-delphi-and-delphi-xe-versions-and-freepascal`.

# Getting started with the parallel world

I mentioned multithreaded programming a lot in the previous chapter, so it is not hard to guess where that path is taking me next. Multithreaded programming, or multithreading, is the art of running multiple parts of your program at the same time.

Multithreading is definitely **not** my first choice for improving existing code. It is hard to write multithreaded programs, and very simple to introduce problems that are then hard to find. Multithreaded programs are also very hard to debug.

To understand multithreading we should first know the processes and threads. In general terms, a process equates to a running program. A process encompasses application code, loaded in memory, and all the resources (memory, files, windows, and so on) used by the program.

A thread, on the other hand, represents a state of the program's execution. A thread is nothing more than the current state of the CPU registers, variables local to the thread (`threadvar` statement introduces them), and the stack belonging to this thread. (Actually, the stack is part of the process' memory, and the thread only owns the *stack pointer* register.)

Every process starts with one thread that makes the process execute. We call it a *main thread*. Additional threads that are created from the code are called *background threads*.

I said before and I'll repeat it here—adding multithreading to your code can create more problems than it is worth. That's why you should know about the problems before you learn how to do multithreading.

The first rule in Delphi is always: *Never access the UI from a background thread.* This is so important that I'll repeat it again.

 Never access the user interface from a background thread!

If the code is running in a background thread, and definitely needs to access the user interface, you have to use mechanisms that take a part of the code (an anonymous method) and execute it in the main thread. I'm talking about `TThread.Synchronize` and `TThread.Queue`.

The next problem appears when two threads are accessing the same data structure at the same time. It is not really surprising that you should not read from a TList when another thread is deleting elements from the same list, but it may shock you to know that problems can also appear when one thread is reading from a simple int64 variable while another thread is writing to it.

Don't think that the first example (simultaneous access to a list) is purely theoretical. I recently fixed a similar example in my code (yes, it happens to the best of us). One thread was reading from a TFileStream and sending data to a web server. Another thread calculated the progress, and in that calculation called the TFileStream.Size function (they were different threads because I was using the asynchronous mode of the WinHTTP API). In my defense, I know very well that it is not a good idea, but, well, mistakes happen.

What's the problem with calling Size? Its implementation. When you read from Size, the GetSize method (shown following) calls Seek three times. Imagine what happened when one thread read from a stream and another changed the current position at the same time:

```
function TStream.GetSize: Int64;
var
  Pos: Int64;
begin
  Pos := Seek(0, soCurrent);
  Result := Seek(0, soEnd);
  Seek(Pos, soBeginning);
end;
```

To solve such issues, we typically introduce *locking*. This technique creates a sort of barrier that allows only one thread at a time to enter a critical path through the code. *Critical sections* are the standard locking mechanism, but we can also use *mutexes* and *semaphores*, although both are slow and more useful when synchronizing multiple processes.

Delphi also offers two mechanisms that are slightly faster than critical sections—TMonitor and TSpinLock. In situations when threads are mostly reading from shared data and rarely writing to it, the badly-named TMultiReadExclusiveWriteSynchronizer can be used. You can also refer to it with an alias, which is much simpler to type—TMREWSync. It's just too bad that the implementation of this mechanism is terribly slow and that pure critical sections typically operate faster.

When you need to use locking, you should use TMonitor or TSpinlock.

Locking techniques introduce at least two problems to the program. They lead to slower operations, and they can result in *deadlocks* when improperly used. In a deadlocked program, one thread is waiting on another thread, which is waiting on the first one, and all operation stops.

An alternative to locking is *interlocked* (atomic) operations. They are faster than locking but only support a small range of operations—incrementing and decrementing a memory location, modifying a memory location, and *conditionally* modifying a memory location.

The latest variation, `TInterlocked.CompareExchange`, can be used to implement *optimistic initialization*. This mechanism can be used to safely create a shared object or interface. The latter is preferred as it will be safely destroyed at the right time.

Instead of using one of the synchronization techniques described previously, you can introduce *communication* mechanisms to the program. Instead of accessing a shared value, you can use *data duplication* (sending a copy of full or partial input data to each worker thread) and *aggregation* (putting partial results calculated in threads together). Each thread can then work on its own copy of data and doesn't have to use any locking to access it.

 Communication is better than synchronization!

Standard techniques to implement messaging in a Delphi program are Windows messages, `TThread` methods `Synchronize` and `Queue`, and polling in connection with a thread-safe message queue, such as `TThreadedQueue<T>`.

The best way to find problems in a multithreaded application is to do **stress-testing**, repeating multithreaded operations multiple times, and testing your program on only one CPU core (Windows API `SetProcessAffinityMask` will help you with that). You'll be surprised how many problems can be found this way. If at all possible (the implementation may prevent you from doing this), you should also test the code by creating more worker threads/tasks than there are CPU cores in the computer.

Use automated tests as much as possible and you'll be able to trust your code more. Never trust the multithreaded code fully. It actually never fully works; it's just that the bugs are so deeply hidden that they almost never appear.

# Working with parallel tools

There are multiple ways to implement multithreading in an application, and Chapter 6, *Working with Parallel Tools*, dealt with the most basic of them all—TThread. This class was introduced in Delphi 2 where it simply wrapped the Windows CreateThread API. Later, it was enhanced with additional methods and got support for other operating systems but, in essence, it stayed the same good old, stupid, clumsy TThread, which we all learned to love and hate.

Threads created with TThread can be used in two modes. In one, the code has full control over a TThread object—it can create it, tell it to terminate (but the object must observe that and wilfully terminate), and destroy it. In other modes, the code just creates a thread that does its job, terminates it, and is automatically destroyed. The former is more appropriate for service-like operations. You start a thread that then responds to requests, and performs some operations as a response to those requests. When you don't need it anymore, the code destroys the thread. The latter is more appropriate for background calculations. You start a thread, the thread executes some calculation, notifies the main thread of the result, and exits.

Working with the basic TThread object is quite clumsy, so in this chapter I presented a way to combine TThread and a communication channel. While it is simple to send messages from a background thread to the main thread (and I described four such mechanisms in the previous chapter), sending messages to a thread is hard.

I introduced a DHPThreads unit, which implements the TCommThread class representing a thread with a two-way communication channel, which can transfer TValue records to and from the thread. To use this thread, you had to write its Execute method in a fairly specific way, which limits its use.

To simplify the code, I introduced a more capable TCommTimerThread that shows how to work with threads on a more abstract level. You no longer override the Execute method as with the standard TThread mechanism, but merely introduce simple *event handlers*. The base class runs the Execute loop, processes messages, handles timers, and calls event handlers when appropriate. One event handler processes messages while another handles timer events.

If you approach multithreading that way, you move from the standard *big block of code* way to a modular event-driven architecture. This simplifies the programming logic, reduces the quantity of shared data, and makes multithreading a safer and more pleasant experience.

# Exploring parallel practices

The last example is also a demonstration of the current trend in multithreaded programming. Instead of working directly with threads, we try to put as much of the ugly multithreading *plumbing* into ready-to-use components. The first level of such abstraction is replacing threads with *tasks*.

A thread is just an operating system concept; one that allows executing multiple parts of a process simultaneously. When we program with threads, we have to handle all the cumbersome minutiae related to managing operating system threads.

A task, on the other hand, is the part of code that we want to execute in parallel. When we are working with tasks, we don't care how threads are created and destroyed. We just tell the system that we want to run the task and it does the rest.

The task is a useful step forward, but, for the majority of users tasks are still too low-level. That is why parallel programming libraries that support specialized building blocks (which I like to call *patterns*) have appeared for all major programming languages.

The first pattern that I looked into was *Async/Await,* a concept that (to my knowledge) first appeared in C#. It enables you to execute an anonymous method in a background thread. When the background thread finishes its work, the pattern executes a second anonymous method in the main thread. This allows us to clean up after the worker and to update the user interface—something that we must never do from a background thread! This pattern is not a lot different from a task that calls `TThread.Queue` at the end. The main difference is that, in the latter case, we have to write all the necessary code while Async/Await implements as much of the infrastructure as possible, and you only have to provide the appropriate anonymous methods.

Another interesting pattern is *Join*. It creates a task, wrapping multiple anonymous procedures. Join executes each procedure in its own thread. More specifically, it *should* do that, but the implementation from the built-in Parallel Programming Library is broken in the latest Delphi edition, Tokyo. `Chapter 7`, *Exploring Parallel Practices*, included two different workarounds for the bug.

The next pattern I created from scratch was *Join/Await*. It extended the Join concept with a simple-to-use termination event that executes in the main thread. This pattern is also capable of catching exceptions in worker code and presenting them to the termination event.

Another simple and interesting pattern is *Future*. It starts a calculation in a background thread and then enables you to access the result in the main thread. The Parallel Programming Library's implementation does not implement a notification handler that would notify the main thread when computation is finished, but that is easily fixed by using any of the messaging mechanisms I described before.

Also from the Parallel Programming Library comes *Parallel for*. This very powerful pattern allows you to convert a normal `for` loop into a parallel version. The pattern starts multiple workers, and processes just a part of the `for` range in each one. This pattern waits for a parallel loop to finish execution (which blocks the main thread), but that can be easily fixed by wrapping Parallel for in a Future or Async/Await pattern.

There are many other patterns that help you write multithreaded code, but they are not implemented in Delphi's parallel library. Instead of writing them yourself, which may be a very hard task, you should look at existing libraries. My OmniThreadLibrary (`www.omnithreadlibrary.com`), for example, implements patterns such as *Background worker*, *Timed task*, *Fork/Join*, and more.

One of those patterns is the very useful *Pipeline*, which can be used to parallelize tasks that can be split into *processing stages*. This pattern runs each stage in its own thread and connects them with communication queues. As each stage is working on its own copy of the data, there's no need for locking and all the troubles that come with it.

If you have to write multithreaded code, patterns are definitely the way to go. By implementing the most complicated parts of the infrastructure internally, they help you focus on the important part—the problem-specific code.

# Using external libraries

Sometimes, performance problems are too hard to be solved in code. Maybe the problem lies in a specific domain that requires specialized technical knowledge to be solved efficiently. Or maybe the compiler is generating code that just doesn't cut it.

In both cases, the answer is the same—if you can't solve it internally, find a better solution and use it as an external module. If you can get a DLL, great! Using DLLs from a Delphi application is a breeze. Lots of times, however, you'll have to use either *object files* generated with a C compiler, or C++ *libraries*.

While the former can be used directly in Delphi, there are usually several obstacles to overcome. Firstly, the object file has to be in the correct format. The 32-bit Delphi compiler can link OMF and COFF formats (generated by the Embarcadero's and Microsoft's compiler, respectively), while the 64-bit Delphi compiler can only link COFF format files.

Secondly, the object file may refer to external methods that you have to write. If they come from Microsoft's standard *msvcrt* library then you can resolve the problems by adding `System.Win.Crtl` to the `uses` list. Other times, you'll have to write the necessary code in your application. Just remember, C uses the `cdecl` calling convention, not standard Delphi `pascal` convention or `stdcall` used for Windows DLLs.

Sometimes, you have to link to multiple object files that contain circular references. In the simplest scenario, object file A refers to a function implemented in object file B, while file B refers to a function implemented in file A. In such cases, we have to help the compiler a little by providing a simple `external` declaration for one of the functions.

While linking to C object files is hard, but at least possible, linking to C++ object files or libraries can present an impossible mission. C++ files usually contain language-specific features such as classes, streams, and strings, and Delphi has no idea how to handle them. A proper approach is to write a piece of software in C++—a proxy DLL that accepts Delphi calls and passes them to the C++ library. All the knowledge of complicated C++ stuff, such as objects, can stay hidden inside this proxy library.

There's one other option to speed up the program that I didn't cover in `Chapter 8`, *Using External Libraries*, and that is *GPU programming*. Modern graphics cards have powerful processors that can be used for generic programming—provided that you know how to program them. This is not a simple job, and if you want to go that way, you'll need to do some serious studying. If you are interested, you should start with the `OpenCL` framework, which is supported by all important graphics card manufacturers.

# Final words

Before I leave you for good, I would like to say a few parting words.

It is obvious that you want to learn, otherwise you wouldn't have made it to this very last page. Don't stop here! While this book contains lots of interesting information, it is by no means a definitive work. There is so much more to be learned, so much more to find!

Let this be your guiding line—never stop learning. Learn what others have to say, even if they contradict something I have said in this book. Maybe they are right and I am wrong. Follow what other languages are doing and what libraries exist for them. That is the source of many great ideas. Write good code. Write bad code. Find why it is bad and fix it. Never stop moving.

Explore. Experiment. Evolve!

# Other Books You May Enjoy

If you enjoyed this book, you may be interested in these other books by Packt:

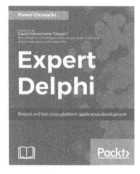

**Expert Delphi**
Paweł Głowacki

ISBN: 978-1-78646-016-5

- Understand the basics of Delphi and the FireMonkey application platform as well as the specifics of Android and iOS platforms
- Complete complex apps quickly with access to platform features and APIs using a single, easy-to-maintain code base
- Work with local data sources, including embedded SQL databases, REST servers, and Backend-as-a-Service providers
- Take full advantage of mobile hardware capabilities by working with sensors and Internet of Things gadgets and devices
- Integrate with cloud services and data using REST APIs and scalable multi-tier frameworks for outstanding multi-user and social experience
- Architect and deploy powerful mobile back-end services and get super-productive by leveraging Delphi IDE agile functionality
- Get to know the best practices for writing a high-quality, reliable, and maintainable codebase in the Delphi Object Pascal language

# Leave a review - let other readers know what you think

Please share your thoughts on this book with others by leaving a review on the site that you bought it from. If you purchased the book from Amazon, please leave us an honest review on this book's Amazon page. This is vital so that other potential readers can see and use your unbiased opinion to make purchasing decisions, we can understand what our customers think about our products, and our authors can see your feedback on the title that they have worked with Packt to create. It will only take a few minutes of your time, but is valuable to other potential customers, our authors, and Packt. Thank you!

# Index

www.ingramcontent.com/pod-product-compliance
Lightning Source LLC
Chambersburg PA
CBHW080621060326
40690CB00021B/4774